Removing the Confusion on the Ruling of Shaving and Shortening the Beard According to the Ḥanafī School

رفع المرية
في قص اللحية
وحلقها عند الحنفية

*Rafʿ al-Mirya fī Qaṣṣ al-Liḥya
wa-Ḥalqihā ʿand al-Ḥanafiyya*

A bilingual treatise

By Shaykh Ṣalāḥ Abū al-Ḥājj

Translated by
Siddiq Adam Mitha

SUNNI PUBLICATIONS

ISBN 978-90-79294-350

Removing the Confusion on the Ruling
of Shaving and Shortening the Beard
According to the Hanafi School
A bilingual treatise

رفع المرية في قص اللحية وحلقها عند الحنفية

Shaykh Salah Abu al-Hajj

الدكتور صلاح أبو الحاج

Translation by:
Siddiq Adam Mitha

Cover Design by:
Sunni Publications

Cover Art by:
Sunha Paul Kim
Abu Hanifa Mosque, Baghdad

Printed by:
IngramSpark

Published by:
Sunni Publications
Rotterdam, the Netherlands
www.sunnipubs.com
info@sunnipubs.com

TRANSLITERATION TABLE

ا/آ/ى	ā	ظ	ẓ
ب	b	ع	ʿ
ت	t	غ	gh
ث	th	ف	f
ج	j	ق	q
ح	ḥ	ك	k
خ	kh	ل	l
د	d	م	m
ذ	dh	ن	n
ر	r	ه	h
ز	z	و	w/ū
س	s	ي	y/ī
ش	sh	ة	a
ص	ṣ	ء	ʾ
ض	ḍ	أ	a/u
ط	ṭ	إ	i

HONORIFIC PHRASES

﷾	Exalted and Sublime is He
ﷺ	Allah's prayers and salutations be upon him
ﷷ	Peace be upon him
ﷷ	Peace be upon them
﵁	May Allah be pleased with him
﵁	May Allah be pleased with her
﵁	May Allah be pleased with them both
﵁	May Allah be pleased with them

TABLE OF CONTENTS

فهرس المحتويات

About the Author

HAYKH ṢALĀḤ MUḤAMMAD ṢĀLIM ABŪ AL-ḤĀJJ was born in Amman, Jordan, in the year 1974 CE. He completed his early education in Jordan, where he studied with local teachers and finished his secondary education. He then continued his studies by enrolling at the College of Daʿwa & Uṣūl al-Dīn at al-Balqa Applied University gaining his bachelor's degree in 1997.

His thirst for knowledge continued and he decided to travel to Baghdad, Iraq, where he enrolled at the University of Saddam for Islamic Sciences. Here, he attained a master's degree in Islamic Law in 1999 during which he wrote a detailed thesis on Imam al-Laknawī and his methodology in *fiqh* which gained wide acclaim and was later published. At the same university in 2002, he completed his PhD in which he researched and verified a manuscript of *Sharḥ al-Wiqāya*, an important and monumental work in the Ḥanafī school.

During his time in Baghdad, Shaykh Ṣalāḥ also had the privilege of studying a traditional curriculum with many of the leading scholars of Iraq. His teachers included Shaykh Bakr al-Mawṣilī, Shaykh Qāsim al-Ṭā'ī, Shaykh Sājid ʿAbd al-Qādir, Shaykh Mawlūd al-Turkī, Shaykh Muḥammad Ramaḍān al-Kurdī and Shaykh ʿAbd al-Malik al-Saʿdī. He was authorized to teach and received his *sanad* in Fiqh and the Islamic Sciences from Shaykh Qāsim al-Ṭā'ī in 2005.

ولد الدكتور صلاح محمد سالم أبو الحاج في العاصمة الأردنية عمان عام 1974. أتم الدكتور صلاح تعليمه الابتدائي والثانوي في الأردن ثم التحق بكلية الدعوة وأصول الدين بجامعة البلقاء التطبيقية، حيث نال على شهادة البكالوريوس عام 1997.

استمر تعطشه للعلم بعد ذلك فقرر السفر إلى بغداد حيث التحق بجامعة صدام للعلوم الإسلامية ونال فيها على شهادة الماجستير في الشريعة الإسلامية، ناقش فيها الإمام اللكنوي ومنهجه الفقهي. وقد نال بحثه استحسانا واسعا وتم طبعه ونشره. ثم نال على درجة الدكتوراه من نفس الجامعة في عام 2002 ، حيث بحث وحقق في رسالته مخطوطة من كتاب شرح الوقاية، وهو أحد أهم الكتب في المذهب الحنفي.

خلال مكوثه في بغداد ، حظي الدكتور صلاح بفرصة دراسة المناهج التقليدية مع كبار العلماء في العراق. وكان من أساتذته الشيخ بكر الموصلي والشيخ قاسم الطائي والشيخ ساجد عبد القادر والشيخ مولود التركي والشيخ محمد رمضان الكردي والشيخ عبدالملك السعدي. ونال على إجازته وسنده في الفقه والعلوم الإسلامية من الشيخ قاسم الطائي عام 2005.

Shaykh Ṣalāḥ's passion for knowledge and his exceptional intelligence and ability has made him one of the most respected and widely recognised scholars in the field of Ḥanafī *fiqh* and *uṣūl*. His opinions and discourses are highly regarded by both teachers and students of knowledge from all around the world. He has published many important works in the Ḥanafī school and has numerous, articles, research papers, and manuscript verifications. Some of his most important works include *Minna al-Fattāḥ*, which is a commentary on *Marāqī al-Falāḥ*, *al-Madkhal ilā al-Fiqh al-Ḥanafī*, *Masār al-Wuṣūl ilā 'Ilm al-Uṣūl*, *Ghāya al-'Ināya 'alā 'Umda al-Ri'āya* and *Is'ād al-Muftī 'alā Sharḥ 'Uqūd Rasm al-Muftī*.

Shaykh Ṣalāḥ continues to work tirelessly, teaching students from all backgrounds and is a staunch proponent for Sunni orthodoxy in the study and practice of Islam. He is currently the Dean of the Ḥanafī Fiqh College at the World Islamic Sciences and Education University in Jordan where he has developed a unique programme that combines both the classical and the contemporary, attracting hundreds of students from all around the globe. He is also the founder of the Anwār al-'Ulamā' Centre from where he teaches many of his lessons and also shares research articles and answers online. Shaykh Ṣalāḥ continues to inspire a whole generation of students of the Sacred Law and remains a source of inspiration and guidance for aspiring students everywhere.

وقد أصبح الدكتور صلاح من أكبر العلماء تقديرا وسيطا في مجال الفقه الحنفي والأصول، وذلك نتيجة لقدراته وشغفه بالعلم وذكائه الحاد. وتحظى آراؤه وخطاباته بتقدير كبير من قبل كل من المعلمين وطلبة العلم من جميع أنحاء العالم. له العديد من الأعمال الهامة في المذهب الحنفي كما له العديد من المقالات والأبحاث والتحقيقات من أهمها: منة الفتاح وهو شرح لمراقي الفلاح، والمدخل إلى الفقه الحنفي، ومسار الوصول إلى علم الأصول وغاية العناية على عمدة الرعاية وإسعاد المفتي على شرح عقود رسم المفتي.

يواصل الدكتور صلاح العمل بتفانٍ على تدريس الطلبة من جميع الخلفيات، و هو من كبار الداعين إلى اتباع النهج السني في دراسة الإسلام وممارسته. كما يشغل حاليًا منصب عميد كلية الفقه الحنفي في جامعة العلوم الإسلامية العالمية في الأردن حيث طور برنامجًا فريدًا من نوعه يجمع الأصالة والحداثة معا، مما جذب مئات من الطلاب من جميع أنحاء العالم. كما أنه مؤسس مركز أنوار العلماء حيث يقوم بتقديم العديد من دروسه، ويشارك مقالاته وأبحاثه ويجيب على الاستفسارات عبر الإنترنت. يواصل الدكتور صلاح إلهام جيل كامل من طلاب الشريعة ويظل مصدر إلهام وتوجيه لكثير من الطلبة الطموحين من كل مكان.

INTRODUCTION

In the name of Allah, the Lord of Mercy, the Giver of Mercy.

All praise belongs to Allah ﷻ, Lord of the worlds. And may blessings and salutations be upon the liege-lord of all the Messengers and the leader of those guided rightly, and upon his family, companions and all those who follow him in excellence until the Day of Judgement.

There is no doubt that the issue of shaving and shortening the beard has become an oft-discussed topic within both academic and social circles due to the spread of Western culture in the Muslim world and shaving essentially having become common practice everywhere. This has meant that most Muslims have, in some way, been affected by this issue. Perhaps only those who are obviously religious, with this being evident in their character and behaviour, are the ones who strive to keep the beard in accordance with the Prophetic directive.

However, even these people face an additional hurdle, which is whether or not to shorten the beard. This means whether or not to lengthen it to the sunna fist-length, as has been related in various Prophetic traditions [*aḥādīth*]. A beard of such length is ultimately only kept by a small number of individuals.

All of the above has in turn resulted in tens of books and articles being written specifically on the issue of the beard, citing frequently the Prophetic traditions that command one to lengthen or grow the beard [*iʿfāʾ al-liḥya*]. Surprisingly, all of these works report consensus [*ijmāʿ*] from the four schools of law on the necessity [*wujūb*] of keeping the beard, and by extension, making it unlawful [*ḥarām*] to shave or even shorten it. They assert, at times, that shaving or shortening the beard is imitative [*tashabbuh*] of non-Muslims, sometimes it is seen to be imitative of females, and at other times it is thought to detract from one's social integrity [*murūʾa*].

مقدمة

بسم الله الرحمن الرحيم

الحمد لله ربّ العالمين، والصَّلاة والسلام على سيد المرسلين، وإمام المهتدين، وعلى آله وصحبه ومَن تبعه بإحسان إلى يوم الدِّين.

وبعد:

فإنَّ موضوع حلق اللحية وتقصيرها من أكثر الموضوعات جدلاً في الأوساط العلمية والاجتماعية، بسبب انتشار الثقافة الغربية بين المسلمين، وشيوع أمر الحلق للحية، حتى ابتلي به عامة المسلمين، إلا مَن كان التدين ظاهراً في سلوكه، فإنَّه يحرص على التحلِّي باللحية متابعة منه لهدي المصطفى ﷺ.

وهذا المتدين أيضاً مبتلى بتقصير اللحية فلا يطيل اللحية على الهيئة المسنونة وهي القبضة الواردة في الأحاديث إلا النزر اليسير جداً.

وتسبب هذا في ظهور عشرات الكتب في موضوع اللحية خاصة، وهذه الكتب والأبحاث عموماً تنقل الإجماع من المذاهب الأربعة على وجوب اللحية، فيحرم حلقها أو تقصيرها، وتُكثِر من ذكر الأحاديث الواردة في أمر النبي ﷺ بإعفاء اللحية، وتبيّن أنَّ الحلق والتقصير من التشبه بغير المسلمين تارة، وتشبه بالنساء تارة أُخرى، وأنَّه خارم للمروءة أيضاً.

This strict approach to the issue has regrettably flared up much discord [*fitna*] between the general Muslim populace, such that someone who shortens or shaves his beard is often prevented from leading the prayer in some countries. Muslims can be found feuding, cursing and belittling each other in mosques, especially in places like India, Pakistan, Europe and America.

It is extremely perplexing to find Muslims expending all their energy on matters which are differed upon and concern themselves with the outward and superficial, leaving the inner and core matters. This means that customary practices like the beard, clothing, covering the head, and using prayer beads have become the primary focus of the Muslim community. This has meant that they have abandoned matters which affect them without disagreement, like the spread of obscenity, moral depravity, the ruin of their countries, and deviation from correct thought, methodology and education, as was taught by the Messenger ﷺ.

Restricting Islam to secondary and disputed matters has been a major factor in the deviation of the *umma* and in occupying Muslims from their main role of disseminating the guidance of Islam to the whole of mankind, and it is unfathomable that these teachings would be restricted only to outward appearances and customary practices [*'ādāt*].

In fact, the Messenger ﷺ was sent to the most well-known of all Arabs who covered their heads, lengthened their beards and even wore long Arabian garments. However, he ﷺ sanctioned these established practices of theirs because they are all related to the customs of a people. Thus, if the teachings of Islam were only related to these outward matters of appearance, then it would seem that the Arabs were in no need of them, as they were already in adherence to them even before the coming of the Messenger ﷺ.

وأثار هذا التَّشدُّد فتناً كثيرةً بين المسلمين عموماً، حتى منعوا المقصِّر أو الحالق من الإمامة في الصلاة في بعض البلاد، وتنابذ المسلمون في المساجد بالتشهير والطعن بسبب هذه المسألة لا سيما في أوربا وأمريكا والهند وباكستان.

وهذا أمر في غاية العجب أن يصرف المسلمون جلَّ اهتمامهم في المسائل الخلافية، وأن يصبح اهتمام المسلمين بالقشور والمظاهر، ويتركوا اللبَّ والباطن، وتصبح مسائل العادات: كاللحية واللباس وتغطية الرأس والسُّبحة هي قضايا المسلمين الرئيسية، ويتركون قضاياهم الكلية في انتشار الفحشاء والفسق وضياع البلاد وانحراف الفكر والمنهج والتربية عمّا كانت عليه في هدي النبي ﷺ.

وإنَّ حصر الإسلام بهذه الأمور الجزئية والخلافية كان سبباً في حرف الأمّة عن طريقها، وإشغالٌ للمسلمين عن وظيفتهم الرئيسية في حمل هدي الإسلام للبشرية جمعاء، فهل يعقل أنَّ هدي الإسلام محصور بهذه الشكليات والعادات.

فها هو النبي ﷺ يُبعث بين أظهر العرب وهم يَلتحون ويغطّون رؤوسهم ويلبسون الثوب، وأقرَّهم على ما هم عليه؛ لأنَّها من عادات الناس، فلو كانت هداية الإسلام بهذه الأمور لما احتاج العرب لهداية الإسلام؛ لأنَّهم كانوا يمارسونها قبل مجيء النبي ﷺ.

And, if there was a specific dress code in Islam, then we would have clearly come across it, either in the Prophetic traditions or the books of the jurists. However, from the outset, Islam entered many lands, but left the people of those lands upon their customary practices relating to clothing, covering the head and other similar matters. This is because the Messenger of Allah ﷺ was not sent to disseminate or propagate the culture of the Arabs in relation to appearance and dress, rather, it is simply recommended [*mustaḥabb*] for the Muslims to follow the acts of the Messenger ﷺ which emanate from his natural state [*afʿāl al-jibilliyya*].

Therefore, one must understand that the point of reference for these outward appearances (like the length of the beard) is the customary practices of a people. A Muslim is encouraged to appear refined and elegant in these types of matters, making sure not to resemble non-Muslims. Through this, the effect of religion can manifest on his behaviour and he may thereby taste the sweetness of faith in his distinction as a Muslim.

Placing the beard under the rubric of customary practices confers upon it the same legal rulings as other customary acts. Depending on the evidence, it will either be recommended, sunna or otherwise. This is because customary practices usually differ in their legal rulings depending on which foundation [*aṣl*] they are derived from—as will be explained in the following sections.

ولو كان للإسلام هيئة خاصّة للباس لوجدناها مبيَّنة في أحاديث النَّبيِّ ﷺ وفي كتب الفقهاء، ولكنَّ الإسلام دخل عامّة البلاد من فجر الإسلام، ومع ذلك تُرك كلُّ قوم على ما هم عليه من الهيئة المعتادة من اللباس والتَّغطية للرأس وغيرها؛ لأنَّ النَّبيّ ﷺ لم يرسل لنشر ثقافة العرب في اللباس والهيئة، وإنَّما يستحب لكافة المسلمين الاقتداء بأفعال النبي ﷺ الجبلية.

فعلم أنَّ هذه الهيئات كمقدار اللحية مرجعها لعادات النَّاس، وإنَّما رغَّب المسلم بالتهذيب في مثل هذه الأمور، وأن تكون حسنة، وأن لا يتشبّه بغير المسلمين؛ ليظهر أثر الدِّين على سلوكه ويشعر بحلاوة الإيمان في تميِّزه كمسلم.

وادراج اللحية في العادات يعطيها أحكام العادات على حسب قيام الدليل لها من حيث الاستحباب أو السنية أو غيرها؛ لأن العادات تتفاوت في حكمها بحسب الأصل الذي بنيت عليه، كما سيظهر في المباحث التالية.

The aforementioned brings to light the importance of this treatise in discussing a critical issue that concerns the general Muslim populace, that is whether shaving or shortening the beard is considered lawful or unlawful, and how it should be kept. The treatise also contains an invitation to Muslims to leave secondary matters of dispute—like the one at hand—which relate to the customs and culture [*'urf*] of a people, since doing so would then allow them to direct their attention and efforts to the worthy concerns of the Muslims and Islam.

Moreover, this treatise also demonstrates the philosophy and methodology of *fiqh* (Islamic jurisprudence) in interacting with legal issues in a logical, intellectual, lawful and principled way.

The primary question that this treatise seeks to answer is the following: Is shaving or shortening the beard to less than a fist-length unlawful according to the Ḥanafī school?

This, in turn gives rise to some other secondary questions:

Do the 'derivation principles' [*uṣūl al-istinbāṭ*] in the Ḥanafī school indicate towards the beard being necessary, sunna or recommended?

Is shaving or shortening the beard considered to be from that which is imitative of non-Muslims?

Is shaving or shortening the beard considered to be from that which detracts from one's social integrity?

Is shaving or shortening the beard considered to be from that which is imitative of females?

Is shaving or shortening the beard considered to be from that which has become a 'general necessity' [*'umūm al-balwā*]?

وهذا يظهر أهمية هذا البحث في مناقشته لمثل هذه المسألة الشائكة التي تهمّ عامّة المسلمين من جهةِ الحِلِّ والحرمة والهيئة التي يكون عليها، وتدعو إلى ترك المسلمين لمثل هذه الجزئيات الخلافية؛ لأنَّ مرجعها لعادة الناس وأعرافهم، بحيث تتوجَّه طاقاتهم إلى همّ الإسلام والمسلمين، وتظهر لنا فلسفة الفقه في التَّعامل مع المسائل بطريقة منطقيّة عقليّة شرعيّة منضبطة.

وتكمن مشكلة البحث في الإجابة عن سؤال رئيس، وهو هل حلق اللحية أو تقصيرها أقل من قبضة محرم عند الحنفية؟ ويتفرع عليه أسئلة فرعية:

هل أصول الاستنباط للحنفية تدلّ وجوب اللحية أم سنيتها واستحبابها؟

هل يُعَدُّ حلق اللِّحية أو تقصيرها من التَّشبُّه بغير المسلمين؟

هل حلق اللحية أو تقصيرها من خوارم المروءة؟

هل حلق اللحية من التشبه بالنساء؟

هل يعتبر حلق اللحية أو تقصيرها مما تعم به البلوى؟

LITERATURE REVIEW

Previous studies and tracts relating to the issue of the beard are many, yet there are no specialised studies that clarify its ruling in the Ḥanafī school, or analyse and verify the statements of the jurists, clarifying the causal factors [*ʿilal*] these statements were derived from. Rather, existing studies merely implicitly mention the unlawfulness of shaving or shortening the beard according to the Ḥanafī school. Below are some examples of these other studies:

1. ***Qaṭʿ al-Mariyya fī Bayān Madhhab al-Shāfiʿiyya fī Ḥalq wa-Taqṣīr al-Liḥya*** (*Removing the Doubt with Regards to the Issue of Shaving and Shortening the Beard in the Shāfiʿī School*) by Dr Amjad Rashid

In his treatise Dr Amjad clarifies that lengthening the beard is an emphasised sunna [*sunna muʾakkada*] in the Shāfiʿī school, meaning that the one who shaves or shortens his beard without any valid excuse is not sinful but has committed an offensive act.

2. ***Ifāda Dhawī al-Afhām anna Ḥalq al-Liḥya Makrūh wa-laysa bi-Ḥarām*** (*Notifying those with Sound Intellect that Shaving the Beard is Offensive but not Unlawful*) by ʿAbd al-ʿAzīz al-Ghumārī

He establishes in it that the command [*amr*] transmitted in various traditions regarding the issue of lengthening is merely by way of recommendation and nothing else, and that the correct opinion with regards to shaving the beard is that of it being offensive but not unlawful.

3. ***Al-Ḥujja al-Dāmigha ʿalā Buṭlān Daʿwā man Zaʿama anna Ḥāliq al-Liḥya Malʿūn wa-Ṣalātuhu Bāṭila*** (*Compelling Proof of the Invalidity of the Claim of those who Allege that the one who Shaves the Beard is Accursed and his Prayer is Invalid*) by ʿAbd al-Ḥayy al-Ghumārī

He establishes in it that lengthening the beard is sunna.

الدراسات السابقة

كثرت الكتب والأبحاث في مسألة اللحية، إلا أنَّه لم توجد أي دراسة متخصصة في حكم اللحية عند الحنفية بتحرير أقوالهم وتحقيقها وبيان العلل التي بنيت عليها، وإنَّما يذكر في ضمن الدراسات حرمة حلقها وتقصيرها عند الحنفية ، ومن هذه الدراسات:

1. قطع المرية في بيان مذهب الشافعيّة في حلق وتقصير اللحية: للدكتور أمجد رشيد، أثبت فيها أنَّ إعفاء اللحية سنة مؤكدة عند الشافعية، فمَن حلقها أو قصَّرها من غير عذرٍ لم يأثم ولكنَّه ارتكب مكروهاً.

2. إفادة ذوي الأفهام أنَّ حلق اللحية مكروه وليس بحرام: لعبد العزيز الغماري، أثبت فيها أنَّ الأمر الوارد في الإعفاء على سبيل الاستحباب لا غير، والصواب القول بكراهة حلقها لا حرمته.

3. الحجة الدامغة على بطلان دعوى مَن زعم أنَّ حالق اللحية ملعون وصلاته باطلة: لعبد الحي الغماري، أثبت فيها أنَّ إعفاء اللحية سنة لا غير.

4. ***Wujūb I'fā' al-Liḥya wa-Taḥrīm Ḥalqihā wa-Taqṣīrihā*** (*The Necessity of Leaving the Beard and the Unlawfulness of Shaving or Shortening it*) by 'Abd al-Raḥmān al-'Āṣimī al-Ḥanbalī

The title is self-explanatory in terms of what the tract establishes.

5. ***Adilla Taḥrīm Ḥalq al-Liḥya*** (*Evidences to Prove the Unlawfulness of Shaving the Beard*) by Muḥammad al-Muqaddam

The title is self-explanatory in terms of what the tract establishes.

6. ***Al-Radd 'alā man Ajāza Tahdhīb al-Liḥya*** (*Refuting those who Permit Trimming the Beard*) by Maḥmūd al-Tuwayjirī

Its subject matter is evident from the title.

7. ***Al-Ḥilya fī I'fā' al-Liḥya*** (*The Adornment in Leaving the Beard*) by 'Abd al-Laṭīf al-Balūshī

He strives to prove that shaving the beard is unlawful according to the *mujtahid* scholars (independent jurists) of the Muslim *umma*: Abū Ḥanīfa, Mālik, al-Shāfi'ī and Aḥmad.

8. ***Ḥukm al-Shar' fīl-Liḥya wal-Azyā' wal-Taqālīd wal-'Ādāt wa-Ibṭāl Za'm annahā Maḥḍu Ashkāl Madaniyya wa-min al-Shu'ūn al-Shakhsiyya Yaḥkumuhā al-'Urf wal-'Āda*** (*The Legal Ruling with Regards to the Beard, Dress, Tradition, and Customary Practice in the Sacred Law, and the Refutation of those who Claim it is Purely a Social or Personal Matter that is Governed by Culture and Custom*) by 'Uthmān al-Ṣāfī

Its subject matter is evident from the title.

4.وجوب إعفاء اللحية وتحريم حلقها وتقصيرها: لعبد الرحمن العاصمي الحنبلي (ت1392هـ)، وعنوانه يبين مضمونه.

5.أدلة تحريم حلق اللحية: لمحمد المقدم، وعنوانه يوضح مضمونه.

6.الرد على من أجاز تهذيب اللحية: لحمود التويجري، وموضوعها ظاهرٌ من عنوانها.

7.الحلية في إعفاء اللحية: لعبد اللطيف البلوشي، وسعى في إثبات أنَّ حلق اللحية محرمة عند أئمة المسلمين المجتهدين أبي حنيفة ومالك والشافعي وأحمد.

8.حكم الشرع في اللحية والأزياء والتقاليد والعادات وإبطال زعم أنَّها محض أشكال مدنية ومن الشؤون الشخصية يحكمها العرف والعادة: لعثمان الصافي، ومن اسمه يظهر مضمونه.

9. ***Al-Liḥya fī al-Kitāb wal-Sunna wa-Aqwāl Salaf al-Umma***
(*The Beard in the Qur'ān and Prophetic traditions, and the
Statements of the Early People from the umma*) by Muḥammad
Ḥassūna

He cites that there is consensus from all four schools of law on
the unlawfulness of shaving the beard.

10. ***Al-Jāmi' fī Aḥkām al-Liḥya*** (*A comprehensive Look at the
Legal Rulings Related to the Beard*) by 'Alī al-Rāzikhī

He also mentions that there is consensus of all the four
schools of law on the impermissibility of shaving the beard.

11. ***Ish'ār al-Ḥarīṣ 'alā 'Adam Jawāz al-Taqṣīṣ min al-Liḥya
li-Mūkhālafatihi al-Tanṣīṣ*** (*The Notification of the one who is
Covetous upon the Unlawfulness of Cutting the Beard due to it
Contradicting Scripture*) by 'Abd al-Karīm al-Ḥamīd

He strives to prove in it the unlawfulness of cutting the beard.

12. ***Wujūb I'fā' al-Liḥya*** (*The Necessity of Leaving the Beard*) by
Muḥammad Zakariyyā al-Kāndahlawī

He states that there is consensus upon leaving the beard and
the unlawfulness of shaving it.

13. ***Ārā' al-'Ulamā' fī-Ḥalq wa-Taqṣīr al-Liḥya*** (*The Opinions of
the Scholars Regarding the Shaving and Shortening of the
Beard*) by Muḥyī al-Dīn 'Abd al-Ḥamīd

He reports from the various schools of law the unlawfulness of
shaving the beard.

14. ***Ḥukm al-Liḥya fīl-Islām*** (*The Legal Ruling of the Beard in
Islam*) by Muḥammad al-Ḥāmid

He declares that there is consensus of the four schools of law
upon the necessity of keeping a beard and the unlawfulness of
shaving it.

9.اللِّحية في الكتاب والسنة وأقوال سلف الأمة: لمحمد حسونة، نقل اتفاق المذاهب الأربعة على تحريم الحلق.

10.الجامع في أحكام اللحية: لعلي الرازخي، وذَكر اتفاق المذاهب الفقهية على حرمة حلق اللحية.

11.إشعار الحريص على عدم جواز التقصيص من اللحية لمخالفته التنصيص: لعبد الكريم الحميد، سعى لإثبات حرمة القص للحية.

12.وجوب إعفاء اللحية: لمحمد زكريا الكاندهلوي، ذكر اتفاق المذاهب على توفير اللحية وحرمة حلقها.

13.آراء العلماء في حلق وتقصير اللحية: لمحيي الدِّين عبد الحميد، نقل فيه عن المذاهب الفقهية حرمة حلق اللحية.

14.حكم اللحية في الإسلام: لمحمد الحامد، ذكر فيه اتفاق المذاهب الأربعة على وجوبها وحرمة حلقها.

PREFACE
THE MOTIVE FOR WRITING THIS TREATISE ACCORDING TO AND WITHIN THE ḤANAFĪ SCHOOL

In my endeavour to reach the objective, the treatise has been divided into a preface, five sections and a conclusion.

Section One: The Derivation Principles [uṣūl al-istinbāṭ].

This section covers seven topics:

- The beard is considered from the additional sunnas [sunan al-zawāʾid].
- Contextual factors regarding the basis of the legal command [maḥall al-amr].
- A lack of warning [waʿīd] with regards to the command to keep a beard.
- Specifying the generic [takhṣīṣ al-ʿumūm] that has been transmitted with regards to the beard.
- The narrator acting contrary to his own narration regarding the beard.
- Some of the companions acting contrary to the tradition of the beard.
- Primordiality [fiṭra] is from the Sunna.

Section Two: Differing from Non-Muslims.

This section covers four topics:

- The types of imitation [tashabbuh].
- The defining principles of imitation.
- The types of Imitation and their legal rulings.
- Imitation and the beard.

تمهيد: في سبب كتابة البحث على المذهب الحنفي

وسعياً لتحقيق المقصود قسمت البحث إلى تمهيد وخمسة مباحث:

المبحث الأول: من جهة أصول الاستنباط، وفيه سبع مطالب:

- المطلب الأول: اللحية من سنن الزوائد.

- والمطلب الثاني: قرينة محلّ الأمر.

- والمطلب الثَّالث: عدم الوعيد في الأمر باللِّحية.

- والمطلب الرابع: تخصيص العموم الوارد في اللَّحية.

- والمطلب الخامس: عمل الرواي مخالف لمرويه في اللِّحية.

- والمطلب السادس: مخالفة بعض الصحابة لحديث اللِّحية.

- والمطلب السابع: الفطرة هي السنة.

المبحث الثاني: من جهة مخالفة غير المسلمين، وفيه أربع مطالب:

- المطلب الأول: أنواع التَّشبُّه.

- والمطلب الثاني: ضوابط التَّشبُّه.

- والمطلب الثالث: حالات التَّشبُّه وحكمها.

- والمطلب الرابع: التَّشبُّه في اللحية.

Section Three: Acting Contrary to Social Integrity [*murū'a*]

This section covers four topics:

- The linguistic and technical definitions of social integrity.
- The importance of social integrity.
- The effect of social integrity in the Ḥanafī school.
- The relation between the beard and social integrity.

Section Four: Imitating Females when Shaving the Beard.

This section covers four topics:

- Imitating females and its intended meaning.
- Imitation and its prohibition in the Sunna.
- The legal ruling of imitating females in the Ḥanafī school.
- The relationship between imitating females and shaving the beard.

Section Five: General Necessity [*'umūm al-balwā*]

This section covers three topics:

- The intended meaning of 'general necessity'.
- The legal ruling of the beard according to the Shāfi'ī and Mālikī schools of Law.
- Textual references from the Ḥanafī school with regards to shaving and shortening the beard.

Conclusion: Some of the Most Important Outcomes

والمبحث الثَّالث: من جهة مخالفة المروءة، وفيه أربع مطالب:

- المطلب الأول: تعريفة المروءة لغةً واصطلاحاً.

- والمطلب الثاني: مكانة المروءة.

- والمطلب الثالث: أثر المروءة في المذهب الحنفي.

- والمطلب الرابع: علاقة اللِّحية بالمروءة.

المبحث الرابع: التشبه بالنساء في حلق اللِّحية، وفيه أربع مطالب:

- المطلب الأول: المقصود بالتَّشبه بالنِّساء.

- والمطلب الثاني: المنع من التَّشبه بالنِّساء في السُّنة.

- والمطلب الثالث: حكم التَّشبُّه بالنِّساء عند الحنفية.

- والمطلب الرابع: علاقة التشبه بالنساء بحلق اللِّحية.

المبحث الخامس: من جهة عموم البلوى، وفيه ثلاث مطالب:

- المطلب الأول: المقصود بعموم البلوى.

- والمطلب الثاني: حكم اللحية عند الشافعية والمالكية.

- والمطلب الثالث: حلق اللحية وقصُّها في كتب الحنفية.

وخاتمة في أبرز النتائج.

In this treatise, I have focused on explaining the legal ruling with regards to shaving and shortening the beard according to and within the Ḥanafī school, for the following reasons:

1. My speciality and area of expertise being the instruction of the Ḥanafī school at various levels.

2. One of the issues facing some of the publications written on this topic is the frequent citation—by various writers—of the unlawfulness of shaving and shortening the beard from the various schools of law. This problem essentially returns back to many of the writers lacking speciality in one of the schools of law, or not deferring to specialists in some of the schools. This has no doubt led to a lack of scholarly precision when analysing the various schools, and in recognising the settled upon legal verdict [*muftā bihi*] as opposed to other lesser opinions. Generic passages are quoted that seem to coincide with what the researcher is claiming. This is why, when citing positions from the Mālikī and Shāfiʿī schools, I have deferred the matter to specialists in each respective school, seeking their opinion and ensuring to quote their judgements alongside the actual text citations [from the books of the school] which are indicative of that. Through this method I have hoped to arrive at the correct opinion in each school. I also encourage all researchers and writers to defer to the specialists in each school when quoting from the school.

3. To correct the mistake which many of the scholars have fallen into when claiming the unlawfulness of shaving and shortening the beard according to the Ḥanafī school.

اقتصرت في بحثي على بيان حكم الحلق والتقصير للحية في المذهب الحنفي للأسباب الآتية:

١. تخصصي بدراسة المذهب الحنفي في المراحل المختلفة.

٢. إنّ من أسباب المشكلة في الكتب المؤلّفة في الموضوع هو نقل عامّة الباحثين عن المذاهب حرمة حلق أو قص اللحية بسبب عدم تخصّصهم في أحد هذه المذاهب أو عدم رجوعهم إلى متخصصيين فيها، مما تسبب في عدم الدقّة العلمية في تحرير كلّ مذهب، ومعرفة المفتى به من غيره، وإنَّما نقل بعض العبارات العامة التي توافق زعم الباحث؛ لذلك عندما نقلت عن الشافعية والمالكية رأيهم في المسألة رجعت إلى علمائهم المتخصصين في مذهبهم وسألتهم ودونت رأيهم مع عبارات المذهب الدالة على ذلك، تحرياً في الوصول إلى الصواب في كل مذهب؛ لذلك أتمنى على الباحثين دائماً الرجوع إلى علماء المذاهب عند النقل عنها.

٣. تصويب الخطأ الذي وقع فيه الباحثون في كتبهم في نقل حرمة ذلك الحلق والقصّ عن الحنفية.

4. To correct the misunderstanding of some of the passages found in the books of the Ḥanafī school on this issue, in which the apparent meaning is taken without exploring the causal factor [*'illa*], despite the fact that there are numerous other statements which actually state the opposite, making the beard a sunna or recommended. This type of error, in understanding only part of the greater picture, is fairly common, as is brought to one's attention by Ibn 'Ābidīn in his books: *Sharḥ 'Uqūd Rasm al-Muftī*, *Nashr al-'Urf* and *Tanbīh al-Wulāt wal-Ḥukkām*.

5. As a means to egress from the widespread fanaticism that is present in India, Pakistan, Bangladesh, South Africa and various mosques in Europe and the United States, that are essentially managed by individuals who originate from one of the aforementioned places. This is as a result of the well-known ruling—which states that to keep a beard is necessary and that it is unlawful to shave or shorten it less than a fist-length— being widespread. They have been confused by their literal understanding of certain traditions and unclear passages, even in the presence of passages from many of the reliable books of law which clearly indicate that leaving the beard to a fist-length is sunna and not necessary.

6. To refute the precept upon which the honourable and blessed Shaykh Muḥammad Zakariyyā al-Kāndahlawī built his treatise: **Wujūb I'fāʾ al-Liḥya** (*The Necessity of Leaving the Beard*), as this treatise has had an enormous impact on spreading the fanaticism that we see amongst some in the Ḥanafī school; it proves true the saying, '*when a scholar slips, the entire world slips* [*zallat al-'ālim, zallat al-'ālam*].'[1] Al-Sarakhsī states that, 'the slip of a scholar is a cause for the tribulation of a people, as it has been said, "If a scholar slips, then due to his error the entire world slips [*in zallat al-'ālim zallat bi-zallatihi al-'ālam*]."'[2]

---

[1] *Mirqāt al-Mafātīḥ* (1:334)
[2] *Al-Mabsūṭ* (16:62)

4.تصحيح الخطأ في فهم بعض العبارات الواردة في كتب الحنفية في المسألة بحيث فهمت على ظاهرها بدون النظر لعلتها، رغم وجود عبارات أخرى على عكسها تشهد بسنية اللحية واستحبابها، ومثل هذا الخطأ في فهم بعض العبارات يحصل كثيراً في الكتب، كما نَبَّه على ذلك ابنُ عابدين في «شرح عقو رسم المفتي» و«نشر العرف» و«تنبيه الولاة والحكام».

5.الخروج من هذا التَّشدُّد الشَّائع في بلاد الهند وباكستان وبنغلادش وجنوب إفريقيا والمساجد التي يشرف عليها أهل هذه البلاد في أوروبا وأمريكا، بسبب شيوع حكم وجوب اللحية وحرمة الحلق والقصّ لأقلّ من قبضة، اغتراراً بظاهر الأحاديث وبعض العبارات الموهمة لذلك، رغم وجود عبارات فقهية في عامة الكتب المعتمدة، صريحة بالتكلم عن القبضة المسنونة وليس الواجبة.

6.ردّ الوجوه التي بنى عليها فضيلة الشيخ المبارك محمد زكريا الكاندهلوي رسالته في «وجوب إعفاء اللحية»، حيث كان لهذه الرسالة الأثر الكبير في شيوع مثل هذا التشديد عند بعض الحنفية، وهذا مصداق المثل الشائع: زلة العالِم زلة العالَم[1]، قال السَّرَخْسيُّ: «فزلة العالِم سبب لفتنة الناس كما قيل: إن زل العالِم زل بزلته العالَم»[2].

---

(1) ينظر: مرقاة المفاتيح1: 334. المبسوط

(2) المبسوط 16: 62

7. A call to stay firm upon the way of the Ḥanafī jurists when extrapolating and deriving rulings from their foundations and causal factors. These foundations and causal factors are the aggregation of a great amount of Qur'anic verses, Prophetic traditions and traditions related from the companions. Therefore, this way has a greater priority in the Ḥanafī school over the way of the Hadith jurists [muḥaddithī al-fuqahā'] who try to favour legal rulings derived from solitary chain traditions [ḥadīth āḥād]. The school of the jurists from the Ḥanafīs have a complete and integrative way of understanding and working with Prophetic traditions, in terms of understanding their soundness and weakness, and from the point of their acceptance and rejection. I have stopped briefly to mention some of these points when discussing the traditions related to the beard. Al-Jaṣṣāṣ states, 'I do not know anyone from the jurists who depended upon the way of the Hadith scholars [muḥaddithīn] or considered their foundation [uṣūl].'[1]

There is very little doubt that the formulation of independent judgement [ijtihād muṭlaq] by those who do not have the ability to do so is from one of the main factors that has led to this fanaticism concerning the subject of the beard. It would be more fitting and beneficial to society if we directed our efforts to developing the school, its legal rulings and the formulation of independent judgement by way of extrapolation—as is the way of the school of the jurists.

---

[1] *Sharḥ Mukhtaṣar al-Ṭaḥāwī* (4:244)

7.الدَّعوة للتَّمسُّك بمدرسةِ الفقهاء عند الحنفية في بناء الأحكام على عللها وأصولها؛ لأنَّ هذه العلل والأصول جامعة لعدد كبير من الآيات القرآنية والأحاديث النبوية والآثار عن الصحابة، فهي أحقّ بالتقديم من مدرسة محدثي الفقهاء عند الحنفية التي تعمد للترجيح أحياناً بظاهر حديث آحاد؛ لأنَّ لمدرسة الفقهاء منهج متكامل في التعامل مع الأحاديث من حيث التصحيح والتضعيف والقَبول والردّ ـ عرجت على ذكر بعضه في مناقشة أحاديث اللحية ـ، قال الجصاص[1]: «لا أعلم أحداً من الفقهاء اعتمد طريق المحدثين ولا اعتبر أصولهم».

وإنَّ من أسباب هذا التَّشدُّد في موضوع اللحية هو الاجتهاد المطلق ممن ليس من أهل الاجتهاد، فلو صرفنا جهدنا لتحرير المذاهب ومسائلها والاجتهاد بطريق التَّخريج فيها، كما هو منهج مدرسة الفقهاء؛ لكان أولى وأنفع للمجتمع.

---

[1] في شرح مختصر الطَّحاوي 244:4.

SECTION ONE
THE DERIVATION PRINCIPLES [*UṢŪL AL-ISTINBĀṬ*]

The Prophetic traditions that command one to lengthen the beard (which will be mentioned further on in the treatise) have been transmitted using five different expressions; Ibn 'Abd al-Barr states, 'This has resulted in five narrations: *a'fū, awfū, arkhū, arjū* and *waffirū*; all of them meaning: to leave it as it is.'[1]

Our discussion in the following chapters will be whether the Ḥanafī principles of legal theory [*qawā'id al-uṣūl*] indicate keeping a beard to be necessary or sunna.

Some of the topics that we will try to explore further in the following chapters are: the additional sunnas [*sunan al-zawā'id*] and sunnas of guidance [*sunan al-hudā*] of the Messenger ﷺ, what the command [*amr*] can be built upon, the concept of warning [*wa'īd*] in the command, specifying the generic [*takhṣīṣ al-'ām*], the companions acting contrary to the legal command and the meaning of primordiality [*fiṭra*].

---

[1] *Al-Istidhkār* (3:151)

المبحث الأول

من جهة أصول الاستنباط

وردت روايات الأحاديث في الأمر بإطلاق اللحى بخمسة ألفاظ، وستأتي أثناء البحث، قال ابنُ عبد البر[1]: «فحصل خمس روايات: أعفوا وأوفوا وأرخوا وأرجوا ووفروا، ومعناها كلُّها: تركها على حالها».

وستكون مناقشتنا لها من جهة قواعد الأصول عند الحنفية هل تفيد وجوب اللحية أم السنية، فنطرح قضية سنن الزوائد وسنن الهدى، ومحلّ الأمر، والوعيد في الأمر، وتخصيص العام، ومخالفة الراوي لمرويه، ومخالفة الصحابة للأمر، ومعنى الفطرة، في المطالب الآتية:

CHAPTER ONE
THE BEARD IS FROM THE ADDITIONAL SUNNAS
[*SUNAN AL-ZAWĀ'ID*] OF THE MESSENGER ﷺ

The legal theorists in the Ḥanafī school have categorised the practices of the Messenger ﷺ into two: the sunnas of guidance [*sunan al-hudā*] and the additional sunnas [*sunan al-zawā'id*]. Ṣadr al-Sharī'a states, 'The sunna of guidance when left results in sin and offense; for example: the congregational prayer, the calls to prayer (*adhān* and *iqāma*) and other similar acts. The additional sunnas, however, when left, do not result in sin and offense; for example, the practice of the Messenger ﷺ related to his food, drink, clothing, standing and sitting.'[1]

We find that the sunnas of guidance of the Messenger ﷺ are those things that relate to the establishment of the rites [*sha'ā'ir*] of religion, like the congregational prayer and the call to prayer. However, it is important to be aware that anything that enables or assists in the completion of a necessary [*wājib*] or obligatory [*farḍ*] matter also falls under the same rubric—as, the Sunna is essentially anything through which a necessary component of desired worship [*'ibāda maqṣūda*] like the prayer and Ḥajj can be perfected. Anything through which an obligatory act can be perfected is considered to be necessary [*wājib*]. The Sunna in supporting acts of worship [*'ibādāt ghayr al-maqṣūda*]—for example in the ritual ablution [*wuḍū'*]—is anything through which an obligatory act can be perfected (as there are no necessary acts therein), like the washing of each limb three times.[2]

---

[1] *Al-Tawḍīḥ* (2:248-251), *Fawātiḥ al-Raḥamūt* (1:57) & others
[2] *Ḥāshiya al-Ṭaḥṭāwī 'alā al-Marāqī* (1:71), *al-Hadiyya* (p. 13) & *Majma' al-Anhur* (1:161)

المطلب الأول

اللحية من سنن الزوائد

قسم أصوليو الحنفية السنن إلى قسمين: سنن هدى، وسنن زوائد.

قال صدر الشريعة[1]: «سنَّةُ الهدى: وتركُها يوجب إساءة وكراهية: كالجماعة والأذان والإقامة ونحوها. وسنَّةُ الزَّوائد: وتركها لا يوجب ذلك: كسنن النبي ﷺ في طعامه وشرابه ولباسه وقيامه وقعوده».

حيث جَعل سنن الهدى ما تعلَّق بإقامة شعائر الدِّين كالجماعة والأذان، ويندرج تحتها ما كان طريقاً لتحقيق إكمال الواجبات أو الفروض؛ لأنَّ السُّنَّةَ لإكمال الواجب في العبادات المقصودة كالصَّلاة والحجّ، والواجب لإكمال الفرض فيها، وتكون لإكمال الفرض في العبادات غير المقصودة كالوضوء لعدم وجود واجب فيه، كما في تثليث الغَسل لأعضاء الوضوء[2].

---

(1) ينظر: التوضيح 2: 248-251، وانظر: فواتح الرحموت 1: 57، وغيره.

(2) ينظر: الطحطاوي على المراقي 1: 71، والهدية 13، ومجمع الأنهر 1: 161.

The additional sunnas of the Messenger ﷺ are those things that relate to his natural disposition in matters like his food, drink and clothing. Consequently, some of the desired acts of worship—that do not reach the rank of obligation, necessity, or emphasis in the Sunna—fall under this same rubric. Ibn Nujaym states, 'It is as if they meant by additional sunnas those practices that are not emphasised, and therefore, they are sometimes labelled as sunna, but other times as being recommended [*mustaḥabb*] and at other times as being preferred [*mandūb*]. However, the jurists have differentiated between each of these three saying, "Whatever the Messenger ﷺ did persistently only leaving it sometimes—without an excuse—is considered a sunna. Whatever he ﷺ did, but not persistently, is recommended if the performance and leaving of the act are equal; and it is preferred [*mandūb*] if his ﷺ leaving of the act is more than his ﷺ performance of the act, such that he ﷺ may have performed the act simply one or two times." However, the legal theorists do not differentiate between the preferred and recommended.'[1]

Nonetheless, Ibn ʿĀbidīn brings to attention the fact that, even though the additional sunnas of the Messenger ﷺ are considered to be customary [*ʿurf*], doing them with sincere intention propels them to the sphere of worship [and thus one is rewarded for their performance]. Likewise, the consistency of the Messenger ﷺ upon some additional sunnas in the realm of worship makes them from his customary practice;[2] and so he states that, 'There is no difference between the optional [*nafl*] and additional sunnas—in terms of the legal ruling—as there is no offense in leaving either one of them. However, the difference is that the former is from the acts of worship and the latter from custom. However, it has been mentioned that the difference between acts of worship and customs is a sincere intention—as is mentioned in *al-Kāfī* and other places. All the actions of the Messenger ﷺ can be included in this as has been clarified in its section.'

---

[1] *Fatḥ al-Ghaffār* (p. 66)
[2] [That is, an act he ﷺ did persistently]

وجَعل سنن الزَّوائد ما تعلّق بأفعال النَّبيّ ﷺ الجبليّة من أكل وشرب ولباس، ويندرج تحتها بعض الأفعال والأقوال في العبادات المقصودة مما لم يبلغ رتبة الفرضية والوجوب والسُّنَّة المؤكَّدة، قال ابنُ نُجيم[1]: «كأنَّهم أرادوا بسنن الزَّوائد السُّنن التي ليست بمؤكدةٍ، فتارةً يُطلقون عليها اسم السُّنَّة، وتارةً المستحبّ، وتارةً المندوب، وقد فَرَّق الفقهاء بين الثَّلاثة فقالوا: ما واظب النَّبيُّ ﷺ على فعله مع ترك ما بلا عذر سُنَّة، وما لم يواظب مُستحبٌّ إن استوى فعلُه وتركُه ﷺ، ومندوبٌ إن ترجَّح تركُه على فعله ﷺ بأن فعله مَرَّةً أو مَرَّتين، والأصوليون لم يفرقوا بين المستحبّ والمندوب».

ونبَّه ابنُ عابدين على أنَّ سننَ الزَّوائد وإن كانت من العادات لكن اشتمالها على الإخلاص يدرجها في العبادات، وكذلك مواظبة النَّبيّ ﷺ على بعض الزَّوائد من العبادات يجعلها من عادته ﷺ، فقال: «لا فرق بين النَّفل وسنن الزَّوائد من حيث الحكم؛ لأنَّه لا يُكره ترك كلّ منهما، وإنَّما الفرق كون الأول من العبادات والثاني من العادات، لكن أُورد عليه أنَّ الفرق بين العبادة والعادة هو النيَّة المتضمنة للإخلاص، كما في «الكافي» وغيره، وجميع أفعاله ﷺ مشتملة عليها كما بين في محلّه.

---

[1] ينظر: فتح الغفار ص66.

'And I say, many have used, "the prolongation of his ﷺ recitation, his bowing and prostration," as an example of additional sunna—and there is no doubt that these are considered from the acts of worship. Therefore, the meaning of additional sunnas being customary is that: the Messenger ﷺ persisted upon it until it became his custom and thus was never left—except on a few occasions, as the Sunna is a path that is tread in the religion—it is in itself considered to be worship, and has been named customary for the reason we have mentioned. Also, because it is not from those things that perfectively complete religion or from its holy rites, then it was given the name of *additional* sunnas as opposed to the sunnas of *guidance* which are emphasised and close to being necessary, with the one leaving it being considered sinful as leaving it is seen to be from belittling religion.'[1]

From those actions that are from his ﷺ natural disposition, is eating with the right hand—which is recommended.[2] Ibn Nujaym states, 'It is fine for one to assist himself with his left hand because his ﷺ persistence upon something does not necessarily result in it becoming a sunna, unless it was performed as an act of worship. If it was performed as a customary act then it is considered recommended or preferred, but not sunna, like wearing a long Arabian garment and eating with the right hand. The persistence of the Messenger ﷺ in eating with the right hand comes under the second category, and is thus not regarded to be from the level of a sunna act.'[3]

---

[1] *Radd al-Muḥtār* (1:103)

[2] Al-ʿIrāqī states, 'Eating and what it involves, and eating with the right hand, are considered by most of the scholarly folk to be recommended. This opinion has been clearly expressed by al-Ghazālī and al-Nawawī. Al-Shāfiʿī in *al-Umm* regarded it to be necessary, and likewise al-Ḥāfiẓ in *al-Fatḥ* has preferred its necessity due to traditions related in [Ṣaḥīḥ] *Muslim* that warn those who eat with their left hand.' (*ʿUmda al-Qārī* (9:654), *Takmila Fatḥ al-Mulhim* (4:4) & others)

[3] *Al-Baḥr al-Rāʾiq* (1:29) & others

وقد مثَّلوا لسُنَّة الزَّوائد أيضاً: «بتطويله ﷺ القراءة والركوع والسجود»، ولا شَكَّ في كون ذلك عبادة، وحينئذٍ فمعنى كون سُنَّة الزَّوائد عادة: أنَّ النَّبيَّ ﷺ واظب عليها حتى صارت عادة له ولم يتركها إلا أحيانا؛ لأنَّ السُّنة هي الطَّريقة المسلوكة في الدِّين، فهي في نفسها عبادة، وسُميت عادةً لما ذكرنا، ولما لم تكن من مكمِّلات الدِّين وشعائره سُميت سنة الزَّوائد، بخلاف سُنَّة الهدى، وهي السُّنن المؤكَّدة القريبة من الواجب التي يُضلَّل تاركها؛ لأنَّ تركَها استخفافٌ بالدِّين...». [1]

ومن الأفعال الجبليّة: الأكل باليمين، فهو مستحبٌّ [2]، قال ابنُ نجيم [3]: «لا بأس بأن يستعين بيساره؛ لأنَّ مواظبته ﷺ لا تفيد السُّنية إلا إذا كانت على سبيل العبادةً وأما إذا كانت على سبيل العادة فتفيد الاستحباب والنَّدب لا السُّنية: كلبس الثوب والأكل باليمين، ومواظبة النبي ﷺ على التيامن كانت من قبيل الثاني فلا تفيد السُّنية».

---

[1] ينظر: رد المحتار 1: 103.

[2] قال العراقي: الأكل مما يليه والأكل باليمين حمله أكثر أصحابنا على الندب، وبه صرَّح الغزالي والنووي، ونص الشافعي في الأم على وجوبه، ورجح الحافظ في الفتح 9: 522 الوجوب؛ لما في أحاديث مسلم من الوعيد على الأكل بالشمال. ينظر: عمدة القاري 9: 654، وتكملة فتح الملهم 4: 4، وغيرهما.

[3] ينظر: البحر الرائق 1: 29، وغيره.

This is despite the presence of a Prophetic command; the Messenger of Allah ﷺ said, 'If any one of you eats, then let him eat with his right [hand], and if anyone of you drinks then let him drink with his right [hand], as Satan eats with his left [hand] and drinks with his left [hand].'[1]

With regards to the tradition: 'A man ate with the Messenger of Allah ﷺ with his left hand, so he ﷺ (the Messenger) said to him, "Eat with your right [hand]," to which he replied, "I cannot," whereupon he ﷺ said, "May you not be able to! It was arrogance that prevented him, and thus did not raise it up to his mouth."'[2]

Then, the Messenger ﷺ makes a prayer against him, praying that he never has the ability to use his right hand; however, it may be that he came to know—whether by revelation or other means—that the man had actually lied with regards to his excuse, and therefore, the only reason that prevented him [from raising his right hand] was his arrogance. Qāḍī 'Iyāḍ was of the firm opinion that he was from the hypocrites.[3]

All in all, it is noteworthy that the beard is not in any way more significant than eating with the right hand.

In an attempt to solidify and support this idea, another example mentioned by some of the authors of the relied upon legal manuals [*mutūn*] in the school is the washing of the limbs by beginning with the right side [*tayāmun*][4] when making ritual ablution. This is recommended and not sunna, despite the Messenger of Allah ﷺ being persistent upon it, and his ﷺ statement, 'When you perform the ritual ablution, then start with your right side.'[5]

---

[1] *Ṣaḥīḥ Muslim* (3:1598), *Ṣaḥīḥ Ibn Ḥibbān* (12:30) & others
[2] *Ṣaḥīḥ Muslim* (3:1599) & others
[3] *Takmila Fatḥ al-Mulhim* (4:6) & others
[4] *Al-Wiqāya* (2:24), *al-Niqāya* (1:57), *al-Multaqā* & others
[5] *Ṣaḥīḥ Ibn Ḥibbān* (3:370) (Shaykh Shu'ayb al-Arnā'ūṭ states, 'It is a sound tradition.') & *Sunan Ibn Mājah* (1:141)

وهذا الاستحباب رغم وجود الأمر النَّبويّ قال ﷺ: «إذا أكل أحدكم فليأكل بيمينه، وإذا شرب فليشرب بيمينه، فإنَّ الشَّيطان يأكل بشماله ويشرب بشماله»[1].

وما روي: «أنَّ رجلاً أكل عند رسول الله ﷺ بشماله، فقال: كل بيمينك، قال: لا أستطيع، قال: لا استطعت، ما منعه إلا الكبر، قال: فما رفعها إلى فيه»[2]، فدعا الرسول ﷺ عليه بأن لا يتمكن أبداً من استخدام اليمين، فلعلَّه لما عَلِم بالوحي أو غيره بأنَّه كذب في هذا الاعتذار، ولم يحمله على ذلك إلا الكبر، وجزم القاضي عياض بأنَّه كان منافقاً[3].

وليس الحال في اللحية بأقوى من الأكل باليمين.

ومثال آخر في تأكيد هذه الفكرة ورسوخها في المذهب: ذكر أصحاب المتون التيامن[4] في غسل الأعضاء من مستحبات الوضوء لا من سننه، مع مواظبة النَّبيّ ﷺ على ذلك، وقوله ﷺ: (إذا توضَّأتم فابدؤوا بميامنكم)[5].

---

[1] ينظر: صحيح مسلم 3: 1598، وصحيح ابن حبان 12: 30، وغيرهما.

[2] ينظر: صحيح مسلم 3: 1599، وغيره.

[3] ينظر: تكملة فتح الملهم 4: 6، وغيره.

[4] ينظر: الوقاية 2: 24، والنقاية 1: 57، والملتقى 1: 16، وغيرها.

[5] ينظر: صحيح ابن حبان 3: 370، وقال الشيخ شعيب: حديث صحيح، وسنن ابن ماجه 1: 141.

Ṣadr al-Sharīʿa complies by stating, 'The Sunna is whatever the Messenger ﷺ was persistent upon but left sometimes. If the persistence was with regards to an act of worship, then it is from the sunnas of guidance. However, if it was with regards to culture or customary matters then it is from the additional sunnas, like the wearing of Arabian garments, eating with the right hand, entering with the right foot first and the like. Our discussion is about the first category; however, the persistence of the Messenger ﷺ upon using the right side is regarded to be from the second category.'[1]

The following tradition related by ʿĀʾisha affirms the fact that beginning acts with the right side was from the customs of the Messenger of Allah ﷺ; ʿĀʾisha states, 'The Messenger of Allah ﷺ liked beginning with the right side when wearing his ﷺ sandals, when walking, when making ablution and in all of his ﷺ affairs.'[2]

Even when there is a command to begin with the right side—and the actions of the Messenger ﷺ whilst making the ritual ablution corroborate that—the legal status is dropped from being sunna to recommended, like the other actions of ablution. This is ultimately due to it being placed under the rubric of customs and not worship.

---

[1] *ʿUmda al-Riʿāya* (1:308)
[2] *Ṣaḥīḥ al-Bukhārī* (168) & *Ṣaḥīḥ Muslim* (268)

فأجاب صدر الشريعة: «السُّنَّةُ ما واظبَ عليه النَّبيُّ ﷺ مع التَّركِ أحياناً، فإن كانت المواظبةُ المذكورةُ على سبيلِ العبادةِ فسننُ الهدى، وإن كانت على سبيلِ العادةِ فسننُ الزَّوائد، كلبسِ الثِّياب، والأكل باليمين، وتقديمِ الرِّجلِ اليُمْنى في الدُّخول، ونحو ذلك، وكلامُنا في الأوَّل، ومواظبةُ النَّبيِّ ﷺ على التَّيامنِ كانت من قبيلِ الثَّاني»[1].

ويشهد إلى أنَّ التيامن كان عادة للنبي ﷺ: ما روي عن عائشة رضي الله قالت: (كان رسول الله ﷺ يحب التَّيمُّن في تنعُّله، وترجُّله، وطُهوره، وفي شأنه كله)[2].

فمع وجود الأمر بالتَّيامن، وكذلك فعله في داخل الوضوء، إلا أنَّ رتبتَه نزلت عن بقيت أفعال الوضوء من السُّنيَّة إلى الاستحباب؛ لكونه يندرج تحت العادات لا العبادات.

---

[1] ينظر: عمدة الرعاية 1: 308.

[2] ينظر: صحيح البخاري ر168، وصحيح مسلم ر268.

And if we consider the matter of the beard, we will not find that its status is higher than that; it is not an act of worship but instead one of custom. Therefore, it falls under the additional sunnas rather than [the sunnas] of guidance. The additional sunnas are those generally referred to as being recommended. Al-Laknawī said: "The additional sunna is what was consistently practiced as a custom. It is equivalent to the recommended in that one is rewarded for it but not blamed for leaving it. Persisting in beginning with the right side is of the second category, so it is not a confirmed [mu'akkada] sunna but rather recommended [mustaḥabb]."[1]

As a result of this discussion, we can evaluate that the beard and the lengthening of it would be deemed to be from the recommended acts. However, this does not negate the statement of some who said that, 'The sunna-length is a fist-length,' as the jurists are usually quite lenient with using the term sunna to actually mean recommended, and vice versa, as can be identified in the sunnas and recommendations of wuḍū'. This ruling is derived by employing *this* causal factor only; though, it may be possible by juxtaposing it with other causal factors—as will follow—for it to reach the level of an emphasised sunna; and Allah ﷻ knows best.

---

[1] *'Umda al-Ri'āya* (1:309)

وإن تأمَّلنا الأمر في اللحية فلن نجد أنَّ رتبته أعلى من ذلك، فلن تكون عبادة، بل هي من العادات فحسب، وبالتالي تلحق بسنن الزَّوائد لا الهدى، وسُنن الزَّوائد هي التي يُعبَّر عنها بالاستحباب عادة، قال اللكنوي[1]: «السنةُ الزائدة، وهي التي واظبَ عليها على سبيلِ العادة، وهي تساوي الاستحبابَ في أنَّه يثابُ عليها ولا يلامُ تاركها، والمواظبةُ على التَّيامنِ من القسمِ الثَّاني، فلا يكون سنَّة مؤكَّدة، بل مُستحبّاً».

فعلى هذه المناقشة تكون اللِّحية في نفسها وإطالتها من المستحبّات، وهذا لا يخالف قولهم: «القدر المسنون مقدار القبضة»؛ لأنَّ الفقهاء يتساهلون في إطلاق كل من السُّنة على المستحب والمستحب على السُّنة، كما في سنن الوضوء ومستحباته، وهذا الحكم من خلال هذه العلَّة، ويمكن باقتران علل أُخرى معها ـ كما سيأتي ـ تصل إلى رتبة السنّة المؤكدة، والله أعلم.

---

(1) ينظر: عمدة الرعاية 1: 309.

CHAPTER TWO
CONTEXTUAL FACTORS REGARDING THE BASIS OF THE LEGAL COMMAND [*MAHALL AL-AMR*]

The majority of the previous studies have used the maxim: '*The command implies necessity [al-amr yufid al-wujūb]*' indiscriminately, without taking into consideration any contextual issues which would move it away from implying necessity.

One of these contextual issues is the very critical question of what the legal command can be built upon. This is a matter that many are unfortunately ignorant of when examining the legal command and thereby deciding indiscriminately that it implies necessity—which is the well-known ruling. Little attention is paid to whether the basis of the legal command can actually permit or allow the ruling of necessity since the Sacred Law [*sharī'a*] has been revealed to promote ease and lighten difficulty. Allah ﷻ says, ❴*God wants ease for you, not hardship,*❵[1] and, ❴*He has chosen you and placed no hardship in your religion.*❵[2] These are some of the maxims that legal rulings are generally built upon, as can be seen in the maxim: '*hardship procures ease [al-mashaqqa tajlib al-taysīr].*' The following are some examples of 'hardship procuring ease':

The Messenger of Allah ﷺ commanded in various traditions to pray in congregation in the mosque; Abū Hurayra ؓ narrates, 'A blind man came to the Messenger ﷺ and said, "Messenger of Allah, there is no guide available to direct me to the mosque," and so, he asked the Messenger ﷺ for a concession, such that he would be allowed to pray in his house, to which the Messenger of Allah ﷺ granted him the concession. When the man turned away, he ﷺ called him and asked, "Do you hear the call to prayer?" He replied saying, "Yes," to which the Messenger ﷺ said, "Respond to it."'[3]

---

[1] [*The Qur'an, A new translation by M. A. S. Abdel Haleem,*
The Cow, 2:185 (p. 20)]
[2] [Ibid., The Pilgrimage, 22:78 (p. 214)]
[3] *Ṣaḥīḥ Muslim* (1:452)

المطلب الثاني
قرينة محلّ الأمر

إنَّ عامة الدِّراسات السابقة عندما طرحت قاعدة: الأمر يفيد الوجوب، طبقتها على إطلاقها بدون النظر إلى أي قرائن في الباب تكون صارفة له عن الوجوب.

فمن القرائن المهمَّة هي قضية محلّ الأمر، فهذه مسألة هامّة جداً يغفل عنها عندما ينظر للأمر بأنَّه يفيد الوجوب كما هو مشهور، ولا ينتبه هل محلّ الأمر يحتمل الوجوب أم لا؟ لأنَّ الشريعة نزلت للتيسير ورفع الحرج: {يريد الله بكم اليسر ولا يريد بكم العسر}، و{ما جعل عليكم في الدين من حرج}، فهذه قواعد تنبني عليها الأحكام الشرعية عموماً، كما في قاعدة: «المشقة تجلب التيسير».

ومن أمثلة ذلك:

أمر النبي ﷺ بالجماعة في المسجد في أحاديث عديدة منها: عن أبي هريرة ﷺ قال: «أتى النبي ﷺ رجل أعمى، فقال: يا رسول الله، إنَّه ليس لي قائد يقودني إلى المسجد، فسأل رسول الله ﷺ أن يرخص له، فيصلي في بيته، فرخص له، فلمّا ولى، دعاه، فقال: هل تسمع النداء بالصلاة؟ قال: نعم، قال: فأجب»[1].

---

[1] ينظر: صحيح مسلم 1: 452.

On the authority of Abū Hurayra ﷺ who said, 'The Messenger of Allah ﷺ said, "By Him ﷻ in whose hand is my soul, I had intended to command someone to gather firewood, then command for the call to prayer to be made, and then command someone to lead the prayer; I would then go from behind and burn the houses down of anyone who did not attend the congregational prayer. By Him ﷻ in whose hands is my soul, if any one of them knew there would be a bone with some meat remaining upon it or the two hooves of a sheep or goat, he would have attended the *'ishā'* prayer."'[1]

Despite the command to pray the prayer in the mosque and the presence of serious warnings, we find that the relied upon [*mu'tamad*] position in the Ḥanafī school is of the congregational prayer being sunna—and this is the opinion of the majority of the considered legal manuals.[2] The rationale behind this is that the basis upon which the ruling has been built cannot allow for it to be necessary, due to the immense difficulty that would be caused to the Muslim populace, by making it necessary to pray every prescribed daily prayer in the mosque.

---

[1] *Ṣaḥīḥ al-Bukhārī* (1:231)

[2] This is what the author of *al-Wiqāya* (2:130), Maḥmūd Burhān al-Sharī'a al-Maḥbūbī is upon, and it is also the opinion al-Qudūrī has chosen in his *Mukhtaṣar* (p. 10). The authors of *al-Hidāya* (1:55), *al-Īḍāḥ* (back of 5th folio), *al-Mukhtār* (1:78), *al-Kanz* (p. 17), *al-Multaqā* (1:15), *al-Durar* (1:84) and *al-Tanwīr* (1:371) are also of this opinion. Shurunbulālī has also verified this opinion in his commentary upon *Durar al-Ḥukkām* (1:84). The opinion that calls for its necessity is merely an isolated opinion in the school that is preferred by Ibn Nujaym, the author of *al-Baḥr al-Rā'iq* (1:365), and by al-Samarqandī, the author of *al-Tuḥfa* (1:227), where he states, 'Some of our companions have called it an emphasised sunna but both mean the same.'

1.2 قرينة محلّ الأمر

وعن أبي هريرة ﵁، قال ﷺ: «والذي نفسي بيده لقد هممت أن آمر بحطب فيحطب ثم آمر بالصلاة فيؤذن لها ثم آمر رجلاً فيؤم الناس، ثم أخالف إلى رجال فأحرق عليهم بيوتهم، والذي نفسي بيده لو يعلم أحدهم أنَّه يجد عرقاً سميناً أو مرماتين حسنتين لشهد العشاء»[1].

فرغم الأمر بالصَّلاة في المسجد وكلِّ هذا الوعيد الشَّديد نجد أنَّ المعتمد في المذهب الحنفيّ أنَّ صلاة الجماعة سنةّ، واختاره عامة المتون المعتبرة في المذهب[2]، والسَّببُ في ذلك: أنَّ المحلَّ لا يحتمل الوجوب؛ لما فيه من التكليف الشَّديد على المسلمين بوجوب صلاة المكتوبات في المساجد.

---

[1] ينظر: صحيح البخاري 1: 231.

[2] وهو ما ذهب إليه صاحب الوقاية2: 130، واختاره القدوري في مختصره ص10، وصاحب الهداية1: 55، والإيضاح ق16/ب، والمختار1: 78، والكنز ص13، والملتقى 1: 15، والدرر 1: 84، والتنوير 1: 371، وصححه الشرنبلالي في حاشيته على الدرر 1: 84، والقول بالوجوب مجرد قول في المذهب رجَّحه صاحب البحر1: 365، واختاره صاحب التحفة1: 227 وقال: وقد سماها بعض أصحابنا سنة مؤكدة وكلاهما واحدة.

If it was necessary, then there would not remain any actual difference between the prescribed prayers and the Friday prayer, which is necessary for one to pray in a mosque. Allah ﷻ says, ❴*When the call to prayer is made on the day of congregation, hurry towards the reminder of God.*❵[1] In this verse, there would have been no need to specify the Friday prayer as it would have become necessary if the call to prayer was made for any prayer.

And where is the beard in relation to the prayer, when the latter is one of the desired objectives of religion. Despite being so, it is considered to be sunna, and from the sunnas of guidance, just as the Messenger of Allah ﷺ informed us: on the authority of 'Abdullah b. Mas'ūd ﷺ who said, 'I have seen a time where no one stayed away from the prayer except a hypocrite whose hypocrisy was well known, or an ill person. However, if the ill person could walk between two people (with the help of two persons with one on each side) he would come to prayer.' And he [further] said, 'The Messenger of Allah ﷺ taught us the sunnas of guidance, among which is prayer in a mosque, in which the call to prayer is called.'[2] And while this latter issue is from the sunnas of guidance, the beard is from the additional sunnas.

Following are some examples which illustrate how the basis of the legal command is considered:

Allah ﷻ says, ❴*You who believe, when you contract a debt for a stated term, put it down in writing.*❵[3] The Qur'anic command here to write down the appointed term for debts is regarded as being recommended and is seen as counsel, but it is not considered to be necessary.[4] This is because the writing down of transactions every time they occur is thought to be immensely difficult.

---

[1] [*The Qur'an, A new translation by M. A. S. Abdel Haleem,*
The Day of Congregation, 62:9 (p. 372)]
[2] *Ṣaḥīḥ Muslim* (1:453)
[3] [*The Qur'an, A new translation by M. A. S. Abdel Haleem,*
The Cow, 2:282 (p. 32)]
[4] *Badā'i' al-Ṣanā'i'* (2:252)

2.1 قرينة محلّ الأمر

ولو كانت واجبة لم يبقَ فرقاً عملياً بين الصلاة المكتوبة وبين صلاة الجمعة التي يلزم أداؤها في المسجد، قال تعالى: ﴿إذا نودي للصلاة من يوم الجمعة فاسعوا إلى ذكر الله﴾، ولم يكن حاجة لتخصيص صلاة الجمعة، ولزم أن يكون إذا نودي للصلاة مطلقاً.

فأين الأمر باللِّحية من الأمر بالصلاة، التي هي من الأمور المقصودة في الدِّين، وهي مع ذلك سُنّة، فهي من سنن الهدى، كما أخبر النبي ﷺ، قال ابن مسعود ﷺ: «لقد رأيتنا وما يتخلف عن الصَّلاة إلا منافق قد علم نفاقه، أو مريض إن كان المريض ليمشي بين رجلين حتى يأتي الصلاة، وقال: إنَّ رسول الله ﷺ علمنا سنن الهدى، وإنَّ من سُنن الهدى الصَّلاة في المسجد الذي يؤذن فيه»[1]، في حين أنَّ اللِّحية من سُنن الزَّوائد.

ومن أمثلة مراعاة محل الأمر، قال تعالى: ﴿يَا أَيهَا الَّذين آمنُوا إِذا تداينتم بدين إِلَى أجل مُسَمّى فاكتبوه﴾ الْبَقَرَة 282، فهذا الأمر القرآني يفيد الاستحباب والإرشاد لا الوجوب[2]؛ لأنَّ الكتابة في المعاوضات مطلقاً تكليف شديد.

---

[1] ينظر: صحيح مسلم 1: 453.

[2] ينظر: بدائع الصنائع 2: 252.

Likewise, the witnessing of all contracts except the marriage contract is recommended, despite the presence of a command. Allah ﷻ says, ❨*Call in two men as witnesses,*❩[1] and He ﷻ says with regards to the issue of a revocable divorce [*ruj'a*], ❨*Call two just witnesses from your people.*❩[2] Al-Kāsānī states, 'There is no disagreement that the witnessing of all contracts is not a condition [of validity], however, it is recommended and preferred.'[3]

The basis of the legal command is a factor which prevents the command from inferring the ruling of necessity. The intention of this discussion is for one to be aware that not every command implies necessity, but rather it is critical that one examines any contextual factor surrounding it, especially the basis of the legal command: can it permit the command to infer necessity or not? It will become clear during the following discussions that the basis of the command in this case (which is the beard) cannot allow the ruling of necessity, due to the beard not actually being from the primary objectives of religion; and Allah ﷻ knows best.

If we were to derive the ruling from this foundation [*aṣl*], then there is nothing preventing the beard from being an emphasised sunna [*sunna mu'akkada*].

---

[1] [*The Qur'an, A new translation by M. A. S. Abdel Haleem,*
The Cow, 2:282 (p. 32)]
[2] [Ibid., Divorce, 65:2 (p. 378)]
[3] *Badā'i' al-Ṣanā'i'* (2:252)

وكذلك الإشهاد على سائر العقود ما عدا النكاح فهو على الاستحباب، رغم وجود الأمر، قال تعالى: {واستشهدوا شهيدين من رجالكم}[البقرة: 282] وقال ﷺ في باب الرَّجعة {وأشهدوا ذوي عدل منكم}[الطلاق: 2]، قال الكاساني[1]: «ولا خلاف في أنَّ الإشهاد في سائر العقود ليس بشرط، ولكنَّه مندوب إليه ومستحب».

ومحلُّ الأمر يندرج تحت القرائن التي تكون صارفة للأمر عن إفادة الوجوب، والمقصود هاهنا: التنبيه على أنَّه ليس كل أمر مطلقاً محمول على الوجوب، بل لا بُدَّ من الالتفات للقرائن حوله لا سيما المحلّ، هل يحتمل الوجوب أو لا؟ وسيظهر معنا فيما يأتي أنَّ محلّ الأمر في البحثـ وهو اللحية ـ لا يحتمل الوجوب؛ لعدم كونها مقصوداً أصليّاً في الدِّين، والله أعلم.

وعلى هذا الأصل لا يمتنع أن تكون اللُّحية سنة مؤكدة.

---

[1] ينظر: بدائع الصنائع 2: 252.

CHAPTER THREE
A LACK OF WARNING [*WA ʿĪD*] WITH REGARDS TO
THE COMMAND TO KEEP A BEARD

One of the well-known definitions for necessity is: 'an action whose performance is more fitting than its non-performance with a command to not leave its performance established by indecisive evidence [*dalīl ẓannī*].' Whereas the sunna is defined as: 'an action whose performance is more fitting than its non-performance, *without* the presence of any prohibition when leaving the act; although, this is only if the act is from those things that are objectively sought and followed in the religion; otherwise, it is considered to be optional [*nafl*] or recommended.'[1]

This definition distinguishes between the necessary and the sunna by stipulating the presence of a prohibition when leaving the act. That prohibition is communicated by warnings of punishment with Hellfire if the act is left. The sunna, on the other hand, encourages one to perform the act, but without any such warnings of punishment with Hellfire.

Consequently, what has been related with regards to the beard from the Messenger of Allah ﷺ is from recommendation and encouragement, as to keep a beard is regarded as the most complete outward appearance for a male. On the authority of Ibn ʿUmar ؓ who said, 'The Messenger ﷺ commanded to shorten the moustaches and leave the beard.'[2]

The Messenger ﷺ did not, upon leaving the beard, infer any punishment of Hellfire. Therefore, according to the previous definitions, the beard is closer to the definition of the emphasised sunna and not necessity, as the traditions call towards encouragement and preference rather than punishment.

---

[1] *Al-Tawḍīḥ* (2:248-251), *Fawātiḥ al-Raḥamūt* (1:57) & others
[2] *Ṣaḥīḥ Muslim* (1:222)

المطلب الثَّالث

عدم الوعيد في الأمر باللحية

من التعريفات المشهورة للواجب: وهو ما كان الفعل أولى من الترك مع منع الترك الثابت بدليل ظني، أمّا السنة: وهو ما كان الفعل أولى من الترك بلا منع الترك، وهذا إذا كان الفعل طريقة مسلوكة في الدِّين، وإلا فنفل ومندوب[1].

فهذا التعريف يميز الواجب عن السنة بوجود المنع من الترك، وذلك بالوعيد في العقاب بالنَّار إن ترك، أمّا السُّنّة فهي تشمل على جانب التَّرغيب بالفعل بلا وعيد بالعقاب بالنار.

وما ورد في اللحية عن النَّبيِّ ﷺ من بابالندب والترغيب فيها؛ لأنَّها الصِّفة الأكمل للرَّجل، فعن ابن عمر ﵄ قال: (أمر ﷺ بإحفاء الشوارب، وإعفاء اللِّحية)[2].

ولم يُرتّب النَّبيِّ ﷺ على ترك اللِّحية عقاباً من نار، فكانت اللحيةُ على التَّعريف السابق أقرب للسُّنّة المؤكدة لا للوجوب؛ لاشتمال الأحاديث على التَّرغيب والأَوليّة لا العقاب.

---

[1] ينظر: التوضيح 2: 248-251، وانظر: فواتح الرحموت 1: 57، وغيره.

[2] ينظر: صحيح مسلم 1: 222.

CHAPTER FOUR
SPECIFYING THE GENERIC [*TAKHṢĪṢ AL-ʿUMŪM*]
THAT HAS BEEN TRANSMITTED
WITH REGARDS TO THE BEARD

It is well known in the Ḥanafī school that each and every component of the generic [*ʿām*] is regarded as definitive [*qaṭʿī*] before it is specified. However, after it has been specified then it becomes presumed [*ẓannī*].[1] Therefore, the affirmed command present in: *aʿfū, awfū, arkhū, arjū and waffirū*, with regards to the beard is definitive. On the authority of Ibn ʿUmar ﷺ who said, 'The Messenger of Allah ﷺ said, "Cut your moustaches short and lengthen [*aʿfū*] your beards."'[2]

However, through the actions and speech of the Messenger ﷺ that has been related to us, we see examples that imply specificity, as in shortening the beard from both its length and width. Abū Quḥāfa ﷺ relates that, 'He was brought to the Messenger of Allah ﷺ whilst his beard had grown in length and width, and the Messenger ﷺ said, "If only you were to take from it," and he ﷺ pointed with his ﷺ hand towards the ends of his ﷺ beard.'[3]

---

[1] *Khulāṣa al-Afkār* (p. 20)
[2] *Ṣaḥīḥ al-Bukhārī* (7:160) & *Ṣaḥīḥ Muslim* (1:222), whose words are: ʿaḥfū al-shawārib...'
[3] *Āthār Abū Yūsuf* (p. 234) & *Musnad Abū Ḥanīfa* (transmitted by al-Ḥaṣkafī)

المطلب الرابع

تخصيص العموم الوارد في اللِّحية

معلومٌ أنَّ العامَّ عند الحنفيّة قطعيٌّ في تناول أفراده قبل التَّخصيص، أمّا بعد التَّخصيص فيكون ظنيّاً[1]، فالأمرُ الثَّابت من: أعفوا وأوفوا وأرخوا وأرجوا ووفروا، يثبت في مدلول اللِّحى على سبيل القطع، فعن ابن عمر ﷺ قال ﷺ: «أنهكوا الشَّوارب وأعفوا اللِّحى»[2].

وورد في قول النَّبيّ ﷺ وفعله ما يدلّ على التَّخصيص بأن يؤخذ من عرض اللحية وطولها، فعن أبي قحافة ﷺ أنَّه أتى به النَّبيّ ﷺ ولحيته قد انتشرت فقال: «لو أخذتم وأشار بيده إلى نواحي لحيته»[3].

---

[1] ينظر: خلاصة الأفكار ص20.

[2] ينظر: صحيح البخاري7: 160، وصحيح مسلم1: 222، ولفظه: (أحفوا الشوارب...).

[3] ينظر: الآثار لأبي يوسف ص234، ومسند أبي حنيفة رواية رواية الحصكفي (ر7).

In addition, on the authority of ʿUmar b. Hārūn, narrating from Usāma b. Zayd, who narrates from ʿUmar b. Shuʿayb, who narrates from his father, who narrates from his grandfather ﷺ that, 'The Messenger of Allah ﷺ used to trim his beard both from its length and width.'[1]

This specification ultimately removes the text from its definitiveness to presumption; subsequently shifting the derived ruling to a lesser status. Thus, if the definitive text inferred necessity, a presumptive one would, for example, infer sunna.

To follow are narrations related from the companions ﷺ, with regards to how they trimmed their beard, thereby removing the text from its generality. As long as trimming the beard is extensively affirmed, to determine *how much* is trimmed is an issue which ultimately oscillates between sunna and preference [*istiḥbāb*] from one perspective, and from another perspective it is a matter which varies from one custom to another depending on the culture and tradition of a people, and Allah ﷺ knows best.

---

[1] *Sunan al-Tirmidhī* (5:94). Al-Tirmidhī states, 'This is an odd [*gharīb*] tradition. I heard Muḥammad b. Ismāʿīl say, "ʿUmar b. Hārūn was fit for narrating traditions, I do not know any tradition narrated by him which does not have a foundation"—or said—"or that he is the only one who transmits it, except this tradition: '...that the Messenger of Allah ﷺ used to trim his beard both from its length and width.' We have not heard this tradition except from the narration of ʿUmar b. Hārūn." I saw him have a good opinion of ʿUmar; I also heard Qutayba say, "ʿUmar b. Hārūn was a bearer of Prophetic traditions."'

1.4 تخصيص العموم الوارد في اللِّحية

وعن عمر بن هارون عن أسامة بن زيد عن عمرو بن شعيب عن أبيه عن جده ﷺ: «أنَّ النَّبيَّ ﷺ كان يأخذ من لحيته من عرضها وطولها»[1].

وهذا التخصيص يُخرج النصّ عن قطعيته إلى الظَّنّ، فتقل رتبة الحكم المأخوذ إلى درجة أقل، فلو كان في قطعيته يفيد الوجوب ففي ظنيته يفيد السُّنية مثلاً.

وسيأتي نصوص عن الصَّحابة ﷺ في إخراج النَّصّ عن عمومه بأخذهم من لحاهم.

وطالما أنَّ أصل الأخذ ثابت بطريقة مستفيضة، صار التَّقدير بهيئةٍ منه دون هيئة مسألةٌ تدور بين السُّنية والاستحباب من جهةٍ، ومتفاوتةٌ من عرفٍ إلى عرفٍ على حسب عادات النَّاس من جهة أخرى، والله أعلم.

---

[1] ينظر: سنن الترمذي 5: 94، وقال الترمذي: هذا حديث غريب، وسمعت محمد بن إسماعيل، يقول: «عمر بن هارون مقارب الحديث لا أعرف له حديثاً ليس له أصل – أو قال – ينفرد به، إلا هذا الحديث: كان النبي ﷺ يأخذ من لحيته من عرضها وطولها، لا نعرفه إلا من حديث عمر بن هارون، ورأيته حسن الرأي في عمر: وسمعت قتيبة، يقول: عمر بن هارون كان صاحب حديث».

CHAPTER FIVE
THE NARRATOR ACTING CONTRARY
TO HIS OWN NARRATION REGARDING THE BEARD

In the Ḥanafī school, the narrator acting contrary to what he has narrated lowers the weight of the narration, since he has contradicted it *after* having narrated it. In this situation, we consider what he actually did and *not* what he narrated. Essentially, the upright [*'adl*] and trustworthy [*mu'taman*] narrator acting contrary to a narration that he has related from the Messenger of Allah ﷺ points towards the fact that he (the narrator) believes, according to his understanding, that the initial ruling has either been abrogated, or that there may be some type of inconsistency, or that the tradition has been specified in some way for a certain situation, or that the narration is not fully established, or to some other valid reasoning[1] for not acting upon the tradition. It is crucial to recognise that if his contradiction of the tradition was due to a lack of concern, carelessness or an indifference to it, then he would fall from his lofty position [of being a trustworthy narrator] and no longer be considered upright, but that is *incomprehensible* with regards to the reality of a companion.

An example of the above is a tradition related by Abū Hurayra ﷺ, in which he states that, 'The Messenger of Allah ﷺ said, "If a dog drinks from any of your vessels then let him wash it seven times."'[2]

---

[1] *'Aqd al-Jumān* (p. 399)
[2] Ṣaḥīḥ al-Bukhārī (1:75), Ṣaḥīḥ Muslim (1:234) & others

المطلب الخامس

عمل الرَّواي مخالف لمرويه في اللحية

إنَّ عمل الرَّاوي بخلاف المرويّ يسقط اعتباره عند الحنفية، بأن يعمل الرَّاوي بعدما روى حديثاً بخلاف ما رواه؛ لأنَّ الرَّاوي إذا عمل بخلاف ما روى، فالعبرة عند الحنفية بما رأى لا بما روى؛ لأنَّ الرَّاوي العدل المؤتمن إذا رَوَى حديثاً عن رسول الله ﷺ وعَمِل بخلافه دلَّ ذلك على شيءٍ ثبت عنده من نسخٍ أو مُعارضةٍ أو تخصيصٍ أو لكونِهِ غيرِ ثابت أو غير ذلك من الأسباب[1]، وإن خالف لقلَّة المبالاة به أو لغفلتِه فقد سقطت عدالته، وهذا بعيدٌ عن حالِ الصحابيّ.

فمثلاً في حديث أبي هريرة ﵁، قال ﷺ: (إذا شرب الكلب من إناء أحدكم فليغسله سبعاً)[2].

<hr>

[1] ينظر: عقد الجمان ص399.

[2] ينظر: صحيح مسلم 1: 234، وصحيح البخاري 1: 75، وغيرهما.

This tradition implies that it is incumbent to wash any vessel seven times after a dog has lapped up from it; however, we find that the narrator Abū Hurayra ؓ actually contradicts his own narration and washes the vessel 'three times.'[1] This is a clear indication that the washing of a vessel seven times has been abrogated as we have a good opinion of Abū Hurayra and do not suspect in any way that he would leave that which he has heard, except due to something of the same strength.

In another tradition Ibn 'Abbās ؓ relates, 'The Messenger of Allah ﷺ said, "Whoever changes his religion, then kill him."'[2] However, we find that this tradition is actually particular for males only, since the narrator, Ibn 'Abbās ؓ, actually issues a contradictory legal verdict, where he states, 'Do not kill women when they apostate from Islam, however, imprison them and call them to Islam—compelling them therein.'[3]

---

[1] There is a suspended [*mawqūf*] tradition to Abū Hurayra ؓ in *Sharḥ Maʿānī al-Āthār* (1:22) where he relates, 'If a dog laps up in a vessel then pour the contents out and wash it three times.' (It is also mentioned in the *Sunan al-Dāraquṭnī* (1:66) and al-ʿAynī has verified it in his *ʿUmda al-Qārī* (3:40) saying, '...Shaykh Taqī al-Dīn states in *al-Imām*, "This is a sound transmission."') Supporting it further is what Abū Hurayra ؓ relates from the Messenger ﷺ that, 'When a dog laps up in a vessel then one should wash it three, five or seven times.' (*Sunan al-Dāraquṭnī* (1:65)).
[2] *Ṣaḥīḥ al-Bukhārī* (6:2524) & *al-Muwaṭṭaʾ* (3:324)
[3] *Muṣannaf Ibn Abī Shayba* (5:564) & *Sunan al-Kubrā* of al-Bayhaqī (8:353). It has been mentioned in *al-Dirāya* (2:136), 'The narration is elevated [*marfūʿ*] by Ibn 'Abbās which states, "Do not kill a woman if she apostates." Al-Dāraquṭnī believes it is not sound, as in it is 'Abdullah b. 'Īsā, and he was a liar. Al-Ṭabarānī relates from Muʿādh that the Messenger ﷺ said to him when sending him to Yemen, "If any woman apostates from Islam then invite her to it [again], if she then repents then accept it, however, if she refuses then imprison her," but its chain is weak.'

1.5 عمل الرَّاوي مخالف لمرويه في اللحية

فأفاد لزوم غسل الإناء من شرب الكلب سبع مرات، لكنَّ رواي الحديث خالف مرويه، فقد غسل أبو هريرة ﷺ: (ثلاث مرّات)[1]، فثبت بذلك نسخ السَّبع؛ لأنا نحسن الظَّن به، فلا نتوهم عليه أن يترك ما سمعه إلاَّ على مثله.

وفي حديث ابن عباس ﷺ، قال ﷺ: (مَن بدَّل دينه فاقتلوه)[2]، فإنَّه مُختصٌّ بالرِّجال؛ لأنَّ راويه ابن عَبَّاس ﷺ قد أفتى بخلافه، فقال: (لا يقتلن النِّساء إذا هنّ ارتددن عن الإسلام ولكن يحبسن ويدعين إلى الإسلام فيجبرن عليه)[3].

---

[1] ينظر: شرح معاني الآثار 1: 22، فعن أبي هريرة ﷺ موقوفاً: «إذا ولغ الكلب في الإناء فأهرقه ثم اغسله ثلاث مرّات» في سنن الدارقطني 1: 66، وصحّحه العيني في عمدة القاري 3: 40: «وقال الشيخ تقي الدِّين في الإمام: هذا إسناد صحيح». ويؤيده أيضاً ما رواه أبو هريرة ﷺ عن النبي ﷺ: «في الكلب يلغ في الإناء أنه يغسله ثلاثاً أو خمساً أو سبعاً» في سنن الدارقطني 1: 65.

[2] ينظر: صحيح البخاري 6: 2524، والموطأ 3: 324.

[3] ينظر: مصنف ابن أبي شيبة 5: 564، والسنن الكبرى للبيهقي 8: 353، وقال في الدراية 2: 136: «عن ابن عباس رفعه لا تقتلوا المرأة إذا ارتدت، قال الدارقطني لا يصح وفيه عبد الله بن عيسى وهو كذاب، وروى الطبراني عن معاذ أنَّ النبي ﷺ قال له حين بعثه إلى اليمن: أيما امرأة ارتدت عن الإسلام فادعنها فإن تابت فاقبل منها وإن أبت فاستتبها، وإسناده ضعيف».

If the narrator issues a legal verdict in contradiction to the accrual narration, then this is an indication that from its outset it was specified or abrogated.[1]

It is important to understand that the issue of the beard does not differ greatly from the issue of a dog lapping up in a vessel or the issue of female apostasy. Some of the most prominent narrators of the traditions regarding the beard were well known for trimming that which was in excess of a fist-length. Ibn ʿUmar narrates from the Messenger of Allah ﷺ, 'Differ from the disbelievers; make profuse the beards [*waffirū al-liḥā*] and trim the moustaches,' and Ibn ʿUmar ؓ himself would grasp a fistful from his beard and trim anything that exceeded it when performing the Ḥajj or lesser pilgrimage [*ʿumra*].[2]

The term '*waffirū al-liḥā*' [in the above tradition] (pronounced by doubling the *fāʾ*) means to leave something free and ample. The term *al-liḥā* (pronouncing the *lām* with either a *kasra*[3] or *ḍamma*[4]) is the plural of the word *liḥya* (pronounced with a *kasra* on the *lām* only), which is anything that grows on the cheeks and chin.[5]

From those that have also narrated traditions regarding the beard is Abū Hurayra ؓ; he states, 'The Messenger of Allah ﷺ said, "Shorten your moustaches and lengthen your beards, and differ from the Magians."'[6] However, the narrator acts contrary to that which he has narrated since he was known to trim his beard. Abū Zurʿa narrates, 'Abū Hurayra ؓ would take a fistful from his beard and then trim anything that exceeded it.'[7]

---

[1] *Khulāṣa al-Dalāʾil* (p. 1180)
[2] *Ṣaḥīḥ al-Bukhārī* (7:160)
[3] To provide the vowel *i*
[4] To provide the vowel *u*
[5] *Irshād al-Sārī* (8:464)
[6] *Ṣaḥīḥ Muslim* (1:222)
[7] *Fatḥ al-Qadīr* (2:348)

5.1 عمل الرَّاوي مخالف لمرويه في اللحية

والرَّاوي إذا أَفْتَى بخلاف الرِّواية يدلّ على الاختصاص ابتداء أو على انتساخه[1].

وقضية اللِّحية لا تختلف عن ولوغ الكلب وردّة المرأة، فأبرز رواة حديث اللِّحية اشتهر عنه أخذه ما زاد على القبضة، فعن ابن عمر عن النَّبيّ ﷺ: «خالفوا المشركين وفِّروا اللحى وأحفوا الشوارب»، وكان ابن عمر ﷺ إذا حجّ أو اعتمر قبض على لحيته، فما فضل أخذه[2].

ومعنى «وفِّروا اللحى» ـ بتشديد الفاء ـ أي اتركوها موفَّرة، واللِّحى ـ بكسر اللام وتُضمّ ـ جمع لحية، بالكسر فقط اسم لما ينبت على العارضين والذَّقن[3].

ومِمن روى أحاديث اللحية أبو هريرة ﷺ، قال ﷺ: «جزوا الشوارب وأرخوا اللحى خالفوا المجوس»[4]، وقد خالف مرويه وأخذه من لحيته: فعن أبي زرعة قال: «كان أبو هريرة ﷺ يقبض على لحيته ثم يأخذ ما فضل عن القبضة»[5].

---

(1) ينظر: خلاصة الدلائل على القدوري ص1180.

(2) ينظر: صحيح البخاري 7: 160.

(3) ينظر: إرشاد الساري 8: 464.

(4) ينظر: صحيح مسلم 1: 222.

(5) ينظر: مصنف ابن أبي شيبة 13: 112.

And so, we have two narrators: Ibn ʿUmar and Abū Hurayra ﷺ, who both contradict their narration by trimming their beards; however, what is considered is their action, and not the actual narration. This is implementation of the prior mentioned principle in the Ḥanafī school which states: '*The consideration is for that which has been acted on (seen) and not for that which has been narrated.*' Ibn al-Humām, regarding the traditions of the beard states, 'This is the least of what can be understood in the chapter [that is, to take whatever exceeds a fist-length] *if* we do not regard them [*aḥādīth*] to be abrogated, since this is our principle when the narrator acts contrary to his narration; in addition, other than the narrator have also acted contrary to these narrations.'[1]

This demonstrates that shortening the beard in and of itself was actually permissible, with the amount shortened being referred back to the companions' ﷺ own independent judgement, which was based on their understanding of social integrity in the time they were in; and Allah ﷻ knows best.

---

[1] *Fatḥ al-Qadīr* (2:348)

فهِا هم رواة الحديث ابن عمر وأبو هريرة ﷺ يخالفون ما رووه ويأخذون من لحاهم، فيكون المعتبر فعلهم ورأيهم لا روايتهم على قاعدة الحنفية: العبرة بما رأى لا بما روى، قال ابنُ الهمام[1] في أحاديث اللحية: «فأقلُّ ما في الباب إن لم يحمل على النَّسخ كما هو أصلنا في عمل الراوي على خلاف مرويه مع أنَّه روي عن غير الراوي».

وهذا يدلّنا على أنَّ الأخذ بنفسه جائزٌ، والتقدير اجتهاد من الصحابة ﷺ مرجعه للعرف والمروءة في زمانهم، والله أعلم.

---

[1] ينظر: فتح القدير 2: 348.

Chapter Six
Some of the Companions Acting Contrary to the Tradition of the Beard

When we find several companions ﷠ acting in contradiction to an apparent and clear tradition, such that there is no possibility of them being unaware of it, then the tradition is critiqued. This is why they said, 'The action of another companion in contradiction to it (the tradition) lowers its status of consideration.' This is, however, different to when the actual narrator himself contradicts what he has related, as in that instance the tradition is not considered at all.[1]

For example, the tradition in which 'Ā'isha ﷢ relates that, 'Abū Ḥudhayfa b. 'Utba adopted Sālim, whilst Sahla bt. Suhayl was the wife of Abū Ḥudhayfa ﷠. She came to the Messenger of Allah ﷺ and said, "Messenger of Allah, we used to see Sālim as a child and he would enter [my house], and we only have one room, so what is your opinion regarding him?" The Messenger of Allah ﷺ said, "Breastfeed him," and so she breastfed him five feeds, making him unmarriageable as a result and he thus became her milk child."[2]

---

[1] *Nūr al-Anwār* (2:27-28), *Ifāḍa al-Anwār* (p. 186) & *Sharḥ Ibn Malak* (2:648)
[2] *Al-Mustadrak* (2:17), *Ṣaḥīḥ Ibn Ḥibbān* (28:10) & *al-Muntaqā* (1:173)

المطلب السادس

مخالفة بعض الصحابة لحديث اللِّحية

إنَّ مخالفةَ بعضِ الصحابة ﵃ العملَ بالحديث إذا كان ظاهراً لا يحتمل الخفاءَ عليهم يورث الطعن فيه؛ لذلك قالوا: عمل صحابيّ آخر بخلافه يسقطه عن درجة الاعتبار، بخلاف عمل الصحابي نفسه بخلاف مرويه فإنَّه يجعله غير معتبر أصلاً[1].

فمثلاً: حديث عائشة ﵂ أنَّ أبا حذيفة بن عتبة تبنى سالماً، وإنَّ سهلةَ بنت سهيل كانت تحت أبي حذيفة ﵁ فجاءت رسول الله ﷺ، فقالت: يا رسول الله، إنا كنا نرى سالماً ولداً، وكان يدخل عليَّ وليس لنا إلاَّ بيتٌ واحد، فماذا تَرَى في شأنه؟ فقال رسول الله ﷺ: (أرضعيه، فأرضعته خمس رضعات، فحرم بهنّ، وكان بمنزلة ولدها من الرضاعة)[2].

---

[1] ينظر: نور الأنوار 2: 27-28، وإفاضة الأنوار ص186، وشرح ابن ملك 2: 648.

[2] ينظر: المستدرك 2: 177، وصححه، وصحيح ابن حبان 10: 28، والمنتقى 1: 173.

The apparent understanding of the tradition is that by breastfeeding an adult he or she becomes unmarriageable, just like when a child is breastfed. However, this tradition was in contradiction to the actions of the majority of the companions ﷺ, and thus, it was understood to be specific to the issue of Sālim ﷺ. Moreover, it also conflicts with other traditions such as:

It is reported from 'Alī ﷺ that he said, 'There is no breastfeeding after having been weaned.'[1]

It is reported from Ibn 'Abbās ﷺ that he said, 'There is no breastfeeding after having been weaned for two years.'[2]

It is reported from 'Umar ﷺ that he said, "There is no breastfeeding after being weaned."[3]

---

[1] *Al-Muṣannaf* of 'Abd al-Razzāq (6:416) & *Sunan al-Kabīr* of al-Bayhaqī (7:461). Masrūq relates, "Ā'isha ﷺ said, "The Messenger of Allah ﷺ entered [my house], whilst there was a man sat with me; he was extremely distressed by it to the extent that I saw the anger in his face, so I said, 'Messenger of Allah ﷺ he is my milk brother,' to which the Messenger ﷺ replied, 'Be careful with regards to who you consider your milk siblings, as breastfeeding is from famine [meaning that milk relations are only established when milk is the only food for the child].'"" (*Ṣaḥīḥ al-Bukhārī* (3:170) & *Ṣaḥīḥ Muslim* (2:1078))

It has also been related from Umm Salama ﷺ that, 'The Messenger of Allah ﷺ said, "No one is made unmarriageable by breastfeeding, except if the intestines are filled with milk (a good amount of milk is drank), before the completion of two years and the weaning [of the child]."' (*Sunan al-Nasā'ī al-Kubrā* (3:301) & *Sunan al-Tirmidhī* (3:450), al-Tirmidhī states this is a good and sound tradition).

[2] *Muṣannaf 'Abd al-Razzāq* (7:465)

[3] *Muṣannaf Ibn Abī Shayba* (3:550)

فظاهر الحديث يفيد: أنَّ إرضاع الكبير يحرم من الرِّضاع، كما هو الحال في الصغير، ولكن هذا مخالف لعمل عامة الصحابة ﷺ؛ لذلك جعلوه خاصّاً بسالم ﷺ لمخالفته للآثار الأخرى، فعن عليّ ﷺ قال: (لا رضاع بعد الفصال)[1]، وعن ابن عبَّاس ﷺ قال: (لا رضاع بعد الفصال الحولين)[2]، وعن عمر ﷺ، قال: (لا رضاع بعد الفصال)[3].

---

[1] ينظر: مصنف عبد الرزّاق 6: 416، وسنن البيهقي الكبير7: 461، وعن مسروق قالت عائشة ﷺ: (دخل عليّ رسول الله ﷺ وعندي رجل قاعد فاشتدَّ ذلك عليه ورأيت الغضب في وجهه، فقلت: يا رسول الله، إنَّه أخي من الرضاعة، فقال رسول الله ﷺ: انظرن مَن أخوتكن من الرضاعة، فإنَّما الرضاعة من المجاعة)، في صحيح البخاري 3: 170، وصحيح مسلم 2: 1078، وعن أم سلمة ﷺ قال ﷺ: (لا يحرم من الرضاع إلا ما فتق الأمعاء في الثدي وكان قبل الفطام) في سنن النسائي الكبرى3: 301، وسنن الترمذي 3: 450، وقال: هذا حديث حسن صحيح.

[2] ينظر: مصنف عبد الرزاق7: 465.

[3] ينظر: مصنف ابن أبي شيبة 3: 550.

All in all, we find that the companions ﷺ contradicted the command of leaving the beard without restriction. There are narrations which confirm that the companions ﷺ used to trim their beards. It has been related from Sammāk b. Yazīd that, "Alī ﷺ would trim anything from his beard that was not directly attached to the sides of his face."[1] It has also been related from Qatāda that Jābir ﷺ said, 'We do not take from its length except during the Hajj and lesser pilgrimage.'[2]

Ḥasan al-Baṣrī mentions that the companions ﷺ conceded in trimming anything more than a fist-length, by saying, 'They used to permit trimming from the beard anything that exceeded a fist-length.'[3]

Similarly, Ibrāhīm al-Nakhaʿī mentions, 'They would let their beards grow down in length and trim from its width.'[4]

This concession of trimming the beard was also inherited by the followers [tābiʿīn] from the companions. Aflaḥ relates, 'If Qāsim shaved his head, he would trim his beard and moustache as well.'[5] Furthermore, Abū Hilāl relates, 'I asked Ḥasan and Ibn Sīrīn, who both said, "There is no problem in trimming your beard length-ways."'[6]

---

[1] *Muṣannaf Ibn Abī Shayba* (13:112)
[2] Ibid.
[3] Ibid. (13:113)
[4] Ibid. (13:112)
[5] Ibid.
[6] Ibid.

وخالف الصحابة ﷺ الأمر بإعفاء اللحية مطلقاً، فورد الأخذ من الصحابة ﷺ من لحاهم، فعن سماك بن يزيد، قال: «كان عليّ ﷺ يأخذ من لحيته مما يلي وجهه»[1]، وعن قتادة، قال جابر ﷺ: «لا نأخذ من طولها إلا في حجّ أو عمرة»[2].

وذكر الحسن البصري أنَّ الصحابة ﷺ كانوا يرخصون في ذلك، فقال: «كان يُرخصون فيما زاد على القبضة من اللحية أن يؤخذ منها»[3].

ومثله ذكره إبراهيم النخعي عنهم فقال: «كانوا يَبْطُنُون لحاهم ويأخذون من عوارضها»[4].

وهذا الترخيص بالأخذ من اللحية توارثه التابعون عنهم، فعن أفلح قال: «كان القاسم إذا حلق رأسه أخذ من لحيته وشاربه»[5]، وعن أبي هلال قال سألت الحسن وابن سيرين فقالا: «لا بأس به أن تأخذ من طول لحيتك»[6].

.

---

[1] ينظر: مصنف ابن أبي شيبة 13: 112.

[2] ينظر: المصدر السابق 13: 112.

[3] ينظر: المصدر السابق 13: 113.

[4] ينظر: المصدر السابق 13: 112.

[5] ينظر: المصدر السابق 13: 112.

[6] ينظر: المصدر السابق 13: 112.

All of this indicates to us that to shorten the beard is permissible, and that it is, actually, what has been transmitted from the Messenger ﷺ, companions and those that came after them ﷺ. When we contemplate the causal factor behind shortening the beard, we discover that it is in fact their eagerness to keep their appearance and outward form beautiful and not repulsive. Paying attention to and having concern for one's outward appearance is a desired objective in the Sacred Law *just as* the beautification of the inward is; and Allah ﷻ knows best.

فهذه كلّه يدلّنا على جواز التقصير للحية، وأنَّه هو المأثور عن النَّبيِّ ﷺ والصَّحابة والتابعين ﷺ، وعندما نتأمل في علّة الأخذ نجدها: حرصهم على أن تكون هيئتهم ومظهرهم حسناً لا منفّراً، وإنَّ الاعتناء بالمظهر مقصودٌ في الشريعة، كما أنَّ الشريعة اعتنت بتحسين الباطن، والله أعلم

Chapter Seven
Primordiality [*Fiṭra*] is from the Sunna

In certain narrations, the expression: 'is from primordiality [*min al-fiṭra*]' is employed to describe leaving the beard [*i'fā' al-liḥya*]; however, the intended meaning of primordiality in these traditions is of it being from the sunna.

On the authority of Abū Hurayra ﷺ, the Messenger of Allah ﷺ said, 'From those actions that are considered primordial in Islam: the ritual ablution [*ghusl*] on the day of Friday, cleaning the teeth (using the *siwāk*), trimming the moustache and leaving the beard; verily, the Magians would lengthen their moustaches and trim their beards, so differ from them; trim your moustaches and lengthen your beards.'[1]

---

[1] *Ṣaḥīḥ Ibn Ḥibbān* (2:24). Shaykh Shu'ayb al-Arnā'ūṭ states, 'Ibn Abī Uways, he is: Ismā'īl b. 'Abdullah b. 'Abdullah b. Abī Uways b. Mālik al-Aṣbaḥī b. Ukht (the son of the sister of) Mālik b. Anas. The two Shaykhs used him as a proof, however they did not relate many of his traditions; Bukhari did not relate any of his isolated traditions except two. As for Muslim, he takes even less so than Bukhari; others narrated through him except al-Nasā'ī—as he considered him to be weak. Ibn Mu'īn's statements differ with regards to him, at one point he states, "There is no problem with him," and another point he states, "He is weak." Abu Ḥātim says, "He was truthful, but forgetful." Aḥmad states, "He is fine." Al-Dāraquṭnī states, "I do not choose him for sound [*ṣaḥīḥ*] traditions." Al-Ḥāfiẓ (Ibn al-Ḥajar al-'Asqalānī) in his *Muqaddima al-Fatḥ* (p. 391) decides not to require anything of his traditions except that which is in the *Ṣaḥīḥayn* due to him being rejected by al-Nasā'ī and others; although, if he shared [the narration] with other than him, in that instance he would be considered. His brother is: 'Abd al-Ḥamīd b. 'Abdullah b. 'Abdullah, he is trustworthy and they both agreed upon relating his traditions. The rest of the narrators in the transmission are trustworthy.'

المطلب السابع

الفطرة هي السنة

ورد في بعض ألفاظ الأحاديث «من الفطرة»، وذكر فيها إعفاء اللحية، وكان المقصود بالفطرة فيها هو السنة.

فعن أبي هريرة ﷺ قال ﷺ: «من فطرة الإسلام: الغسل يوم الجمعة، والاستنان، وأخذ الشارب وإعفاء اللحى، فإنَّ المجوس تعفي شواربها وتحفي لحاها فخالفوهم، حفوا شواربكم وأعفوا لحاكم»[1].

---

[1] ينظر: صحيح ابن حبان3: 24، وقال الشيخ شعيب: «ابن أبي أويس: هو إسماعيل بن عبد الله بن عبد الله بن أبي أويس بن مالك الأصبحي ابن أخت مالك بن أنس، احتج به الشيخان إلا أنهما لم يكثرا من تخريج حديثه، ولا أخرج له البخاري مما تفرد به سوى حديثين، وأما مسلم فأخرج له أقل مما أخرج له البخاري، وروى له الباقون سوى النسائي، فإنَّه أطلق القول بضعفه، واختلف فيه قول ابن معين، فقال مرة: لا بأس به، وقال مرة: ضعيف، وقال أبو حاتم: محلة الصدق، وكان مغفلاً، وقال أحمد: لا بأس به، وقال الدارقطني: لا أختاره في الصحيح، واختار الحافظ في «مقدمة الفتح» ص 391 أنَّه لا يحتج بشيء من حديث غير ما في الصحيح من اجل ما قدح في النسائي وغيره إلا أن شاركه فيه غيره، فيعتبر به، وأخوه: اسمه عبد الحميد بن عبد الله ثقة اتفقا على إخراج حديثه، وباقي رجال السند ثقات».

On the authority of ʿĀʾisha ﷺ, the Messenger of Allah ﷺ said, 'Ten things are from primordiality: trimming the moustache, leaving the beard, the *siwāk*, snuffing water, clipping the nails, cleaning between the fingers [*ghasl al-barājim*],[1] plucking the [hair under the] armpits [*natf al-ibṭ*],[2] shaving pubic hair and washing the genitals [*intiqāṣ al-māʾ*].' Zakariyyā states, 'Musʿab said, "I have forgotten the tenth however I think it is the gargling of the mouth."' Qutayba further adds, 'Wakīʿ said, "*intiqāṣ al-māʾ*, that is *istinjāʾ* (washing the genitals)."'[3]

Linguistically, primordiality means: a natural disposition.[4] One of the legal usages of its linguistic meaning is in describing a defect [*ʿayb*] which is that which one's essential primordial disposition is free of, since its presence would be considered a deficiency. And this primordial disposition is, in essence, one's natural disposition, which is the basis of this foundation.[5]

---

[1] Cleaning between the fingers [*ghasl al-barājim*]: this is to clean places where dirt gathers (*Sharḥ Fawāʾid ʿAbd al-Bāqī* (1:126))
[2] Plucking the hair under the armpits [*natf al-ibṭ*]: this is to pluck with one's fingers, as this weakens the hair root (*Sharḥ Fawāʾid ʿAbd al-Bāqī* (1:126))
[3] *Ṣaḥīḥ Muslim* (1:223), *Sunan Abī Dāwūd* (1:14) & *Sunan al-Tirmidhī* (5:91), He said, 'The tradition is good [*ḥasan*].'
[4] *Lisān al-ʿArab* (5:56) & *Mukhtār al-Ṣiḥāḥ* (p. 241)
[5] *Durar al-Ḥukkām* (2:160)

1.7 الفطرة هي السنة

وعن عائشة ﷺ، قالت: قال ﷺ: «عشر من الفطرة: قص الشارب، وإعفاء اللحية، والسواك، واستنشاق الماء، وقص الأظفار، وغسل البراجم[1]، ونتف الإبط، وحلق العانة، وانتقاص الماء»، قال زكريا: قال مصعب: ونسيت العاشرة إلا أن تكون المضمضة زاد قتيبة، قال وكيع: انتقاص الماء: يعني الاستنجاء[2].

والفطرة لغةً: الخِلقة[3]، ومن الاستعمال الفقهي للمعنى اللغوي: أنَّ العيب ما يخلو عنه أصل الفطرة السليمة مما يعد به ناقصاً، والفطرة الخلقة التي هي أساس الأصل[4].

---

[1] وغسل البراجم: أي تنظيف المواضع التي تجمع فيها الوسخ. ونتف الإبط: أي أخذ شعره بالأصابع؛ لأنَّه يضعف الشعر. ينظر: شرح فوائد عبد الباقي 1: 126.

[2] ينظر: صحيح مسلم 1: 223، وسنن أبي داود 1: 14، وسنن الترمذي 5: 91، وقال: حديث حسن.

[3] ينظر: لسان العرب 5: 56، ومختار الصحاح ص241.

[4] ينظر: درر الحكام 2: 160.

The majority of the Ḥanafī jurists like al-Marghīnānī,[1] al-Bābartī,[2] Ibn al-Humām,[3] al-ʿAynī [4] and al-Zaylaʿī,[5] have all interpreted primordiality to mean the sunna.

Primordiality can also sometimes be used to express Islam, creation [*khalq*] or invention [*ihkhtirāʿ*] and originality [*ibdāʿ*]; however, al-Khaṭṭābī states that, 'Most of the scholars have held it to mean the Sunna.'

Ibn al-Ṣalāḥ states, 'There is a problem here; the linguistic understanding of Sunna is far from the linguistic understanding of primordiality. Although it may be that the origin and intended meaning of it is [the construct]: '*sunna al-fiṭra*,' the first word in the construct state [*muḍāf*] having been removed and replaced by the second word [*muḍāf ilayh*]. Al-Nawawī states, 'The interpretation of it [*fiṭra*] as sunna is correct.'[6]

Al-ʿAynī has also clearly expressed that the intended meaning of the term primordiality in traditions that mention lengthening the beard is sunna; he states, 'Primordiality is the sunna, and the interpretation [of its usage in certain traditions] is that these ten acts were considered to be from the sunna of the Prophets we have been commanded to follow—with Ibrāhīm ﷺ being the first one to command us to perform them. The word '*min*' (from) has been used [in the tradition] to mean 'some' [*tabʿīḍ*], as there are many sunnas. [In Arabic] *Iʿfāʾ* is from *aʿfā*; it is said: '*afā al-shayʾ*' if the thing increased and multiplied; it is also said: '*afā al-zarʿ*' (the crops increased) and thus, the term '*iʿfāʾ al-liḥya*' means: to let it fall and make abundant.'[7]

---

[1] *Al-Hidāya* (1:19)
[2] *Al-ʿInāya* (1:56)
[3] *Fatḥ al-Qadīr* (1:228)
[4] *Al-Bināya* (1:313)
[5] *Al-Tabyīn* (1:13)
[6] *Al-Bināya* (1:314)
[7] *Al-Bināya* (1:313)

1.7 الفطرة هي السنة

وفسَّر الفطرة بمعنى السُّنة عامة علماء الحنفية: كالمرغيناني[1]، والبابرتي[2]، وابن الهمام[3]، والعَيني[4]، والزَّيلعيّ[5].

وللفطرة معان بمعنى دين الإسلام، وبمعنى الخلق، وبمعنى الاختراع والإبداع، وقال الخطابي فسَّرها أكثر العلماء بالسُّنة. وقال ابن الصلاح: هذا فيه إشكال؛ لبعد معنى السُّنة من معنى الفطرة في اللغة، فلعل وجهه أنَّ أصله سنّة الفطرة أراد بها فحذف المضاف وأقيم المضاف إليه مقامه. وقال النَّووي: تفسيرها بالسُّنة هو الصواب[6].

وصرَّح العينيّ أنَّ الفطرة يراد بها السُّنة في الحديث الموجود فيه إعفاء اللحية، فقال[7]: «والفطرة: السُّنة، وتأويله أنَّ هذه العشرة من سنن الأنبياء عليهم السلام الذين أمرنا أن نقتدي بهم، وأوَّل مَن أمر بها إبراهيم ﷺ، وكلمة من للتبعيض؛ لأنَّ السُّنن كثيرة، والإعفاء من أعفى...، يقال: عفا الشيء إذا كثر وزاد من ذلك عفا الزرع، وإعفاء اللحية: إرسالها وتوفيرها».

---

[1] ينظر: الهداية 1: 19.

[2] ينظر: العناية 1: 56.

[3] ينظر: فتح القدير 1: 228.

[4] ينظر: البناية 1: 313.

[5] ينظر: التبيين 1: 13.

[6] ينظر: البناية 1: 314.

[7] ينظر: المصدر السابق 1: 313.

This same meaning has been employed in a tradition related by al-'Abbās ﷺ; the Messenger of Allah ﷺ said, 'My nation will continue to be upon primordiality as long as they do not delay the sunset prayer [*maghrib*] to the point where the stars become clear and start to interlace.'[1] Al-'Aynī states, 'The meaning of primordiality is sunna as is mentioned in his ﷺ saying, "Ten things are from primordiality."'[2]

There is also an opinion in the Ḥanafī school which has interpreted the term primordiality mentioned in the tradition to mean 'religion' [*dīn*]. Ibn Nujaym states, 'It would require that every single act enumerated [in the tradition] is from the sunna if [the term] primordiality is interpreted as being the sunna, therefore it is better to interpret it as meaning "religion".'[3]

This shows us that the Ḥanafī jurists understood primordiality to mean the sunna, ultimately supporting and strengthening previously mentioned foundations which effectually determine that the legal ruling of the beard is oscillatory between being sunna and recommendation [*istiḥbāb*] but not necessity [*wujūb*].

Throughout this section we do not discover any indicator in the derivation principles [*uṣūl al-istinbāṭ*] of the Ḥanafī school which support the opinion that makes shaving or shortening the beard unlawful, especially the foundation that is related to the additional sunnas [*sunan al-zawāʾid*] and the sunnas of guidance [*sunan al-hudā*], as its proof is clearer than others in establishing the desired objective, and Allah ﷺ knows best.

---

[1] *Sunan Ibn Mājah* (1:225), *Musnad Aḥmad* (24:493) & *Muʿjam al-Awsaṭ* (2:214). Al-Ṭabarānī states, 'It has not been transmitted from Qatāda except from 'Umar b. Ibrāhīm through an isolated tradition from 'Ibād b. al-'Awām.'

[2] *Al-Bināya* (2:45)

[3] *Al-Baḥr al-Rāʾiq* (1:50)

وجاءت بهذا المعنى في حديث العباس ﷺ قال ﷺ: «لا تزال أمتي على الفطرة ما لم يؤخروا المغرب حتى تشتبك النجوم»[1]، قال العينيّ[2]: «والمراد من الفطرة السُّنة كما في قوله ﷺ: «عشرة من الفطرة» ».

ووجد قول عند الحنفية: بأن تفسر الفطرة في الحديث بمعنى الدِّين، فذكر ابن نجيم[3]: «أنَّ الفطرة إذا فسرت بالسُّنة يقتضي أنَّ جميع المعدود من السنة...، فالأولى في الفطرة تفسيرها بالدِّين».

فهذا يظهر أنَّ علماء الحنفية فهموا الفطرة بمعنى السنة، وهذا يؤيد الأصول السابقة بأنَّ مدار اللَّحية على السنية والاستحباب لا الوجوب.

ومن خلال هذا المبحث لا نجد شيئاً في أصول الاستنباط للحنفية تؤيد مسلك الحرمة للحلق أو التَّقصير للحية، لا سيما أصل سنن الزوائد والهدى، فإنَّ دلالته أوضح من غيره على هذا المقصود، والله أعلم.

---

[1] ينظر: سنن ابن ماجه1: 225، ومسند أحمد24: 493، والمعجم الأوسط2: 214، وقال الطبراني: «لم يروه عن قتادة إلا عمر بن إبراهيم تفرد به عباد بن العوام».

[2] ينظر: البناية 2: 45.

[3] ينظر: البحر الرائق1: 50.

In some of the traditions relating to the beard, the explanation mentioned with regards to letting the beard grow was to differ from the polytheists. It has been related by Ibn 'Umar ﷺ that the Messenger ﷺ said, 'Differ from the polytheists, trim your moustaches and lengthen your beards;'[1] and also in a tradition narrated by Abū Hurayra ﷺ, 'Trim your moustaches and lengthen your beards; differentiate yourselves from the Magians.'[2] Ibn al-Humām states that the sentences: '*differ from the polytheists*' or '*differentiate yourselves from the Magians*' are placed as a way of explaining the reason.[3]

It is clearly stated in the aforementioned traditions that the reason for leaving the beard is so the Muslims can differ from the non-Muslims in all their different types, whether they are the polytheists, Magians or the people of the book. It is narrated by Abū Umāma ﷺ that, 'The Messenger of Allah ﷺ went to a group of elderly Anṣār with white beards and said, "O people of the Anṣār, dye your beards red and yellow [with henna], and thereby differ from the people of the book." We said, "O Messenger of Allah ﷺ, the people of the book wear trousers and they do not wear sarongs," to which the Messenger of Allah ﷺ replied, "Wear trousers and sarongs and differ from the people of the book."'

---

[1] *Ṣaḥīḥ Muslim* (1:222)
[2] Ibid.
[3] *Fatḥ al-Qadīr* (2:348)

المبحث الثاني

من جهة مخالفة غير المسلمين

ورد في بعض روايات حديث اللِّحية بيانٌ للسبب في إعفاء اللحية، وهو مخالفة المشركين، فعن ابن عمر ﷺ قال ﷺ: (خالفوا المشركين أحفوا الشوارب وأوفوا اللحى)[1]، وعن أبي هريرة ﷺ، قال ﷺ: (جزوا الشَّوارب وأرخوا اللحى خالفوا المجوس)[2]، قال ابنُ الهمام[3]: «فهذه الجملة واقعة موقع التَّعليل»: أي جملة: «خالفوا المشركين»، أو «خالفوا المجوس».

وهذا صريحٌ في النَّصّ بأن علَّة الإعفاء هي المخالفة لغير المسلمين على اختلاف أصنافهم من مشركين أو مجوس أو أهل كتاب، فعن أبي أمامة ﷺ قال: (خرج رسول الله ﷺ على مشيخة من الأنصار بيض لحاهم، فقال: يا معشر الأنصار، حمروا وصفروا وخالفوا أهل الكتاب، قال: فقلنا: يا رسول الله، إنَّ أهل الكتاب يتسرولون ولا يأتزرون، فقال رسول الله ﷺ: تسرولوا وائتزروا وخالفوا أهل الكتاب.

---

[1] ينظر: صحيح مسلم 1: 222.

[2] ينظر: المصدر السابق

[3] ينظر: فتح القدير 2: 348.

The narrator said, we then said, "O Messenger of Allah ﷺ, the people of the book wear socks [*khuff*] and they do not wear sandals." The Messenger of Allah ﷺ replied, "Wear socks and sandals and differ from the people of the book." We said, "O Messenger of Allah ﷺ, the people of the book trim their beards and let their moustaches grow." He ﷺ replied by saying, "Trim your moustaches and let your beards grow, and differ from the people of the book."'[1]

Also, 'Ubaydullah b. 'Abdullah b. 'Ubaydullah narrates, 'A man from the Magians, who was clean-shaven with a long moustache, came to the Messenger of Allah ﷺ; the Messenger of Allah ﷺ asked him, "What is this?" To which the man replied, "This is from our religion." The Messenger of Allah ﷺ said, "It is from our religion to trim the moustache and lengthen the beard."'[2]

This necessitates that we define what is meant by 'differ from non-Muslims,' as has been commanded by the Sacred Law. This is because since we are all part of human society, it naturally means that we share many of the characteristics and behaviours particular to all people. Thus, in the following chapters we will discuss the issues surrounding the imitation of non-Muslims.

[1] *Musnad Aḥmad* (36:613) & *Shu'b al-Īmān* (8:396). Al-Haythamī states in *Majma' al-Zawā'id* (5:131), 'The men of Aḥmad are sound except al-Qāsim; he is trustworthy, there is some discussion regarding him, but it is not damaging.'

[2] *Muṣannaf Ibn Abī Shayba* (13:117)

قال: فقلنا : يا رسول الله، إنَّ أهل الكتاب يتخففون ولا ينتعلون، قال: فتخففوا وانتعلوا وخالفوا أهل الكتاب، قال: فقلنا: يا رسول الله، إنَّ أهل الكتاب يقصون عثانينهم ـ أي اللحى ـ ويوفرون سبالهم ـ أي الشوارب ـ قال ﷺ: قصوا سبالكم ووفروا عثانينكم وخالفوا أهل الكتاب)[1].

وعن عبيد الله بن عبد الله بن عبيد الله قال: «جاء رجل من المجوس إلى رسول الله ﷺ وقد حلق لحيته وأطال شاربه، فقال له النبي ﷺ: ما هذا؟ قال هذا في ديننا ﴾ قال : ولكن في ديننا أن نجز الشارب وأن نعفي اللحية»[2].

وهذا يقتضي أن نُحقِّق المقصود بحقيقةِ المخالفة لغير المسلمين المنهيّ عنها من قبل الشَّارع الحكيم؛ لأننا جميعاً من بني الإنسان، وهذا يقتضي التَّوافق في العديد من الصِّفات والسُّلوكيات البشرية، فنعرض هنا ما يتعلق بالتَّشبُّه في المطالب الآتية:

---

[1] ينظر: مسند أحمد36: 613، وشعب الإيمان8: 396، قال الهيثمي في مجمع الزوائد5: 131: «ورجال أحمد رجال الصحيح خلا القاسم، وهو ثقة، وفيه كلام لا يضر».

[2] ينظر: مصنف ابن أبي شيبة13: 117.

Chapter One
Types of Imitation

Linguistically, *tashabbuh* or imitation means the resemblance of a thing to something else.[1] Imitating non-Muslims means to conform to their actions and speech, whether in religious or worldly matters, and this falls into two categories:

1. Blameworthy Imitation

This includes conforming to non-Muslims with intent, in matters which are considered shameful and particular to them initially and are not from those issues related to civil life. The Mufti of Egypt Muḥammad al-ʿAbbāsī al-Mahdī al-Azharī al-Ḥanafī states, 'Imitating the disbelievers can be figurative [*ṣūrī*] as we may act as they act but without intent, or it could be real [*ḥaqīqī*] imitation as we could act with intent to behave like them. Both the figurative and real imitation could be in unlawful or lawful actions. Thus, if one was to imitate them in unlawful actions, one is sinful, regardless of whether one did so with intent or not. And if it was in actions which are lawful, then if one imitated them with intent one is [likewise] sinful, otherwise one is not.'[2]

2. Praiseworthy Imitation

This involves conforming to them with intent in matters which are not part of their religion or rites, nor in matters deemed shameful. This would therefore be in civil and day-to-day matters.

---

[1] *Lisān al-ʿArab* (13:503)
[2] *Al-Fatāwā al-Mahdiyya fīl-Waqāʾiʿ al-Miṣriyya* (5:307-308)

المطلب الأول

أنواع التَّشبُّه

فالتَّشبُّه لغةً: من أَشْبَهَ الشَّيءُ الشَّيءَ: مَاثَلَهُ[1].

والتَّشبُّه بغير المسلمين: هو المماثلةُ لهم في فعل أو قول دينيّ أو دنيويّ، وله نوعان:

1.التَّشبُّه المذموم: وهو قصدُ مماثلتهم فيما هو من شعارهم ابتداءً وكان مستقبحاً في غير الأمور المدنية. قال مفتي مصر مُحمَّد العباسيّ المهديّ الأزهريّ الحنفيّ[2]: «التَّشبُّه بالكفّار قد يكون صوريّاً بأن يفعل كفعلهم من غير قصد التَّشبُّه بهم، وقد يكون حقيقياً بأن يفعل ذلك قاصداً التَّشبُّه بهم، وعلى كلٍّ إمّا أن يتشبّه بهم في محرمٍ أو لا، فإن فعل في الأوَّل فهو آثمٌ مطلقاً قصد أو لم يقصد، وإن فعل في الثّاني إن قصد أثم وإلا فلا...».

2.التَّشبُّه الممدوح: هو مماثلتُهم فيما لا يكون شعاراً لهم قصداً ولا مستقبحاً وكان من الأمور المدنية والحياتية.

---

(1) ينظر: لسان العرب 13: 503.

(2) ينظر: الفتاوى المهدية في الوقائع المصرية 5: 307ـ 308.

This praiseworthy imitation also includes what has been related of the Messenger's ﷺ love of imitating or conforming to the ways of the people of book, as has been narrated by Ibn ʿAbbās ؓ who said, 'The Messenger ﷺ loved conforming to the people of the book in matters in which he did not receive command. The people of the book would let their hair fall over their foreheads while the polytheists would part their hair, so the Messenger ﷺ would let his ﷺ hair fall over his ﷺ forehead and then later he ﷺ began to part it.'[1] The phrase 'conforming to the people of the book in matters in which he ﷺ did not receive command,' means that he ﷺ did not receive command contrary to what the people of the book did; Ibn Malak states, 'It means in matters in which he ﷺ did not receive revelation contrary to what the people of the book practiced.'[2]

We also find the concept of praiseworthy imitation amongst those who were raised and nurtured by the Prophet ﷺ, such as Fāṭima al-Zahrāʾ ؓ who, when Asmāʾ bt. ʿUmays ؓ related to her the wisdom of the use of coffins to bury the dead. This being more modest for a woman, since it would not allow the detail of her form to show, in accordance with the Sacred Law, which strives for modesty for women. Thus, our lady Fāṭima ؓ wished to be buried in a coffin and wrote a bequest to be buried in a coffin upon her death.

Umm Jaʿfar ؓ narrates that, 'Fāṭima, the daughter of the Messenger of Allah ﷺ, said, "Asmāʾ, I dislike how they bury women, they cover them in garments which show their form." Asmāʾ said, "Daughter of the Messenger of Allah ﷺ, shall I tell you of something I saw in Abyssinia? They took some wet palms and made a coffin with it, and then draped material over her once placing her in it." Fāṭima replied, "How wonderful is that practice! It means men can be differentiated from women. If I die, then I want you and ʿAlī to wash me, and do not let anyone else enter."

---

[1] *Ṣaḥīḥ al-Bukhārī* (4:189) & *Ṣaḥīḥ Muslim* (4:1817)
[2] *Mirqāt al-Mafātīḥ* (7:2817)

وهذا التَّشبُّه الممدوحُ يُحمل عليه ما ورد عن النبيِّ ﷺ من محبّته لموافقةِ أهل الكتاب، فعن ابن عبّاس ﷺ قال: (كان النبي ﷺ يُحبُّ موافقة أهل الكتاب فيما لم يؤمر فيه، وكان أهل الكتاب يسدلون أشعارهم، وكان المشركون يفرقون رءوسهم، فسدل النّبي ﷺ ناصيته، ثمّ فرَّق بعد)[1]. ومعنى «موافقة أهل الكتاب فيما لم يؤمر فيه»: أي بشيء من مخالفته، قال ابن ملك: أي فيما لم ينزل عليه حكم بالمخالفة[2].

ونجد تطبيق التَّشبُّه الممدوح ممن تربَّت على يد النَّبيِّ ﷺ، من فاطمة الزهراء ﷺ، عندما أخبرتها أسماء بنت عميس ﷺ بحكمة طيبة من صناعة التَّابوت لدفن الميت، فهو أستر في حَقّ المرأة من تفصيل أعضائها، فكان متوافقاً مع الشَّريعة في تحقيق ستر المرأة، فرغبت السَّيدة فاطمة ﷺ به، وأوصت أن يفعل لها عند موتها.

فعن أم جعفر ﷺ: «إنَّ فاطمةَ بنت رسول الله ﷺ قالت: يا أسماء، إنّي قد استقبحت ما يصنع بالنساء، إنّه يطرح على المرأة الثوب فيصفها، فقالت أسماء: يا بنت رسول الله ﷺ ألا أريك شيئاً رأيته بأرض الحبشة، فدعت بجرائد رطبة فحنتها، ثمّ طرحت عليها ثوباً، فقالت فاطمة: ما أحسن هذا وأجمله يعرف به الرَّجل من المرأة، فإذا أنا مت فاغسليني أنت وعلي، ولا تدخلي علي أحداً.

Thus, when she passed away, ʿĀʾisha, came to the door, and Asmāʾ told her, "Do not enter." ʿĀʾisha complained to Abū Bakr of this saying, "The *Khathʿamiyya* is coming between me and the daughter of the Messenger of Allah ﷺ, and she has made her something resembling a bridal howdah [*hawdaj*]!" Thus, Abū Bakr came, and stood at the door saying, "Asmāʾ, what made you prevent the wives of the Messenger ﷺ from coming to his ﷺ daughter? And what has made you make a bridal *hawdaj*?" Asmāʾ replied, "She (Fāṭima ﷺ) commanded me to not let anyone enter upon her passing, and I told her of this (coffin) whilst she was alive, and she asked me to make her one like it upon her passing. At this, Abū Bakr replied, "Do as you have been commanded!""[1]

---

[1] *Sunan al-Kabīr* of al-Bayhaqī (4:56)

فلمّا توفيت جاءت عائشة تدخل، فقالت أسماء: لا تدخلي، فشكت أبا بكر، فقالت: إنَّ هذه الخثعمية تحول بيني وبين ابنة رسول الله ﷺ، وقد جعلت لها مثل هودج العروس؟ فجاء أبو بكر فوقف على الباب، وقال: يا أسماء، ما حملك أن منعت أزواج النبي ﷺ يدخلن على ابنة النبي ﷺ، وجعلت لها مثل هودج العروس؟ فقالت: أمرتني أن لا تدخلي علي أحداً وأريتها هذا الذي صنعت وهي حيّة فأمرتني أن أصنع ذلك لها، فقال أبو بكر: فاصنعي ما أَمَرَتْك...»[1].

---

[1] ينظر: سنن البيهقي الكبير 4: 56.

Similarly, we see how 'Umar ﷺ did not consider the lengthening of the moustache as blameworthy imitation, since he lengthened his moustache. It has been narrated by 'Āmir b. 'Abdullah b. al-Zubayr that, 'When 'Umar b. al-Khaṭṭāb ﷺ became angry he would twirl his moustache and swell up.'[1] This is despite some narrations appearing to forbid this. It is related by Abū Hurayra ﷺ that, 'The Messenger of Allah ﷺ said, "The polytheists let their moustaches grow, while trimming their beards, so differ from them by trimming your moustaches and leaving your beards."'[2]

It is possible that 'Umar interpreted the prohibition in the tradition to mean that what is done *with* the purposeful intention to follow the polytheists; and 'Umar most certainly did not have this intention.

---

[1] *Al-Mu'jam al-Kabīr* (1:66). Al-Haythamī in *Majma' al-Zawā'id* (5:166) states, 'Its men in the chain are the same as the men of the Ṣaḥīḥ, except 'Abdullah b. Aḥmad, but he is trustworthy and reliable; although 'Āmir b. 'Abdullah b. Zubayr never met 'Umar.'

[2] *Musnad al-Bazzār* (14:390). Al-Haythamī states in *Majma' al-Zawā'id* (5:166), 'It has been narrated by al-Bazzār with two chains. In one of them is 'Amr Ibn Abī Salama; Ibn Mu'īn and others have deemed him to be trustworthy, however Shu'ba and others have deemed him to be inadequate; the rest of the narrators are trustworthy.'

وكذلك وجدنا عمر ﷺ لم يجعل إطالة الشارب من التشبه المذموم حيث أطال شاربه، فعن عامر بن عبد الله بن الزبير: (إنَّ عمر بن الخطاب ﷺ كان إذا غضب فتل شاربه ونفخ)[1]، رغم وجود ظواهر بعض الأحاديث المانعة من ذلك، فعن أبي هُرَيرة ﷺ، قال ﷺ: (إنَّ أهل الشرك يعفون شواربهم ويحفون لحاهم فخالفوهم فاعفوا اللحى وأحفوا الشوارب)[2].

فلعلَّه حمل النهي من النبي ﷺ على القصد لمشابهة المشركين مثلاً، وهو لم يكن يقصد مشابتهم.

---

[1] ينظر: المعجم الكبير 1: 66، قال الهيثمي في المجمع 5: 166: «رجاله رجال الصحيح خلا عبد الله بن أحمد، وهو ثقة مأمون إلا أن عامر بن عبد الله بن الزبير لم يدرك عمر».

[2] ينظر: مسند البزار 14: 390، قال الهيثمي في مجمع الزوائد 5: 166: «رواه البزار بإسنادَين في أحدهما عمرو بن أبي سلمة، وثقه ابن معين وغيره، وضعفه شعبة وغيره، وبقية رجاله ثقات».

Chapter Two
The Defining Principles of Imitation

By contemplating the texts of the Ḥanafī school, we can come to understand the defining principles of 'imitation' the scholars of the Ḥanafī school observed:

1. **Imitation in practices which are from the holy rites of non-Muslims and specific to them, such that it is through these practices that they distinguish themselves from others.**

Thus, whoever follows them in these matters is considered to be of them in his manner and behaviour. Al-Qārī states, 'It is well known that unlawful imitation is considered to be in that which is from their holy rites and specific to them.'[1]

2. **For the act of imitation to not be something that is beneficial to Muslims.**

This is because anything considered thus is something that the Muslims are in need of, and it is not permissible for us to prevent them from it. This includes using cars and aeroplanes, as these are from civil life which involves all people. It does not distinguish a group of people from another, but rather the benefits of it reach everyone.

---

[1] *Mirqāt al-Mafātīḥ* (6:2648)

المطلب الثاني

ضوابط التَّشبُّه

التأمل في عبارة الحنفية يوصلنا إلى ضوابط للتشبه يراعونها، وهي:

1. التَّشبُّه بها هو شعارٌ لهم ومختصٌّ بهم، بحيث يتميَّزون به عن غيرهم: فمَن قلَّدهم بها هو شعارهم نُسِب لهم في سلوكه وتصرفه، قال القاري[1]: «ولا يخفى أنَّ التشبه الممنوع إنَّما هو فيها يكون شعاراً لهم مختصّاً بهم».

2. أن لا يكون المتشبه به مما فيه صلاح العباد والخير لهم: فإنَّ ما كان بهذا الوصف يكون المسلمون بحاجة له، ولا يجوز لنا منعهم منه: كركوب السيارات والطائرات، فهذه من الأمور المدنية لكل البشرية، ولا يختص بها قوم عن قوم، بل ترجع منفعتها لهم جميعاً.

---

[1] ينظر: مرقاة المفاتيح 6: 2648.

Ibn Māza[1] said, 'Hishām said, "I saw Abū Yūsuf wearing sandals held together by nails, and so I asked him, 'Do you not see a problem with wearing sandals with iron nails?' He replied, 'No.' I said, 'Sufyān and Thawr b. Yazīd disliked it as it is imitating of monks.' He replied, 'The Messenger of Allah ﷺ would wear sandals with hair, and these are from the dress of the monks.'"[2]

Through this statement, Abū Yusuf indicated that types of imitating that benefit the Muslims are harmless, thereby considering the wearing of sandals with nails as something that benefits Muslims, since the earth, no doubt, cannot be traversed in long distances without these types of sandals.[3]

Moreover, Abū Yusuf's refusal to accept that sandals made in this way is considered to be imitating the way of the monks indicates the extent of his deep learning and understanding, and therefore, what we can learn from his statement is—as Ibn Māza has mentioned—that: any matter that is shared between all mankind, and is good and beneficial for the Muslims, then we should benefit from the non-Muslims in those matters.

---

[1] *Al-Muḥīṭ al-Burhānī* (5:403)

[2] On the authority of Ibn 'Umar who said, 'I saw the Messenger of Allah ﷺ wear sandals which did not have any hair, and make ritual ablution [*wuḍū'*] in them, and thus I love to wear them.' (*Ṣaḥīḥ al-Bukhārī*, 5:2199, *Ṣaḥīḥ Muslim*, 2:844, *Ṣaḥīḥ Ibn Ḥibbān*, 9:79, *Sunan Abī Dāwūd*, 2:150, *Sunan al-Kubrā* of al-Nasā'ī (5:418) & others)

[3] *Radd al-Muḥtār* (1:624), *Minḥa al-Khāliq* (2:11) & *al-Fatāwā al-Hindiyya* (5:333)

قال ابنُ مازه[1]: «قال هشام: رأيت على أبي يوسف نعلين مخسوفين بمسامير، فقلت: أترى بهذا الحديد بأساً؟ قال: لا، فقلت: إنَّ سفيان وثور بن يزيد كرها ذلك؛ لأنَّ فيه تشبهاً بالرُّهبان، فقال: (كان رسول الله ﷺ يلبس النِّعال التي لها شعر، وأنَّها من لباس الرُّهبان)[2]، فقد أشار إلى أنَّ صورة المشابهة فيها تعلَّق به صلاح العباد لا يضرّ، وقد تعلَّق بهذا النَّوع من الأحكام صلاح العباد، فإنَّ الأرض ممَّا لا يمكن قطع المسافة البعيدة فيها إلا بهذا النَّوع من الإحكام»[3].

ورفض أبو يوسف لكون النعلين بهذا الوصف تشبهاً بالرهبان يدلّ على دقَّة فقهه ورسوخ علمه، فأفيد من كلامه كما ذكر ابن مازه: أنَّ كلَّ ما فيه صلاح العباد والخير لهم مما يشترك به البشر، فعلينا الاستفادة من غير المسلمين في ذلك.

---

(١) ينظر: المحيط البرهاني5: 403.

(٢) فعن ابن عمر رضي الله عنهما، قال: (إني رأيت رسول الله ﷺ يلبس النعال التي ليس فيها شعر، ويتوضأ فيها، فأنا أحب أنَّ ألبسها) في صحيح البخاري 5: 2199، وصحيح مسلم 2: 844، وصحيح ابن حبان 9: 79، وسنن أبي داود 2: 150، والسنن الكبرى للنسائي 5: 418، وغيرها.

(٣) ينظر: رد المحتار1: 624، ومنحة الخالق2: 11، والفتاوى الهندية5: 333.

3. **To purposefully intend 'imitation,' thus it does not suffice to simply appear to be following their ways.**

The appearance of conformity is present in the actions of Muslims and non-Muslims, as they are all human beings, therefore, they all eat, and wear clothes, and live; hence, this is not what is considered unlawful.

Rather, what is unlawful is purposefully intending to imitate non-Muslims. This is because of the impact this can have an impact on one's beliefs, identity and feelings of pride in one's faith, and thereby lose the sweetness of faith. Ibn Nujaym said, 'Know that imitating the people of the book is not offensive in all matters. We eat and drink as they do, however, what is unlawful is that which is related to sinful matters and matters where one purposefully intends to imitate.'[1] This has also been mentioned by Qāḍī Khān in *Sharḥ Jāmiʿ al-Ṣaghīr.*

Ultimately, imitation is something that relates to one's inner belief and heart, rather than to one's actions. Therefore, if there is no belief and no intent, then the action is insignificant.

Ibn ʿĀbidīn commented on the previous quotation by Ibn Māza by saying, 'It also indicates that what is intended by 'imitation' is the actual action itself, as in the appearance of imitation without intent.' Hence, imitating an action without purposeful intent is harmless.[2]

4. **For the imitation of non-Muslims to be at the very beginning before the action becomes part of the culture and customs of Muslims.**

After an action becomes widespread in a community, doing it becomes part of following the customs of the community, rather than imitating non-Muslims. Examples in our time include wearing trousers, shirts, suits and ties, amongst other things.

---

[1] *Al-Baḥr al-Rāʾiq* (2:11)
[2] *Radd al-Muḥtār* (1:624)

3. أن يقصد التَّشبُّه بهم، فلا يكفي مجرد صورة المشابهة بالفعل، فإنَّ وجود صورة المشابهة في الأفعال حاصلة بين المسلمين وغيرهم؛ لكونهم بشرٌ يأكلون ويلبسون ويتعايشون، وليس هذا ممنوعاً، وإنَّما المنع متعلِّق بقصد التَّشبُّه بغير المسلمين؛ لما له من تأثير على اعتقادِه وتميزه وشعوره بالعزَّة، فيفقد حلاوة الإيمان، قال ابن نجيم[1]: «اعلم أنَّ التَّشبُّه بأهل الكتاب لا يُكره في كلِّ شيءٍ، فإنَّنا نأكل ونشرب كما يفعلون، إنَّما الحرام هو التَّشبُّه فيما كان مذموماً وفيما يقصد به التَّشبُّه، كذا ذكره قاضي خان في «شرح الجامع الصغير»»؛ لأنَّ قضيةَ التَّشبُّه متعلِّقة بالاعتقاد والقلب لا بالأفعال، وذكر الأفعال فيها إظهار لما عليه الاعتقاد والقلب، فإن لم يكن به اعتقاد ولا قصد فلا عبرة حينئذٍ بالفعل.

وعلَّق ابنُ عابدين[2] على النَّقل السَّابق عن ابنِ مازه: «وفيه إشارةٌ أيضاً إلى أنَّ المرادَ بالتَّشبُّه أصل الفعل: أي صورة المشابهة بلا قصد» أي أنَّ التَّشبُّه في الفعل بلا قصد لا يَضرّ.

4. أن يكون التَّشبُّه بغير المسلمين ابتداءً قبل أن يصبح عرفاً وعادةً بين المسلمين، فبعد أن ينتشر الفعل في المجتمع يكون حينئذ فعلُها للعرف لا للتَّشبه بغير المسلمين، كما حصل في لباس البنطال والقميص والبدلة والقرافة وغيرها في هذا الزمان.

---

[1] ينظر: البحر الرائق 2: 11.

[2] ينظر: رد المحتار 1: 624.

Whoever wore these garments first would have been considered to have imitated non-Muslims and would have been from those who fell into blameworthy imitation, however, after this, this clothing generally became part of the widespread culture of Arab countries. When one wears them, one no longer thinks of imitating the West, rather, it has become part of the clothing of society. Ibn Ḥajar states, 'There is enough evidence in the practice of the Jews, when once, wearing a head-cap[1] was considered from their rites. This was thereafter no longer considered thus, and therefore became from the permissible practices.'[2]

5. The imitation should not be in illicit, obscene or repugnant actions.

These actions are many, and include: eating and drinking the unlawful, revealing one's private areas, and the widespread practice of adultery. Al-Ḥaṣkafī states, 'Imitating them (non-Muslims) is not offensive in everything, however only in blameworthy actions, and in matters where one purposefully intends to imitate.'[3] Ibn 'Ābidīn said, 'Imitating them, i.e. the Christians, is offensive in blameworthy matters, even if one did not purposefully intend to imitate.'[4]

---

[1] On the authority Anas b. Mālik ؓ who said, 'The Messenger of Allah ﷺ said, "The Jews of Isfahan will follow the *Dajjāl*, seventy thousand of them wearing a head-cap."' (*Ṣaḥīḥ Muslim*, 4:2266)
[2] *Fatḥ al-Bārī* (10:275)
[3] *Al-Durr al-Mukhtār* (1:624)
[4] *Radd al-Muḥtār* (1:648)

فمَن لبسها ابتداءً تشبهاً بغير المسلمين، كان واقعاً في التَّشبُّه المنهيّ عنه، لكن فيما بعد أصبحت هي العرف الشَّائع في بلاد العرب عموماً، ولم يَعُد يخطر بالبال عند لبسها التَّشبُّه بالغرب، وإنَّما أصبحت زِيّ المجتمع، قال ابنُ حجر[1]: «وإنَّما يصلح الاستدلال بقصّة اليهود في الوقت الذي تكون الطيالسة[2] من شعارهم، وقد ارتفع ذلك فيما بعد، فصار داخلاً في عموم المباح».

5. أن لا يكون التَّشبُّه بهم بالفجور والفحشاء والتَّصرُّفات القبيحة، وهذه الأفعال متعددة وكثيرة ومنها: شرب وأكل المحرمات، وكشف العورات، وإشاعة الفاحشة، قال الحصكفيّ[3]: «التَّشبُّه بهم لا يُكره في كلِّ شيءٍ، بل في المذموم، وفيما يقصد به التَّشبُّه». وقال ابن عابدين[4]: «ويكره التشبه بهم ـ أي النصارى ـ في المذموم وإن لم يقصده».

---

(1) ينظر: فتح الباري 10: 275.

(2) عن أنس بن مالك ﷺ قال ﷺ: «يتبع الدجال من يهود أصبهان، سبعون ألفاً عليهم الطيالسة» في صحيح مسلم 4: 2266.

(3) ينظر: الدر المختار 1: 624.

(4) ينظر: رد المحتار 1: 648.

CHAPTER THREE
TYPES OF IMITATION AND THEIR LEGAL RULINGS

1. A person disbelieves by imitating *with* reverence for the action and belittling the religion.

The reason for falling into disbelief is that belittling the religion is akin to mocking it, and this is disbelief. Al-Jaṣṣāṣ says, 'Mocking any of the rites of Islam is considered disbelief.'[1] Allah ﷻ says, ❴*Say, "Were you making jokes about God, His Revelations, and His Messenger?"*❵[2]

And, Qāḍī Khān states, 'If someone buys something on the Persian New Year [*yawm al-nayruz*], and would not have bought it on any other day, intending to revere the day with his purchase as non-Muslims do, then this would be considered an act of disbelief. However, if he purchased this for enjoyment or profit, and not for reverence of the day, then it would not be considered an act of disbelief.'[3]

2. It is necessary [*wājib*] to leave imitation in things which are considered to be from their (non-Muslims) rites.

It is necessary for a Muslim to leave imitating non-Muslims in things which align to the defining principles of blameworthy imitation, which is to have purposeful intent in matters which are from the rites of non-Muslims, and being the first to act before the action becomes part of the customs [*ʿāda*] of the wider community—that is if these matters are not of benefit to Islam— in order to not fall into sin.

---

[1] *Al-Bināya* (9:156)
[2] [*The Qur'an, A new translation by M. A. S. Abdel Haleem*, Repentance, 9:65 (p. 122)]
[3] *Al-Khāniyya (Fatāwā Qāḍī Khān)* (3:578)

المطب الثالث

حالات التَّشبُّه وحكمها

1.يَكفرُ بالتَّشبُّه بقصد التَّعظيم للفعل والاستخفاف في الدِّين، وسببُ هذا الكفر أنَّ الاستخفافَ بالدِّين هو استهزاءٌ بالدِّين، وهذا كفر، قال الجصاص: «الاستهزاء لشيء من الشرائع كفر»[1]؛ لقوله تعالى: {قُلْ أَبِاللَّهَ وَآيَاتِهِ وَرَسُولِهِ كُنْتُمْ تَسْتَهْزِئُونَ}[النور: 65].قال قاضي خان[2]: «رجلٌ اشترى يوم النَّيروز شيئاً لم يشتره في غير ذلك اليوم، إن أراد به تعظيم ذلك اليوم كما يعظِّمه الكفرة يكون كفراً، وإن فعل ذلك لأجل السَّرف والتَّنعم لا لتعظيم اليوم لا يكون كفراً».

2.يجب ترك قصد التشبه بما هو من شعارهم، فيجب على المسلم ترك التَّشبُّه بغير المسلمين فيما تحقَّقت فيه ضوابط التَّشبُّه المذموم من القصد للتشبه فيما هو من شعار غير المسلمين، وفعله ابتداءً قبل أن يصبح عادة للمجتمع، ولم يكن مما فيه صلاح العباد، حتى لا يقع في الإثم.

---

(1) ينظر: البناية9: 156.

(2) ينظر: الخانية 3: 578.

Al-Mahdī al-Ḥanafī states, 'The expression: 'and so he is from them [*fa-huwa minhum*]' means that he is a disbeliever like them if he imitated them in unlawful matters. For example, he revered their celebratory days out of reverence for their religion, or he wore their *zunnār* (a band or rope worn around the waist) or something specific to them, intending with this to belittle Islam. This is how it has been defined by Abū al-Suʿūd and al-Ḥamawī in [his commentary] of *al-Ashbāh*. If it does not fit these criteria, then he is the same as them in sin but not in disbelief.'[1]

3. It is recommended to leave imitating non-Muslims in specific instances.

Instances such as: leaving the customs of non-Muslims during their celebrations or well-known occasions, *even if* they have become familiar or known to Muslims.

This is because of the doubt that is in it. For example, Muslims should not embody the actions of Christians and non-Muslims during the New Year celebrations in order to refrain from being in positions of doubt or suspicion.

Qāḍī Khān[2] states, 'If a Muslim was to gift someone something on the Persian New Year, without intending with it a reverence for the day, but rather simply due to the customs of his community, then this would not be considered an act of disbelief. He **should** not do on this day anything that he would not have done on the day prior or after the day, in order to be vigilant against falling into "imitating" the non-Muslims.'[3]

The word 'should' [*yanbaghī*] in the aforementioned statement implies that it is recommended.

---

[1] *Al-Fatāwā al-Mahdiyya* (5:309)
[2] *Al-Khāniyya* (3:578)
[3] *Al-Baḥr al-Rāʾiq* (8:555)

قال المهدي الحنفي[1]: «ومعنى فهو منهم: أنَّه كافرٌ مثلهم إن تشبَّه بهم فيما هو كفرٌ، كأن عظَّم يوم عيدهم تبجيلاً لدينهم أو لبس زنارهم أو ما هو من شعارهم قاصداً بذلك التشبه استخفافاً بالإسلام، كما قيده به أبو السعود والحموي على «الأشباه»، وإلا فهو مثلهم في الإثم لا الكفر».

3. يُستحبُّ ترك المشابهة في حالات، منها: ترك عادة غير المسلمين في يوم أعيادهم ومناسباتهم المشهورة وإن اعتاده المسلمون؛ لما فيه من الشبهة، فلا يماثل النصارى في أعياد رأس السنة في عاداتهم وأفعالهم تنزهاً عن التُّهم والشبهات. قال قاضي خان[2]: «وإن أهدى يوم النَّيروز إلى إنسانٍ شيئاً ولم يرد به تعظيم اليوم وإنَّما فعل ذلك على عادة النَّاس لا يكون كفراً، وينبغي أن لا يفعل في هذا اليوم ما لا يفعله قبل ذلك اليوم ولا بعده وأن يحترز عن التَّشبُّه بالكفرة»[3]. وكلمة: «ينبغي» تفيد أنَّه يستحب له ترك ذلك.

---

(1) ينظر: الفتاوى المهدية 5: 309.

(2) ينظر: الخانية 3: 578.

(3) ينظر: البحر 8: 555.

4. **The Imitation of non-Muslims is permissible if the aforementioned defining principles are not present in the action.**

If the action has no relationship with their rites or are not matters specific to them—such as using a phone or computer—then it is permissible, as long as one does not purposefully intend to imitate them.

If the act is something that has become widespread in the Muslim community such as wearing shoes with socks underneath, or wearing a suit with a tie, and other things like it, then this is from the permissible actions as long as one does not intend to imitate through them.

4. يُباح التَّشبُّه إن لم يتوفَّر فيه أحد الضَّوابط السَّابقة في التَّشبُّه بغير المسلمين، فإن لم يكن الفعل المتشبه به شعاراً لهم: كاستخدام الكمبيوتر والهاتف، فإنَّه من المباحات إن لم يقصد التشبه بغير المسلمين، وإن كان الفعل المتشبّه شائعاً منتشراً في المجتمع المسلم كلبس جورب وحذاء فوقه أو لبس بدلة مع قرافة لها وأشباهها فإنَّه من المباحات إن لم يقصد التَّشبُّه بهم.

Chapter Four
Imitation and the Beard

After the aforementioned detail regarding the understanding of imitating non-Muslims, we will now discuss the rulings relating to shaving or shortening the beard, based on the foundation [aṣl] of imitation [tashabbuh]. This requires us to implement the aforesaid defining principles and scenarios on the beard, as follows:

Is shaving or shortening the beard considered to be from the rites or matters particular to non-Muslims? The answer to this is that the religious leaders of Judaism, Christianity, polytheists and others are all known for their long beards, and it appears that the practicing followers of those faiths also incline towards the beard, whereas the general majority do not keep the beard, rather this depends on what is fashionable, what they love or revere or what the general feeling is amongst the people. We see this more today than ever, since having a beard has become widespread fashion amongst some non-Muslims in Europe, America and Australia.

Consequently, considering the length or shaving of the beard as being specific to non-Muslims is something which is actually of varied disparity amongst them. Due to this, the action of growing or shaving the beard is not actually an issue of imitation.

As for the principle of *qaṣd* or purposeful intent, then this necessitates that one is sinful if the outward form of act is apparent with the purposeful intent to imitate them through it. This would imply that those that grow their beards imitating their (non-Muslims) religious figures has sinned, and those that shave or shorten their beards imitating non-Muslims in general have also sinned, since the causal factor ['illa]—the purposeful intent to imitate—is present.

المطلب الرابع
التَّشبُّه في اللحية

وبعد هذا التقرير لفكرة التَّشبُّه بغير المسلمين، فما هو الحكم الذي تأخذه اللِّحية في الحلق والقصّ بناءً على أصل التَّشبُّه، ويلزمنا أن نطبق الضوابط والحالات السابقة على مسألة اللِّحية على النحو الآتي:

هل يُعَدُّ حلق اللِّحية وقصّها شعاراً لغير المسلمين؟ والجواب: أنَّ رجال الدِّين من اليهود والنَّصارى والوثنيين وغيرهم يشيع بينهم اللحية وإطالتها، ويظهر أنَّ المتدينين منهم يميلون إلى اللِّحية، والعوام منهم الشائع عندهم عدم إطلاق اللِّحية، لكن يرجع للمزاج والمحبة والموضة في ذلك؛ لا سيما هذه الأيام فقد شاعت موضعة إطلاق اللحية عند غير المسلمين في أوروبا وأمريكيا واستراليا.

وبالتَّالي فاعتبار إطالة اللحية أو حلقها شعاراً لهم متفاوت بينهم، فلم تعد صورة الفعل بالحلق والإطلاق فيها مشابهة أصلاً.

وأمَّا ضابط القصد، فيلزم منه أن يكون الإثم إن كانت صورة الفعل موجودة وهو قصد التَّشبُّه بهم فيه، وهذا يقتضي أنَّ مَن أطلق لحيته تشبهاً برجال الدِّين منهم فهو آثم، ومَن حلق لحيته أو قصَّرها تشبهاً بغير المسلمين آثم أيضاً؛ لوجود العلّة وهي قصد التَّشبُّه.

Regarding the principle of 'who starts imitating first,' then this would mean that whoever imitated non-Muslims by shaving or shortening the beard first would be sinful. However, after this action became widespread in the community and became part of common practice then it is no longer a case of imitating, but rather part of the usage of the society itself. Due to this, the sin of imitation no longer applies, since the causal factor of imitation is not present, and the action is merely part of common custom and practice.

As for the principle of what benefits the Muslims, then this cannot be applied to the beard.

This is also the case for the principle of obscene or illicit action which cannot be applied to the beard.

In summary, the non-existence of the act of imitating in shaving or shortening the beard, and the widespread nature of both of these amongst Muslims, to the extent that it is part of their usage, means that shaving or shortening the beard cannot be considered as imitating non-Muslims. It is considered imitating, if one does these actions purposefully intending the imitation of non-Muslims, and such a person is thereby sinful, whether it is in shaving or shortening the beard.

Applying the scenarios and legal rulings of imitation we see that if one was to intend imitation of non-Muslims whilst intending mockery or belittling of Islam, then it is feared that he has fallen into disbelief. This applies to anyone who mocks a ruling of the Sacred Law, as previously mentioned, and he is sinful for purposefully intending imitation by shaving or shortening the beard. If, however, he does not purposefully intend imitation then it is recommended and sunna for him to lengthen the beard in order to stay out of doubtful matters.

وأمَّا ضابط تحقُّق الفعل ابتداءً، فهذا يقتضي أنَّ مَن تشبه بالحلق أو التقصير ابتداءً هو الآثم، ولكن بعد شيوع هذا الفعل في المجتمع وصيرورته عرفاً شائعاً، فلم يعد يُفعل للتَّشبه أصلاً وإنَّما لكونه عرفاً للمجتمع، فيسقط إثم التَّشبُّه؛ لفقدان علَّة التشبه؛ لكونه عرفاً.

وأمَّا ضابط صلاح العباد، فلا تدخل اللحية تحته.

وأما ضابط الفواحش والفجور، فلا تدخل اللحية تحته أيضاً.

فتحصَّل مما سبق: عدم وجود صورة مشابهة الفعل في حلق اللِّحية أو قصِّها، وشيوع الحلق والتقصير في المجتمع المسلم بحيث صار عرفاً لهم، فمن هذين الجانبين لا يعتبر التَّشبُّه ولا يؤاخذ به، وإنَّما يعتبر فيما لو قصد التَّشبُّه بغير المسلمين فهو آثم سواء كان في الحلق أو التقصير.

وبتطبيق حالات التَّشبُّه وأحكامها يكون من قصد التَّشبُّه بغير المسلمين في حلق اللحية وتقصيرها مُستخفّاً ومُستهزئاً بالإسلام يُخشى عليه الكفر؛ لأنَّ هذا حكم كلَّ مَن يستهزئ بحكم شرعيـ كما سبق ـ ويكون آثماً بقصد التَّشبُّه بهم بالحلق والتَّقصير، وإن لم يقصد التَّشبُّه فمستحبٌّ ومسنونٌ له إطلاق اللِّحية؛ خروجاً من شبهةِ التَّشبُّه.

Thus, we establish that imitating non-Muslims without purposeful intent is inadmissible as a cause for making keeping the beard necessary, upon which[1] there is punishment with Hellfire. Ibn Ḥajar in *Ittikhādh al-Awānī min al-Dhahab* says, 'The causal factor for forbidding the imitation of non-Muslims needs re-visiting, due to their being a threat [of punishment], and by simply imitating it does not lead to this.'[2] Moreover, Ḥarmala states with regards to drinking in gold vessels, 'The prohibition is merely one of slight offense since the causal factor is the imitation of non-Muslims.'[3]

Ibn Ḥajar explicitly states that the causal factor of imitating only comes to a level of being slightly offensive, meaning that it is regarded to be from 'leaving the more appropriate' [*khilāf al-awlā*]. This means, we should not be strict in this issue of shortening or shaving the beard, and Allah ﷻ knows best.

---

[1] [That is, if a necessary act is left.]
[2] *Fatḥ al-Bārī* (10:98)
[3] Ibid. (10:94)

2.4 التَّشبُّه في اللحية

وبهذا يتقرَّر: أنَّ المشابهة بنفسها بغير المسلمين بغير قصد لا تصلح أْتكون سبباً للوجوب الذي يترتب عليه العقاب بالنَّار، قال ابن حجر[1] في اتخاذ الأواني من الذهب: «وقيل: العلَّة في المنع التَّشبُّه بالأعاجم، وفي ذلك نظر؛ لثبوت الوعيد لفاعله، ومجرد التشبه لا يصل إلى ذلك». وقال حرملة في الشرب في آنية الذهب: «النهي فيه للتنزيه؛ لأنَّ علته ما فيه من التشبه بالأعاجم»[2]، وهذا صريحٌ من ابن حجر أنَّ علَّةَ المشابهة مدارها على كراهةِ التَّنزيه، وهي خلافُ الأولى، فينبغي أن لا نُشدِّد في هذه القضية كثيراً، والله أعلم.

---

(1) ينظَر: فتح الباري 10: 98.

(2) المصدر السابق 10: 94.

SECTION THREE
ACTING CONTRARY TO SOCIAL INTEGRITY [*MURŪʾA*]

Before we discuss the relationship between social integrity[1] and the beard, we must first define social integrity both linguistically and technically, and establish the effect social integrity has on rulings in the Ḥanafī school, which will eventually lead us to finally discuss the relationship between the beard and social integrity.

---

[1] [*Murūʾa* is a vast concept which is untranslatable into one or two words. It is considered to be 'the ideals of masculinity, comprising all knightly virtues, especially: manliness, valour, chivalry, generosity and a sense of honour.' (*Hans Wehr*, p. 1058) In this context, however, the term 'social integrity' is perhaps closer to the intended Arabic meaning.]

المبحث الثَّالث

من جهة مخالفة المروءة

يتعيَّن علينا قبل بيان تعلّق اللِّحية بالمروءة، أن نبيِّن المراد بالمروءة لغةً واصطلاحاً، ومكانة المروءة، وأثر المروءة في المذهب الحنفي، وعلاقة اللِّحية بالمروءة في المطالب الآتية:

CHAPTER ONE
THE LINGUISTIC AND TECHNICAL DEFINITIONS
OF SOCIAL INTEGRITY

Linguistically, social integrity or *murū'a* means: perfect masculinity. *Mar'u* in Arabic means 'man' and *mar'a* means 'woman,' and both refer to males and females who have reached maturity.[1] Social integrity can also come to mean 'humanity' [*insāniyya*][2] since one avoids that which is considered by the people of virtue and dignity, to lessen the worth of humanity.[3]

As mentioned, social integrity is also considered to be perfect masculinity. This is because someone who possesses perfect masculinity has within him the most virtuous qualities a man can possess; and if we were to take the meaning of 'humanity', then it is because he has within him the best qualities of humanity. Such a person thus has the best and most perfect qualities of both masculinity and humanity.

The technical definition is similar to the aforementioned. It involves personal qualities which, if someone embodies, means they have beautiful character and customs.[4]

Or is it (social integrity) the self-control which is the pivot from which come forth all good actions which are legally, intellectually and culturally praiseworthy.[5]

---

[1] *Al-Mughrib* (2:262), *Lisān al-'Arab* (1:154) & *al-Muḥīṭ fīl-Lugha* (2:443)
[2] *Mukhtār al-Ṣiḥāḥ* (p. 292) & *Lisān al-'Arab* (1:154)
[3] *Durar al-Ḥukkām* (4:407)
[4] *Al-Miṣbāḥ* (2:569) & *Qurra 'Ayn al-Akhyār* (7:492)
[5] *Al-Ta'rīfāt* (1:210)

المطلب الأول

تعريف المروءة لغةً واصطلاحاً

فالمروءة لغةً: كمال الرُّجولة، والمرأة مؤنث والمرء هو الرَّجل، ويطلقان على البالغ منهما[1]، وهي الإنسانية[2]، فيجتنب عمل شيء يوجب تنزل قدر الإنسانية عند أهل الفضل والكمال[3].

واعتبرت المروءة كمال الرُّجولة؛ لجمع صاحبها أفضل الصفات التي يتحلَّها به الرِّجال، وكانت بمعنى الإنسانية؛ لتوفر أكمل صفات الإنسان فيها، فكان صاحبها محققاً معنى الرُّجولة والإنسانية على الكمال.

واصطلاحاً لها تعاريف متقاربة منها:

آداب نفسانية تحمل مراعاتها الإنسان على الوقوف عند محاسن الأخلاق وجميل العادات[4].

أو هي قوة للنفس مبدأ لصدور الأفعال الجميلة عنها المستتبعة للمدح شرعاً وعقلاً وعرفاً[5].

---

(1) ينظر: المغرب 2: 262، ولسان العرب 1: 154، والمحيط في اللغة 2: 443.

(2) ينظر: مختار الصحاح ص292، ولسان العرب 1: 154.

(3) ينظر: درر الحكام 4: 407.

(4) ينظر: المصباح 2: 569، وقرة عين الأخيار 7: 492.

(5) ينظر: التعريفات 1: 210.

Or for someone to not display something which one has to excuse oneself from, such that it would lessen his position amongst people of intellect; or freeing the self from all blemishes and traits that people consider to be a deficiency.[1]

Or it is praiseworthy silence, protecting the tongue and avoiding foolishness. In other words: elevating the self beyond every lowly quality.[2]

Or it is to do permissible matters, which if one was to leave would be considered blameworthy according to his culture [*'urf*]. An example of this is the wearing of shoes in a country where it would be considered ugly for the likes of him to walk barefoot. It is also to leave permissible matters, which if one was to do would be considered blameworthy; such as eating in the marketplace in Arab culture.[3]

In summary, these definitions demonstrate that social integrity is related to good character, sound behaviour, and virtuous actions based on the culture of that time and place. Therefore, any action that belittles the status of the person in his community is considered to lower his social integrity.

---

[1] *Al-Baḥr al-Rā'iq* (7:92)
[2] *Taysīr al-Taḥrīr* (3:44)
[3] *Sharḥ Ḥudūd Ibn 'Arafa* (p. 44) & *Qawā'id al-Fiqh* (p. 479)

أو أن لا يأتي ما يعتذر منه مما يبخسه من مرتبته عند العقلاء.

أو صيانة النفس عن الأدناس وما يشينها عند الناس[1].

أو السَّمتُ الحسن وحفظ اللِّسان والاجتناب من السُّخف: أي الارتفاع عن كلِّ خُلُق دنيء[2].

أو هي المحافظة على فعل ما تركه من مباح يوجب الذَّم عرفاً: كترك الانتعال في بلد يستقبح فيه مشي مثله حافياً، وعلى ترك ما فعله من مباح يوجب ذمه عرفاً: كالأكل عندنا في السوق[3].

فتحصَّل من هذه التَّعاريف أنَّ المروءةَ متعلِّقةٌ بالأخلاق الحسنة والسُّلوكيات السَّوية والتَّصرُّفات الفاضلة على حسب العرف في ذلك الزَّمان والمكان، فكلُّ ما يُنقص من مرتبة فاعله في مجتمعه يُخِلُّ بمروءته.

---

[1] ينظر: البحر الرائق 7: 92.

[2] ينظر: تيسير التحرير 3: 44.

[3] ينظر: شرح حدود ابن عرفة ص44، وقواعد الفقه ص479.

CHAPTER TWO
THE IMPORTANCE OF SOCIAL INTEGRITY

The definition or understanding of social integrity in the Qur'an, prophetic traditions, and the words of the predecessors encompass all of the linguistic and technical definitions mentioned previously.

Social Integrity in the Qur'an

In the Qur'an, Allah ﷻ states, ❨*God commands justice, doing good and generosity towards relatives, and He forbids what is shameful, blameworthy and oppressive.*❩[1]

This verse indicates that perfect masculinity is a combination of beautiful qualities, and it is necessary for a Muslim to adorn himself with them, and to leave anything contrary to them. Ḥasan said, 'Allah ﷻ has made clear for you what it is (social integrity),' and he then read the verse, ❨*God commands justice, doing good and generosity towards relatives, and He forbids what is shameful, blameworthy and oppressive.*❩'[2]

Social Integrity in the Sunna

On the authority of Abū Hurayra, 'The Messenger of Allah ﷺ said, "The honour of a man is his religion, his social integrity is his intellect and his lineage is his character."'[3] Outward social integrity amongst people is defined by good quality clothing, handsome appearance, eating a variety of food, and being generous in feeding others. All these qualities, however, are easier for wealthy people to achieve.

---

[1] [*The Qur'an, A new translation by M. A. S. Abdel Haleem,*
The Bee, 16:90 (p. 172)]
[2] *Al-Murū'a* (p. 45)
[3] *Ṣaḥīḥ Ibn Ḥibbān* (2:232), *Musnad Aḥmad* (14:381) & *Al-Mustadrak* (1:12). Ḥākim said, 'It is sound upon the conditions of Muslim.'

المطلب الثاني

مكانة المروءة

يدور معنى المروءة في القرآن والحديث والآثار وكلام السلف على ما سَبَق إيراده في التعاريف اللغوية والاصطلاحية للمروءة.

فمن القرآن:

قوله تعالى: ﴿إنَّ الله يأمر بالعدل والإحسان وإيتاء ذي القربى وينهى عن الفحشاء والمنكر والبغي﴾[النحل: 90]، تدلُّ هذه الآية على أنَّ المروءةَ لجمعها الصّفات الحسنة التي ينبغي للمسلم أن يتحلَّى بها، ويترك ما سواها، قال الحسن: «قد فرغ الله ﷻ لك منها ثم قرأ:﴿إن الله يأمر بالعدل والاحسان وايتاء ذي القربى وينهى عن الفحشاء والمنكر والبغي﴾ هذه المروءة»(١).

ومن السُّنّة:

فعن أبي هريرة، قال ﷺ: «كرم المرء دينه، ومروءته عقله، وَحَسَبه خلقه»(٢)، فظاهر المروءة عند الناس حسن الزّي، وجمال الحال، والتوسُّع في الطعام والإطعام، وهذه أحوال مَن اتسع في المال فيمكنه ذلك.

---

(١) ينظر: المروءة ص45.

(٢) ينظر: صحيح ابن حبان2: 232، ومسند أحمد14: 381، والمستدرك1: 212، وقال الحاكم: صحيح على شرط مسلم.

The Messenger of Allah ﷺ said that social integrity was in fact the *intellect*, and it may be that the sagacious one is the one who has the ability and capability for it. Thus, when one's intellect reaches perfection, then so has his social integrity. *Murū'a* comes from the word *mar'u* which means a human being; and a human being is considered the most honoured of all creation.[1]

This is because it is his intellect that distinguishes him above all other creation; it is what helps him overcome all lowly characteristics and desires and leads to the truth of the creation and Creator.[2]

On the authority of 'Alī b. Abī Ṭālib ﷺ who said, 'The Messenger of Allah ﷺ said, "Whoever interacts with people without oppressing them, speaks to them without lying to them, and promises them without breaking his word, then such a person is from those who has perfected his social integrity, his uprightness is apparent, his companionship is incumbent and it is forbidden to speak ill of him in his absence."[3]

'Umar ﷺ relates that the Messenger of Allah ﷺ said, 'Do not hasten to punish a man of social integrity if he is virtuous.'[4] Abū Bakr al-Ṣiddīq ﷺ also relates, 'Do not hasten to punish a man of social integrity as long as it is not an action that requires capital punishment.'[5] This means that people should not hasten to punish someone from whom a wrong action is rare, except in cases of capital punishment from the limits set by Allah ﷻ, meaning that if such a case reached a judge who passed the judgment, then the implementation of that punishment is mandatory.[6]

---

[1] *Ma'ānī al-Akhbār* (al-Kalābādhī) (1:54)
[2] *Sharḥ al-Zurqānī 'alā al-Muwaṭṭa'* (3:59)
[3] *Musnad al-Shihāb* (1:322)
[4] *Sharḥ Mushkil al-Āthār* (6:150)
[5] *Musnad al-Shihāb* (1:422). Al-Haythamī states in *Majma' al-Zawā'id* (6:282), 'It is narrated by al-Ṭabarānī in *al-Ṣaghīr*, in the chain is Muḥammad b. Kathīr b. Marwān al-Fihrī who is considered weak.'
[6] *Fayḍ al-Qadīr Sharḥ al-Jāmi' al-Ṣaghīr* (3:228)

فكان النبي ﷺ أخبر أنَّ المروءة هو العقل، وقد يكون العاقل موسعاً عليه ومقدراً له، فإذا كمل عقل المرء تمَّت مروءته، وذلك أنَّ المروءة اشتقاقها من المرء، والمرء الإنسان، والإنسان إنَّما شرف على سائر الحيوانات[1]: أي لأنَّ به يتميّز عن الحيوانات ويعقل نفسه عن كلِّ خلق دنيء، ويكفها عن شهواتها الرديّة وطباعها الدنية، ويؤدِّي إلى كلِّ ذي حقٍّ حقَّه من الحقِّ والخَلْق[2].

وعن عليّ بن أبي طالب ﵁ قال ﷺ: «مَن عامل الناس فلم يظلمهم وحدثهم فلم يكذبهم، ووعدهم فلم يُخلفهم، فهو ممن كَمُلَت مروءته، وظهرت عدالتُه، ووجبت أخوته، وحَرُمَت غيبتُه»[3].

وعن عمر ﵁ قال ﷺ: «تجافوا عن عقوبة ذوي المروءة، وهو ذو الصلاح»[4]، وعن أبي بكر الصديق ﵁ قال ﷺ: «تجافوا عن عقوبة ذوي المروءة ما لم يكن حداً»[5]، أي لا تؤاخذوه بذنب ندر منه لمروءته إلا في حدّ من حدود الله تعالى، فإنَّه إذا بلغ الحاكم وثبت عنده وجبت إقامته[6].

---

(1) ينظر: معاني الأخبار للكلاباذي 1: 54.

(2) ينظر: شرح الزرقاني على الموطأ 3: 59.

(3) ينظر: مسند الشهاب 1: 322.

(4) ينظر: شرح مشكل الآثار 6: 150.

(5) ينظر: مسند الشهاب 1: 422، وقال الهيثمي في مجمع الزوائد 6: 282: رواه الطبراني في الصغير، وفيه محمد بن كثير بن مروان الفهري وهو ضعيف.

(6) ينظر: فيض القدير شرح الجامع الصغير 3: 228.

It has also been related from the Messenger of Allah ﷺ that he asked a man from Thaqīf, 'O brother from Thaqīf, what is the definition of social integrity amongst your people?' He responded, 'To be upright in religion and in one's social life, to be generous and keep blood ties.' The Messenger of Allah ﷺ replied, 'It is such amongst us too.'[1]

Social Integrity in the Words of the Companions

'Umar ﷺ said, 'The virtue of a believer is his God-consciousness, his religion is his lineage, and his social integrity is his character.'[2] He has made social integrity similar to good character.

---

[1] *Iṣlāḥ al-Māl* (p. 52), *al-Murū'a* (p. 28) & *Ḥilya al-Awliyā'* (3:155)

[2] *Al-Muwaṭṭa'* (3:659), *Sunan al-Dāraquṭnī* (4:467) & *al-Sunan al-Kubrā* by al-Bayhaqī (10:329). Al-Bayhaqī states, 'This chain of this suspended [*mawqūf*] [tradition] is sound.'

وروي عن النَّبي ﷺ أنَّه قال لرجل من ثقيف: «يا أخا ثقيفَ ما المروءة فيكم» ؟ قال: إصلاح الدِّينَ وإصلاح المعيشةَ وسخاء النَّفسَ وصلة الرَّحم. فقال ﷺ: «كذلك هو فينا»[1].

ومن الآثار:

قال عمر ﷺ: «كرم المؤمن تقواه، ودينه حَسَبُه، ومروءته خلقه»[2]، حيث جعل المروءة تتمثَّل بالأخلاق الحسنة.

---

[1] ينظر: إصلاح المال ص52، والمروءة ص28، وحلية الأولياء3: 155.

[2] ينظر: الموطأ3: 659، وسنن الدارقطني 4: 467، والسنن الكبرى للبيهقي 10: 329، وقال البيهقي: هذا الموقوف إسناده صحيح:

Ibn Masʿūd ﷺ said, 'Whoever humbles himself before a rich person and makes himself low out of reverence for him and desire for what he might acquire from him, has lost two thirds of his social integrity and half of his religion.'[1] In this statement, Ibn Masʿūd related the loss of social integrity to one's heart being attached to other than Allah and one desiring what is with other than Allah.

Muʿāwiya ﷺ said, 'Social integrity is made up of four things: uprightness in Islam, upholding people's rights with regards to money, protecting one's brothers and helping your neighbour.'[2]

---

[1] *Shuʿb al-Īmān* (10:503). Al-ʿAjlūnī mentions in *Kashf al-Khafāʾ* (2:287), 'Al-Bayhaqī also relates the following raised [*marfūʿ*] narration from Ibn Masʿūd, "Whoever woke up pain stricken (*maḥzūn*—it has also been narrated with the word *ḥazīn*) because of the world, then he has woke up angry with his Lord; and whoever woke up complaining of an affliction that has befallen him, then he is complaining about his Lord; and whoever enters [the house of] a rich person, humbling himself for him, has lost a third of his religion; and whoever read the Qurʾan but entered the fire, then he is from those who took the verses of Allah ﷻ in ridicule." And al-Ṭabarānī in *al-Ṣaghīr* also relates from Anas, in a raised narration that, "Whoever woke up pain stricken because of the world, then he has woke up angry with his Lord, and whoever woke up complaining of an affliction that has befallen him, then he is complaining about Allah ﷻ; and whoever humbles himself before a rich person to acquire what is in his hand has made Allah ﷻ angry (also narrated with the wording: 'what is in his hands,' has made Allah ﷻ angry). And, whoever is given the Qurʾan but entered the fire then he has been banished by Allah ﷻ (also narrated with the wording: 'to gain virtue that he does not possess, then Allah ﷻ has made his actions futile')." It is mentioned in *al-Maqāṣid* that, "They are both extremely weak," to the point where Ibn al-Jawzī has mentioned them in *al-Mawḍūʿāt* [as fabricated reports]. However, Jalāl [al-Dīn] al-Suyūṭī in *al-Taʿaqqubāt* states, "He is not correct in that, as al-Bayhaqī has narrated it from Ibn Masʿūd and Anas with the words, 'whoever enters [the house of] a rich person, humbling himself for him, has lost a third of his religion.'" He said that in both of them the chain is weak.'
[2] *Al-Murūʾa* (p. 45)

وقال ابنُ مسعود ﷺ: «ومَن خضع لغني ووضع له نفسه إعظاماً له، وطمعاً فيما قِبله، ذهب ثلثا مروءته وشطر دينه»[1]، حيث علَّق زوال المروءة بتعليق القلب بغير الله تعالى، والطَّمع فيما عند غير الله تعالى.

قال معاوية ﷺ: «المروءة في أربع: العفاف في الإسلام، واستصلاح المال، وحفظ الإخوان، وعون الجار»[2].

---

[1] ينظر: شعب الإيمان10: 503، وقال العجلوني في كشف الخفاء 2: 287: «وللبيهقي أيضًا عن ابن مسعود مرفوعًا: من أصبح محزونًا -وفي لفظ حزينًا - على الدنيا أصبح ساخطًا على ربه، ومن أصبح يشكو مصيبة؛ نزلت به؛ فإنما يشكو ربه، ومن دخل على غني فتضعضع له ذهب ثلثا دينه، ومن قرأ القرآن فدخل النار فهو ممن اتخذ آيات الله هزوًا. وللطبراني في الصغير عن أنس رفعه: من أصبح حزينًا على الدنيا؛ أصبح ساخطًا على ربه، ومن أصبح يشكو مصيبة نزلت به؛ فإنما يشكو الله تعالى، ومن تضعضع لغني لينال مما في يده؛ أسخط الله - وفي لفظ ما في يديه فقد أسخط الله عز وجل- ومن أعطي القرآن فدخل النار أبعده الله. وفي لفظ: لينال فضل ما عنده؛ أحبط الله عمله. قال في المقاصد: وهما واهيان جدًا؛ حتى إن ابن الجوزي ذكرهما في الموضوعات؛ لكن قال الجلال السيوطي في التعقبات: ولم يصب في ذلك فقد رواه البيهقي عن ابن مسعود وأنس بلفظ: من دخل على غني فتضعضع له؛ ذهب ثلثا دينه. قال في كل منهما إسناده ضعيف».

[2] ينظر: المروءة ص45.

In this statement he relates social integrity to these praiseworthy traits and behaviours.

From the Sayings of the Predecessors

Al-Aḥnaf said, 'Social integrity is to be patient over that which angers you, and to be silent over your right until it is asked of you.'[1] He also said that it is, 'being learned in the religion, being patient in the face of hardship and being good to one's parents.'[2]

Muhammad b. 'Imrān al-Taymī said, 'There is nothing more difficult to preserve than social integrity. He was asked, "What is social integrity?" He replied, "To not do something in secret which you would be shy to do in public."'[3]

Ibrāhīm al-Nakha'ī said, 'It is not from social integrity to turn your head a lot when walking in the street, or to walk quickly.'[4]

From these traditions and statements on social integrity, we find that its definition varies between time and place. This is because it is based on the culture of the people, and due to this, each person expresses the definition of perfect character or behaviour based on their culture; and Allah ﷻ knows best.

---

[1] *Al-Murū'a* (p. 39)
[2] Ibid. (p. 42)
[3] Ibid. (p. 56)
[4] Ibid. (p. 78)

حيث جعل المروءة متعلِّقةٌ بهذه السُّلوكيات الحسنة والصِّفات الحميدة.

ومن أقوال السلف:

قال الأحنف: «المروءة أن تصبر على ما غاظك وتصمت عمَّا عندك حتى يُلتمس منك»[1]. وقال: «الفقه في الدِّين والصَّبر على النَّوائب وبَرّ الوالدين»[2].

وقال محمد بن عمران التيمي: «ما شيء أشدُّ حملاً من المروءة، قيل: وأي شيء المروءة، قال: أن لا تفعل شيئاً في السرّ تستحي منه في العلانية»[3].

وقال إبراهيم النخعي: «ليس من المروءة كثرة الالتفات في الطريق، ولا سرعة المشي»[4].

ومن خلال هذا العرض للأحاديث والآثار والأقوال في المروءة نجد أنَّها متفاوتةٌ من زمن إلى زمن ، ومن مكان إلى مكان؛ لأنَّ مدارها على العرف، فكلُّ واحدٍ عبَّر عنها على حسب عرفه في أكمل الأخلاق والتَّصرُّفات، والله أعلم.

---

(1) ينظر: المروءة ص39.

(2) ينظر: المصدر السابق ص42.

(3) ينظر: المصدر السابق ص56.

(4) ينظر: المصدر السابق ص78.

CHAPTER THREE
THE EFFECT OF SOCIAL INTEGRITY
IN THE ḤANAFĪ SCHOOL

One who follows the rulings of the Ḥanafī school will recognise the clear effect of social integrity in some of the chapters of *fiqh*. These include, accepting the testimony, the appearance of Muslims like that regarding clothing, and one's manners when dealing with others and taking into consideration their feelings.

However, many behaviours can be considered good and acceptable in one society but not in another, and we have no means of determining what is good and acceptable except through examining the culture of a particular community. Thus, the state of someone's dress is no less important than the state of their mannerisms and speech. Similarly, in order to understand someone's words we generally have to refer to their culture to determine what they meant, as people use words intending a specific meaning.

Social integrity is the standard which differentiates between the praiseworthy and blameworthy behaviours of a Muslim. Someone whose behaviours are praiseworthy are considered so depending on their culture, and likewise if they are considered blameworthy, then this is deemed as a defect or deficiency in his social integrity.

As long as social integrity is considered a constituent of culture, it takes the ruling of culture with respect to its effect on legal rulings. Culture is part of the application aspect of a legal ruling. This is because a legal ruling has two aspects: the aspect of how it is derived [*istinbāṭ*], and this is related to legal theory [*uṣūl al-fiqh*], and the aspect of how it is applied [*taṭbīq*], which is related to the guidelines of a Mufti [*rasm al-muftī*].

أثر المروءة في المذهب الحنفي

المتتبع لفروع المذهب الحنفية يظهر له الأثر الواضح للمروءة في بعض الأبواب الفقهية: كقبول الشهادة، وهيئة المسلم كاللباس، وتصرفاته في كيفية التعامل مع الآخرين ومراعات مشاعرهم.

فكثير من التصرفات تكون حسنة ومقبولة في مجتمع ومعيبة ومنكرة في مجتمع آخر، ولا سبيل لنا لمعرفة ذلك إلا من خلال النظر في عرف ذلك المجتمع، فالحال في اللباس والتصرفات لا يختلف عن الحال في الكلام، فعادة نرجع لتفسير مراد المتكلم من كلامه على حسب عرفه، فهم يطلقون هذا اللفظ ويقصدون به معنى معين.

فالمروءةُ هي الميزانُ للعرف الممدوح من المذموم في التَّصرُّفات الصَّادرة من المسلم، فما كان من التَّصرُّفات ممدوحاً عُدَّ من المروءة، وما كان منها مذموماً عُدَّ من خوارم المروءة.

وطالما أنَّ المروءةَ جزءٌ من العرف، فتأخذ المروءة حكم العرف في التأثير على الأحكام الشرعية، والعرف من الجانب التطبيقي للحكم الشرعي؛ لأنَّالحكم الشرعيّ له طرفان: طرف في كيفيّة استنباطه، ويكون بأصول الفقه، وطرف في كيفيّة تطبيقه ويكون برسم المفتي.

This method of organisation greatly distinguishes legal rulings, since with consideration of the rules of *rasm al-muftī* we can achieve the justice that is required and apply the ruling in a required manner. Ibn 'Ābidīn says, 'From the things that help us recognise that a *mujtahid* (independent jurist) took into consideration the culture of his time, is that if he was here today he would have ruled differently to his first ruling. It is for this reason that from the stipulations of *ijtihād* (independent legal judgement) is for someone to intimately know the customs of the people ['*ādāt al-nās*].

'Many rulings differ due to differing of time, due to changes in the culture of the people, due to necessity, or due to the corruption of the era, to the extent that if the ruling was to remain the same, it would cause harm and difficulty for people. This would be contrary to the purpose of the Sacred Law, which is built upon bringing ease and repelling harm, in order for the world to remain on the best system of organisation and highest perfection.'[1]

Ibn 'Ābidīn also said, 'A judge should have knowledge of general matters but also of the reality and condition of a people. Through this he will be able to distinguish between one who is honest and a liar, and between truthfulness and falsehood, and compare between things, thereby giving the reality the necessary ruling and not making the necessary contrary to the reality.

'This also applies to the Mufti who delivers legal verdicts according to culture; he must know the times and states of the people, and know whether a certain custom is general or specific [to a people or place] and whether it is contrary to the text or not. He must also have graduated at the hands of a skilled teacher, and it is not enough for him to have simply memorised rulings and proofs. a *mujtahid* must know the customs of the people, as mentioned previously, and such is the same for the Mufti.

---

[1] *Nashr al-'Urf* (2:123)

وهذا التَّرتيب يعطي للأحكام الفقهيّة ميزةً عظيمةً جداً بمراعاة قواعد رسم المفتي عند تطبيقها، فيتحقَّق العدل المطلوب، والمطابقة المرجوة، قال ابنُ عابدين[١]: «وكثيرٌ منها ما يُبيِّنُه المجتهدُ على ما كان في عرفِ زمانه بحيث لو كان في زمان العرف الحادث لقال بخلاف ما قاله أوَّلاً؛ ولهذا قالوا في شروط الاجتهاد: إنَّه لا بُدَّ فيه من معرفةِ عادات الناس.

فكثيرٌ من الأحكام تختلفُ باختلافِ الزَّمان؛ لتغيّر عرف أهله، أو لحدوثِ ضرورةٍ، أو فساد أهلِ الزَّمان بحيث لو بقي الحكم على ما كان عليه أوَّلاً للزم منه المشقّة والضّرر بالنّاس، ولخالف الشَّريعة المبنيّةَ على التّخفيف والتّيسير ودفع الضّرر والفساد؛ لبقاء العالم على أتمّ نظام وأحسن إحكام».

وقال أيضاً: «لا بُدَّ للحاكمِ من فقه في أحكام الحوادث الكليّة، وفقه في نفسِ الواقع وأحوال النّاس، يميِّز به بين الصّادق والكاذب، والمحقّ والمبطل، ثمّ يُطابقُ بين هذا وهذا، فيُعطى الواقعَ حكمَه من الواجب، ولا يَجعل الواجبَ مُخالفاً للواقع.

وكذا المفتي الذي يُفتي بالعُرف لا بُدَّ له من معرفة الزّمان وأحوالِ أهلِه ومعرفة أنَّ هذا العرفَ خاصٌّ أو عامٌّ، وأنَّه مخالفٌ للنّصِّ أو لا، ولا بدّ له من التّخرُّج على أُستاذٍ ماهرٍ ولا يَكفيه مجرّدُ حفظ المسائل والدّلائل، فإنَّ المجتهدَ لا بُدَّ له من معرفةِ عاداتِ الناس، كما قدّمناه فكذا المفتي.

____

[١] ينظر: نشر العرف ٢: ١٢٣.

For this reason, in *Muniya al-Muftī*, towards the end, he says, 'If a man memorised all the books of our Imams, he must still train himself upon issuing legal verdicts until he is guided to it. This is because many issues are dealt with according to the customs of the people of the age, in matters which are not contrary to the Sacred Law.'[1]

No doubt one of the most observed principles in *rasm al-muftī* in terms of delivering and applying rulings is looking at the culture of a given society. For this reason, the ruling differs from place to place, and from time to time, depending on the judgment of the people's culture. Al-Juwaynī said, 'Details return back to culture ['urf], and the most knowledgeable of people in culture is the one most knowledgeable in *the fiqh* of *mu'āmalāt* (transactions).'[2]

This is because culture relates to the applicatory side of *fiqh* or law, and it is not related to the derivative side of *fiqh* like many contemporary scholars think. Culture is related to two things:

1. Understanding the intent of the speaker in what he says, since we use words intending a specific meaning, which we have essentially become acquainted with when it is used. If the word is general then it will include other than what one meant, for example: the word 'meat [*laḥm*]' includes the flesh of all animals including birds, cows, sheep, etc. However, when we use it, we may mean beef and mutton rather than poultry. Thus, if a person said, 'I swear by God, I will never eat meat' and then ate chicken, he would not be considered to have broken his oath. This is because culturally, 'meat' does not include chicken. Thus, we have benefitted from the culture regarding what the person intended by a specific word. This example can be used to judge other things.

---

[1] *Nashr al-'Urf* (2:123)
[2] *Nihāya al-Maṭlab* (al-Juwaynī) (11:416)

ولذا قال في آخر «منية المفتي»: لو أنَّ الرَّجلَ حفظ جميعَ كتب أصحابنا لا بُدَّ أن يَتَلْمَذَ للفتوى حتى يهتدي إليها؛ لأنَّ كثيراً من المسائلِ يُجاب عنه على عادات أهل الزَّمان فيما لا يُخالف الشَّريعة» [1].

وإنَّ أكثر قاعدة من الرسم تُراعى في الفتوى والتَّطبيق هي النَّظرُ إلى عرف المجتمع، فيختلف الحكم من مكانٍ إلى مكانٍ وزمانٍ إلى زمانٍ على ما حسب ما يقتضيه عرف النَّاس، قال الجوينيّ [2]: «والتَّعويل في التَّفاصيل على العرف، وأعرف النَّاس به أعرفهم بفقه المعاملات»؛ لأنَّ العرف من الجانب التَّطبيقيّ للفقه، وليس من الجانب الاستنباطيّ للحكم كما يظنّه عامّة المعاصرين، ومَرَدُّ العرف إلى أمرين:

1. فهمُ مراد المتكلِّم من كلامِه، فنحن نستخدم ألفاظ ونريد بها معاني معيّنة تعارفنا في إطلاقها عليها، وإن كان اللَّفظ عامّاً يشمل غيرها، مثل: اللحم يشمل لحم سائر الحيوانات من الطَّيور والبقر والغنم وغيرها، ولكن تعارفنا عند إطلاقها على إرادة لحم البقر والغنم لا الطيور مثلاً، فإذا قال شخص: والله لا آكل لحماً، ثمَّ أكل دجاجاً لا يحنث؛ لأنَّه لا يعتبر لحماً عرفاً، فاستفدنا من العرف معرفة مقصود المتكلِّم من كلامه، وقس عليه.

---

[1] ينظر: نشر العرف 2: 123.

[2] ينظر: نهاية المطلب للجويني 11: 416.

2. Knowing the appropriateness of the context or basis of the causal factor for the legal ruling, as the ruling itself is constant from the legislator, and culture does not change this ruling. However, the ruling is built on a causal factor and this causal factor is in need of a context and basis for its application.

Thus, understanding the culture helps us apply this. For example, with regards to the ruling that only the testimony of an upright witness is accepted, as is mentioned in the Qur'an, ❨*Out of those you approve as witnesses.*❩[1] In this instance, the culture of a people will help determine what is considered upright.

In the time of Abū Ḥanīfa ⚶, people were not in need of being verified in terms of their uprightness. However, in the time of Abū Yūsuf and Muḥammad, the states of people changed.

Consequently, culture does not at all exceed these two definitions. It does not change the legal ruling and rulings are also not derived from it. Rather, it defines the ruling by clarifying the intent of the speaker and to know the suitability of the context to the causal factor of the ruling.

Ensuring that the context is suitable for the ruling is very important. Thus, before applying the ruling we need to know the causal factor and then look at whether the context is suitable for it or not. If it is not suitable then the ruling cannot be applied here.

Therefore, social integrity is categorised under both types of culture, because if social integrity is related to speech then it is related to understanding the intent of the speaker from the words he uses, and in this instance social integrity helps us understand whether the speech of the speaker is something good and praiseworthy or if it is blameworthy.

---

[1] [*The Qur'an, A new translation by M. A. S. Abdel Haleem,*
The Cow, 2:282 (p. 32)]

2.معرفة صلاحيّة المحلّ لعلّة الحكم، فالحكم في نفسه ثابت من الشّارع الحكم، والعرف لا يغيّر الحكم، لكن الحكم مبنيّ على علّة، وهذه العلّة تحتاج إلى محلّ في تطبيقها، فالعرف يساعدنا على تطبيق ذلك، مثاله: أنَّ الحكم عدم قبول إلا شهادة العدل، كما شهد القرآن: {ممن ترضون من الشهداء}[البقرة: ٢٨]، والعرف يُساعدنا في معرفةِ العدل، ففي زمن أبي حنيفة ﷺ لم يَحتج للتّزكية في العدالة؛ لأنَّ النّاس عدول، وفي زمن الصَّاحبين تغيَّرت أحوال النّاس، فنحتاج لتحقُّق علّة الحكم من العدالة بالتَّزكية، فمَن لم يكن عدلاً لا تُقبل شهادته، هذا هو الحكم، ولكن كيف نتعرَّف على العدالة، حيث أمكن ذلك بالعرف.

وبالتالي لا يخرج العرف عن هذين المعنيين البتّة، فلا يكون مُغيّراً للحكم الشَّرعيّ أبداً، ولا تستنبط به الأحكام أيضاً، وإنَّما هو معرّف للحكم ببيان مقصود المتكلّم من كلامه، ومعرفة صلاحيّة المحلّ لعلّة الحكم.

وتَبيَّن أنَّ المحلّ صالح للحكم أمر مهمٌّ جداً؛ إذ نحتاج قبل تطبيق كلِّ حكم أن نتعرَّف على علّته أوَّلاً ثمّ ننظر هل المحلّ مناسب لها أم لا؟ فإن لم يكن مناسباً لها فإنَّ الحكم لا يطبق هنا.

وبالتالي تندرج المروءة تحت نوعي العرف؛ لأنَّ المروءةَ إذا كانت متعلِّقة بالكلام فهي داخلة في فهم مراد المتكلِّم من كلامه، حيث تساعدنا المروءة للوصول إلى ما تكلَّم به المتكلِّم هل هو شيء حسنٌ وممدوحٌ أم أنَّه شيء مذمومٌ.

And if social integrity is related to behaviour and appearance then this would be considered to be within the appropriateness of the context or basis of the causal factor, and thereby social integrity would help us recognise whether these behaviours and appearances are praiseworthy in the community and therefore recommended, or whether it is blameworthy and therefore disliked religiously, thus preventing a person's testimony being acceptable before the law. This is because whosoever performs such blameworthy actions may not refrain from lying or be concerned with what others say of him, and both of these are points of doubt with regards to one's credibility as a witness before the law.

The following are examples of things that demean one's social integrity, such that it would make one's testimony unacceptable, since if one's social integrity is no longer in place, one may not refrain from lying.[1] Such actions prevent the acceptability of a person's testimony even if they are not considered unlawful:[2]

- Relieving oneself outside where one can be seen by the public
- Eating outside in public areas
- Walking in the marketplace bare-chested
- Stretching your legs out in front of people
- Uncovering one's head in situations where doing so would be considered bad etiquette and would lessen one's social integrity or modesty
- For an old man to wrestle juveniles in the mosque

---

[1] *Al-Ikhtiyār* (2:148)
[2] *Al-Baḥr* (7:92)

وإن كانت المروءة متعلِّقة بالتَّصرُّفات والهيئات فهي داخلة فيمعرفة صلاحيّة المحلّ لعلّة الحكم، حيث تساعدنا المروءة في معرفة أنَّ مثل هذا التَّصرُّف والهيئة حسنة في المجتمع فتكون مستحبة، أو هي مذمومة فتكون مكروهة ديانة ومانعة من قبول الشَّهادة قضاءً؛ لأنَّ مَن يفعلها لا يمتنع عن الكذب ولا يُبالي بكلام النَّاس عليه، فيكون متهماً في شهادته.

ومن أمثلة مايكون خارماً للمروءة ـ فلا تقبل شهادة مَن يفعل شيئاً من الأفعال المستخفَّة؛ لأنَّه يسقط المروءة فلا يتحاشى عن الكذب[1]، فما يخل بالمروءة يمنع قبول الشهادة وإن لم يكن محرماً[2] ـ:

- البول على الطريق بحيث يراه الناس.

- والأكل على الطريق.

- والمشي في السوق بالسروال وحده.

- ومد رجله عند الناس.

- وكشف رأسه في موضع يُعَدُّ فعله خفَّة وسوء أدب وقلَّة مروءة وحياء.

- ومصارعة الشيخ الأحداث في الجامع.

---

[1] ينظر: الاختيار 2: 148.

[2] ينظر: البحر الرائق 7: 92.

- Stealing a morsel [of food]
- Excessive jesting leading to frivolous behaviour
- Keeping the company of vulgar people
- Mocking people
- A jurist wearing a *qabā'*[1]
- Racing pigeons[2]

Ibn Nujaym also drew attention to addictions also being reason to cause demeaning of one's social integrity thereby leading to a rejection of his witness statement.[3]

---

[1] [A kind of tunic resembling the kaftan, generally reaching to the middle of the shank divided down the front, and made to overlap the chest (*Lanes Lexicon*, Supplement, p. 2984)]
[2] *Al-Baḥr* (7:92) & *Majmaʿ al-Anhur* (2:200)
[3] *Al-Baḥr* (7:92)

3.3 أثر المروءة في المذهب الحنفي

- وسرقة لقمة.
- والإفراط في المزح المفضي إلى الاستخفاف.
- وصحبة الأراذل.
- والاستخفاف بالناس.
- ولبس الفقيه قباء.
- ولعب الحمام[1].

ونبَّه ابن نجيم[2] على اشتراط الإدمان في خوارم المروءة حتى لا تقبل شهادته.

---

(1) ينظر: البحر الرائق 7: 92، ومجمع الأنهر 2: 200.

(2) ينظر: البحر الرائق 7: 92.

CHAPTER FOUR
THE RELATIONSHIP BETWEEN
THE BEARD AND SOCIAL INTEGRITY

The previous chapters have made clear that social integrity is a part of culture and it is the balance that judges between praiseworthy and blameworthy culture. Social integrity relates to the permissible, and thus people will judge some permissible actions to be beautiful and others to be ugly depending on their culture and customs, and the Sacred Law has given due recognition to this. Ibn Mas'ūd ﷺ said, 'Whatever the Muslims see as good is good with Allah ﷻ, and whatever they see as ugly, it is ugly with Allah ﷻ.'[1]

Applying this to the shaving and shortening of the beard means that it is something that will be judged as either beautiful or ugly by society. Therefore, if shaving or shortening the beard is considered ugly then it will be blameworthy and thereby offensive to the extent that it is considered ugly by society, and so the testimony of a person who shaves or shortens his beard would not be accepted. And if the action is not considered ugly, then it is not offensive, and the witness testimony of such a person would be accepted.

This means that the ruling pertaining to the beard varies from society to society. In societies in which the shaving or shortening of the beard is ugly, it is offensive to do so, and in those that do not consider it ugly, it is not offensive, such as in Turkey and Middle Asia and China. This is because since the issue of the beard is related to culture, the legal ruling will differ according to the culture and the way it relates to social integrity.

---

[1] *Musnad Aḥmad* (1:379), *Musnad al-Ṭayālisī* (p. 33), *al-Muʾjam al-Kabīr* (9:112) & others. He states in *Kashf al-Khafāʾ* (2:221), 'It is suspended [*mawqūf*] and good [*ḥasan*].'

المطلب الرابع
علاقة اللِّحية بالمروءة

تبيَّن لنا مما سبق أنَّ المروءةَ جزء من العرف، وهي الميزان للعرف الممدوح من المذموم، ومرد المروءة إلى الأمور المباحة، فيكون للنَّاس استحسان بعضها أو استقباحه على حسب ثقافتهم وعاداتهم، والشريعةُ المطهرة اعتبرت مثل هذا الاستحسان والاستقباح، قال ابن مسعود ﷺ: «ما رآه المسلمون حسناً فهو عند الله تعالى حسن، وما رآه المسلمون قبيحاً فهو عند الله تعالى قبيح»[1].

وتطبيق هذا الأمر على اللحية حلقاً أو قصّاً يُدخلها في دائرة الأُمور المستحسنة أو المستقبحة في المجتمع، فإن كان حلقها أو قصّها مستقبحاً تكون مذمومة، فيكره الحلق أو القصّ على مقدار الاستقباح له في المجتمع، ولا تقبل شهادة الحالق أو القاصّ، وإن لم يكن حلقُها وقصُّها مستقبحاً في المجتمع فلا يكره الحلق أو القصّ، وتقبل شهادة الحالق والقاصّ لها.

وهذا الأمر يجعل حكم اللحية متفاوتٌ من مجتمع لمجتمع، ففي المجتمعات التي يستقبحون ذلك يُكره، والمجتمعات التي لا تستقبح هذا لا يُكره: كالأتراك وأواسط أسيا والصين؛ لأنَّها لما تعلَّقت بالعرف، فيختلف حكمها على حسب العرف، ومقياس المروءة فيه.

---

[1] ينظر: مسند أحمد 1: 379، ومسند الطيالسي ص33، والمعجم الكبير 9: 112، وغيرها، وقال في كشف الخفاء 2: 221: وهو موقوف حسن.

This was the response of the Mufti of Damascus al-ʿImādī (d. 1171 AH) when asked whether the testimony of a shaved person could be accepted, 'I do not find an explicit text relating to this due to limited time, however, if shaving the beard is considered to detract from social integrity then it prevents its acceptance, and if not, then it would not.'[1]

Like al-ʿImādī, ʿAbd al-Ḥalīm al-Laknawī said something similar in the covering of the head in prayer where he related it to culture and social integrity; he states, 'Praying without covering the head is offensive in societies where the people would not visit their leaders without covering their heads, nor would they even leave their homes. However, in societies where this is not from the customs of the people, it is not offensive. The belief that if the Imam has not covered his head, the prayer of the followers with covered heads will be offensive, has become a common belief amongst the laity. There is no evidence for this belief, so take heed of this.'[2]

This method of arriving at verdicts and rulings indicates a depth of their understanding, and their ability to relate issues to their foundational principles [*uṣūl al-binā*] when issuing rulings. This, in reality, is what *fiqh* is; and Allah ﷻ knows best.

---

[1] *Al-ʿUqūd al-Duriyya fī Tanqīḥ al-Fatāwā al-Ḥāmidiyya* (1:329). Ibn ʿĀbidīn's discussion with regards to it and the author's evaluation of Ibn ʿĀbidīn's discussion will follow later.
[2] *Naf al-Muftī wal-Sāʾil* (p. 38)

3.4 علاقة اللِّحية بالمروءة

وأجاب بهذا مفتي دمشق العِمادي (ت1171هـ) عندما سئل: في شهادة محلوق اللحية هل تقبل أم لا ؟ فقال:«لم أجد نقلاً صريحاً في المسألة مع ضيق الوقت وكثرة الأشغال، فإن كان حلق اللحية يُخل بالمروءة يمنع القبول وإلا فلا»[1].

وما قاله العِمادي في اللحية قال مثله عبد الحليم اللكنوي في تغطية الرَّأس في الصَّلاة حيث أرجعها للعرف والمروءة، فقال: «تُكره الصلاة بدون العمامة في البلاد التي عادة سكانها أنَّهم لا يذهبون إلى الكبراء بدون العمامة، بل ولا يخرجون من بيوتهم إلا متعممين، وأما في البلاد التي لا يعتادون فيها ذلك فلا، وقد اشتهر بين العوامّ أنَّ الإمامَ إن كان غير متعمم والمقتدون متعممين فصلاتُهم مكروهة، وهذا أيضاً خرق من القول لا دليل عليه، فاحفظ»[2].

وهذه الطريقة في تقرير الأحكام تدلُّ على رسوخ قدمهما في التَّخريج، وإرجاعهما المسائل إلى أصول بنائها عند الإفتاء بها، وهذه هو الفقه حقيقة، والله أعلم.

---

[1] ينظر: العقود الدرية في تنقيح الفتاوى الحامدية1: 329، وسيأتي مناقشة ابن عابدين له، ومناقشة الباحث لابن عابدين.

[2] ينظر: نفع المفتي والسائل ص 38.

SECTION FOUR
IMITATING FEMALES AND SHAVING THE BEARD

Before we delve into explaining the relationship between imitating females and shaving the beard in the following chapters, it is important to mention the intended meaning of imitation and the prohibition in imitating that has been mentioned in the sunna and the legal ruling of imitating females in the Ḥanafī school.

المبحث الرابع

التشبه بالنساء في حلق اللحية

يجدر بنا قبل بيان علاقة التَّشبُّه بالنِّساء في حلق اللحية أن نعرض المقصود بالتَّشبه، والمنع من التَّشبه في السنة، وحكم التشبه بالنساء عند الحنفية، وعلاقة التشبه بالنساء بحلق اللحية في المطالب الآتية:

Chapter One
Imitating Females and its Intended Meaning

The intended meaning of the term 'imitating females' is the imitation of females by males in clothes, items of adornment, actions and speech. However, it does not include imitating in those things that are deemed to be considered from righteousness.

Clothing and items of adornment are considered to be from imitation when a male wears that which is specific for females like, the veil, necklaces, bracelets, anklets, earrings and the like. All of these are regarded as inappropriate for men to wear. Likewise, it is considered to be from imitation when females wear things that are considered specific for males like, flat sandals and walking with them in male gatherings, cloaks, headgear, turbans and other similar items, which are regarded as inappropriate for women to wear.

However, it is vital to understand that it is the culture of a people that determines which attire is specific for males and which is specific for females, as according to the Sacred Law it is compulsory for the male to merely cover the area between the navel and the knees, with the legal ruling of anything exceeding that being referred to social integrity. For a female, it is compulsory to cover her whole body except her face and palms, with clothing that does not reveal the shape of her limbs; anything exceeding that is referred again to culture. What is apparent is that when one exceeds that which is compulsory to cover for both males and females, it is essentially culture that judges and delimits what can be worn.

المطلب الأول

المقصود بالتَّشبه بالنِّساء

والمقصود بالتَّشبه بالنِّساء: هو تشبه الرِّجال بالنِّساء في اللِّباس والزِّينة والأفعال والكلام لا التَّشبه في أمور الخير.

ففي اللباس والزِّينة:بأن يلبس الرَّجل الملابس التي تختصّ بالنساء مثل لبس المقانع والقلائد والأسورة والخلاخل والقرط ونحو ذلك مما ليس للرجال لبسه، وكذلك تتشبه النساء بالرجال بأن تلبس ما يلبس الرجال كلبس النعال الرقاق والمشي بها في محافل الرِّجال ولبس الأردية والطيالسة والعمائم ونحو ذلك مما ليس لهن استعماله[1].

وتعيين أنَّ هذا اللباس مختصٌّ بالرجال أو النِّساء راجعٌ لعرف كلِّ قوم، فمن جهة الشَّرع يشترط ستر العورة للرجل ما بين السرّة والركبة وما جاوزه فالحكم فيه للمروءة، وللمرأة يشترط ستر العورة وهي جميع جسمها إلا الوجه والكفين بلباس لا يصف الأعضاء وما جاوزه فالحكم للعرف، فتبيَّن أنَّ ما تجاوز ستر العورة لكلِّ من الرَّجل والمرأة نحتكم فيه للعرف، والعرف يُحدِّد لباس كلِّ منهما.

---

[1] ينظر: عمدة القاري22: 41.

١٥٥

Al-ʿAynī remarks that, 'The manner of dress can differ with the differing culture of each country. There may be people who do not distinguish between the clothing of females and males, however, the females would be distinguished by the *ḥijāb* and lack of exposure.'[1] This is a clear statement by al-ʿAynī that differences in clothing are an issue that is ultimately referred back to culture and therefore, as long as the aforementioned conditions are fulfilled, we should not be overly strict or rigid with regards to it.

With regards to imitating females in one's actions and speech, it is considered to be so when a male performs actions that are specific to females, such as being physically effeminate, or effeminate in speech and gait.[2]

Effeminacy [*inkhināth*] is the affectation of an inclining of the body from side-to-side and of languor. The noun *khunth* is pronounced with the *ḍamma*, and from it the word *mukhannath* is derived. The construct of *khunth* indicates softness and languidness. If one says: '*Takhannatha fī kalāmihī*,' it means he spoke a word in a way that resembles females, in both speech and manner. This can sometimes be due to an inborn disposition and sometimes due to affectation; however, it is the latter that is blameworthy, and not the former. A *mukhannath* can also be used to describe the one with whom anal intercourse is committed.[3]

---

[1] *ʿUmda al-Qārī* (22:41)
[2] Ibid.
[3] Ibid.

1.4 المقصود بالتَّشبه بالنِّساء

قال العَينيّ[1]: «وهيئة اللباس قد تختلف باختلاف عادة كلِّ بلد، فربَّما قوم لا يفترق زيُّ نسائهم من رجالهم، لكن تمتاز النِّساء بالاحتجاب والاستتار»، وهذا صريح من العيني بأنَّ هيئات اللباس المختلفة مسألة عرفية، فيلزمنا أن لا نشدِّد فيها طالما تحقَّقت الشروط السابقة.

وفي الأفعال والكلام:بأن يفعل الرَّجل الأفعال التي هي مخصوصة بالنِّساء كالانخناث في الأجسام والتَّأنيث في الكلام والمشي[2].

والانخناث: وهو التَّثني والتَّكسُّر، والاسم الخُنث بالضمّ، ومنه سمي المخنَّث، وتركيب الخنث يَدلُّ على لين وتكسُّر، وتخنَّث في كلامه أي: تكلَّم بكلام هو الذي يُشبه النِّساء في أقواله وأفعاله وتارةً يكون هذا خلقياً وتارةً تكلُّفاً، وهذا هو المذموم الملعون لا الأوَّل، ويطلق المخنث على الذي يؤتى ويلاط به[3].

____

(1) ينظر: عمدة القاري 22: 41.

(2) ينظر: المصدر السابق

(3) ينظر: المصدر السابق

As for the one who has an inborn disposition towards such behaviour, then he is ordered to abandon it, and to do so gradually. If he fails to comply and persists upon the act, then he is sinful, especially if it seems that he is content and willing in this.

One of the worst acts possible by both men and women, deserving of punishment and considered sinful is a male with whom anal intercourse is committed and a woman who practices lesbianism.[1]

---

[1] *'Umda al-Qārī* (22:41)

أمّا مَن كان ذلك في أصل خلقته، فإنَّه يؤمر بتكلُّف تركه والإدمان على ذلك بالتَّدريج، فإن لم يفعل وتمادى دخله الذَّم، ولا سيما إذا بدا منه ما يدلُّ على الرِّضا.

وأسوأ الأفعال من الرِّجال والنِّساء التي يستحقان عليها الذَّم والعقوبة، هو الرَّجل الذي يؤتي من دبره، والمرأة التي تتعاطى السحق بغيرها من النساء[1].

____

(1) ينظر: عمدة القاري 22: 41.

CHAPTER TWO
IMITATION AND ITS PROHIBITION IN THE SUNNA

There are many traditions that prohibit and reprimand each gender from imitating the other; desiring from each one to stay upon the form that Allah ﷻ created them upon, so that they can perform the duties they have been entrusted with. The following are some examples of these traditions:

1. On the authority of Ibn ʿAbbās ؓ who said, 'The Messenger of Allah ﷺ cursed those men who imitate women, and those women who imitate men.'[1]

Al-Qārī comments, 'These are the men who imitate females in clothing, hair-dyeing, voice, appearance, speech and in all their movement–and composure [...] and these are the females who imitate men in attire, appearance, gait, loud speech and the like. However, this does not include imitating them in judgement and matters related to knowledge, as imitating them therein is considered praiseworthy.'[2]

2. On the authority of Ibn ʿAbbās ؓ who said, 'The Messenger of Allah ﷺ cursed effeminate men, and females who behave like men saying, "Expel them from your houses."'[3]

---

[1] *Ṣaḥīḥ al-Bukhārī* (7:159)
[2] *Mirqāt al-Mafātīḥ* (7:2818)
[3] *Ṣaḥīḥ al-Bukhārī* (7:159)

المطلب الثاني

المنع من التَّشبه بالنِّساء في السُّنة

وردت أحاديث عديدة تنهى كلاً من الجنسين عن التَّشبُّه بالآخر، وتريد من كلِّ واحدٍ منهما أن يبقى على الهيئة التي خلقهالله عليها؛ ليؤدي الوظيفة المناطة به، ومن هذه الأحاديث:

1.عن ابن عباس ﷺ، قال: «لعن رسول الله ﷺ المتشبهين من الرِّجال بالنساء، والمتشبهات من النِّساء بالرِّجال»[1].

قال القاري[2]:«المتشبهين بالنساء من الرِّجال في الزي واللباس والخضاب والصوت والصورة والتكلم وسائر الحركات والسكنات....، والمتشبهات بالرِّجال من النساء: زياً وهيئةً ومشيةً ورفع صوت ونحوها لا رأياً وعلماً، فإنَّ التشبه بهم محمود».

2.وعن ابن عبَّاس ﷺ، قال: «لعن النَّبيُّ ﷺ المخنثين من الرِّجال، والمترجلات من النِّساء، وقال: أخرجوهم من بيوتكم»[3].

---

[1] ينظر: صحيح البخاري 7: 159.

[2] ينظر: مرقاة المفاتيح 7: 2818.

[3] ينظر: صحيح البخاري 7: 159.

Al-'Aynī states, 'Females behaving like men [*mutarajjilāt*] are: females imitating men and displaying manly traits; in reality it is the opposite of being effeminate [*mukhannithūn*] as they imitate females.'[1]

The intended meaning of, 'expel them from your houses' is to remove them from one's residential area and city. Abū Hurayra ﷺ is reported to have said, 'An effeminate man came to the Messenger of Allah ﷺ with hands and feet dyed with henna. The Messenger of Allah ﷺ proclaimed, "What is this!?" To which he replied, "Messenger of Allah ﷺ it is in imitation of women," at which he ﷺ commanded for him to be expelled to al-Naqī'. They (the companions) asked, "Messenger of Allah ﷺ, shall we not kill him?" He ﷺ replied saying, "I have been prohibited from killing those who pray."'[2]

3. On the authority of Ibn Abī Malīka who said, 'It was said to 'Ā'isha ﷺ, "There is a woman who wears sandals," to which she said, "The Messenger of Allah ﷺ cursed women who behave like men."'[3]

'Women who behave like men' are those women who imitate men in their speech and dress. It has been said that 'Ā'isha was 'manly in opinion [*rajula al-ra'iy*], meaning that her judgement was like that of men. Consequently, imitation in judgement and matters related to knowledge is not blameworthy.[4]

---

[1] *'Umda al-Qārī* (14:22) & *'Umda al-Ri'āya* (22:42)
[2] *Sunan Abū Dāwūd* (4:282) & *Sunan al-Dāraqutnī* (2:399)
[3] *Sunan Abū Dāwūd* (4:60), *Musnad al-Bazzār* (17:40) & *Shu'b al-Īmān* (10:225). Al-Qārī states in *Mirqāt al-Mafātīh* (7:2836) that, 'Its chain is good.'
[4] *Mirqāt al-Mafātīh* (7:2836)

2.4 المنع من التَّشبه بالنِّساء في السُّنة

وقال العيني: «والمترجلات أي: النساء الشبيهات بالرِّجال المتكلفات في الرُّجولة وهو بالحقيقة ضد المخنثين؛ لأنَّهم المتشبهون بالنساء»[1].

ومعنى أخرجوهم من بيوتكم: أي من مساكنكم ومن بلدكم، فعن أبي هريرة ﵁: (أنَّ النبي ﷺ أتي بمخنث قد خضب يديه ورجليه بالحناء، فقال النبي ﷺ: ما بال هذا؟ فقيل: يا رسول الله، يتشبه بالنساء، فأمر به فنفي إلى النقيع، فقالوا: يا رسول الله، ألا نقتله؟ فقال: إني نهيت عن قتل المصلين)[2].

3. وعن ابن أبي مليكة، قال: قيل لعائشة ﵂: (إنَّ امرأةً تلبس النعل، فقالت: لعن رسول الله ﷺ الرجُلة من النساء)[3].

والرجُلة من النساء: المتشبهة في الكلام واللباس بالرجال، ويقال: كانت عائشة رجُلة الرأي أي رأيها رأي الرجال، فالتشبه بالرأي والعلم غير مذموم[4].

____

[1] ينظر: عمدة القاري 24: 14، وعمدة الرِّعاية 22: 42.

[2] ينظر: سنن أبي داود 4: 282، وسنن الدارقطني 2: 399، والنقيع ناحية عن المدينة وليس بالبقيع.

[3] ينظر: سنن أبي داود 4: 60، ومسند البزار 17: 40، وشعب الإيمان 10: 225، وقال القاري في مرقاة المفاتيح 7: 2836: إسناده حسن.

[4] ينظر: مرقاة المفاتيح 7: 2836.

4. On the authority of Abū Hurayra ﷺ who said, 'The Messenger of Allah ﷺ cursed men who wear women's clothes, and women who wear men's clothes.'[1]

5. On the authority of 'Abdullah b. 'Amr ﷺ who said, 'The Messenger of Allah ﷺ said, "Any woman who imitates men and any man who imitates women are not from us."'[2] This means that the one who is from our party and follows our path does not perform actions like that.[3]

---

[1] *Sunan Abū Dāwūd* (4:60), *Sunan al-Kubrā* by al-Nasā'ī (8:297), *Ibn Ḥibbān* (13:62), *Musnad Aḥmad* (14:61) & *Al-Mustadrak* (4:214). Al-Ḥākim said, 'It is sound [*ṣaḥīḥ*] upon Muslim's conditions.'

[2] *Musnad Aḥmad* (11:461) & *al-Mu'jam al-Kabīr* (13:461). Al-Haythamī states in *Majma' al-Zawā'id* (8:103), 'It has been narrated from Aḥmad. [With regards to] al-Hudhalī, I do not know him, but the rest of the narrators are trustworthy. Al-Ṭabarānī has narrated it in brief, and dropped the doubtful al-Hudhalī; thus, upon this all of the men in the chain of Ṭabarānī are upright.'

[3] *Al-Taysīr Sharḥ al-Jāmi' al-Ṣaghīr* (2:329)

2.4 المنع من التَّشبه بالنِّساء في السُّنة

4. وعن أبي هريرة ﷺ، قال: «لعن رسول الله ﷺ الرَّجل يلبس لبسة المرأة، والمرأة تلبس لبسة الرَّجل»[1].

5. وعن عبد الله بن عمرو ﷺ قال ﷺ: «ليس منَّا مَن تشبّه بالرِّجال من النِّساء، ولا من تشبّه بالنِّساء من الرِّجال»[2]: أي لا يفعل ذلك من هو من أشياعنا المقتفين لآثارنا[3].

---

[1] ينظر: سنن أبي داود 4: 60، والسنن الكبرى للنسائي 8: 297، وصحيح ابن حبان 13: 62، ومسند أحمد 14: 61، والمستدرك 4: 214، وقال الحاكم: صحيح على شرط مسلم.

[2] ينظر: مسند أحمد 11: 461، والمعجم الكبير 13: 461، وقال الهيثمي في مجمع الزوائد 8: 103: «رواه أحمد. والهذلي لم أعرفه، وبقية رجاله ثقات. ورواه الطبراني باختصار، وأسقط الهذلي المبهم، فعلى هذا رجال الطبراني كلهم ثقات».

[3] ينظر: التيسير بشرح الجامع الصغير 2: 329.

CHAPTER THREE
THE LEGAL RULING OF IMITATING FEMALES IN THE ḤANAFĪ SCHOOL

The issue of 'imitating females' does not differ significantly from the issue of social integrity, in that both come under the rubric of culture. Social integrity is one of the components of culture, which we use to formulate legal opinions—as has been discussed in the previous chapter dedicated to social integrity.

One of the intended aspired meanings of the Sacred Law is to establish a distinction between men and women, and to seek to make that a reality, as has been mentioned in the previously cited traditions.

We find that many of the *Ḥanafī* jurists formulated numerous legal rulings based upon these very meanings, with their objective being to differentiate between the male and female. This is so that it could be a means for the two genders to achieve a sense of harmony in marriage and strengthen their attraction and desire for each other. It is believed that positives and negatives attract, but two positives repel each other. Thus, with this understanding the Sacred Law has paid huge importance in trying to distinguish the male from the female in actions, speech and movements, hoping to achieve through this continual and lasting attraction between the two genders.

It is worth mentioning that the Ḥanafī jurists have made the causal factor of the ruling of severely offensive or offensive (depending on the situation) for many rulings relating to imitation of one gender of the other. This is sometimes referred to as effeminacy or beautifying, which are both traits specific to women. Examples of this are: preventing men from chewing gum, wearing saffron, dyeing their hands and feet, beautifying themselves through oiling the moustache and eyebrows, and plucking their eyebrows and cheeks.

المطلب الثالث

حكم التَّشبُّه بالنِّساء عند الحنفية

إنَّ حال التَّشبُّه بالنِّساء لا يختلف كثيراً عن حال المروءة في كونهما يندرجان تحت العرف، فهي أحد مفردات العرف الذي نحتكم إليه ـ كما سبق الكلام في المروءة ـ.

ومن المعاني المقصودة في الشريعة المطهرة هو تقرير اختلاف الرِّجال عن النِّساء، والسعي لتحقيق ذلك، كما هو مذكور في الأحاديث السالفة.

وهذا المعنى بنى عليه الحنفية العديد من فروعهم، والقصد هو التميز بين الرَّجل والمرأة؛ ليحصل التجانس بينهم بعد الزواج وتقوى رغبة كلّ واحد منهما في الآخر، فالسالب والموجب يتجاذبان، والموجب والموجب يتنافران، ولتحقيق التجاذب المستمر بين الرَّجل والمرأة اهتمت الشريعة بأن يتميز كلُّ واحد منهما عن الآخر بمظهره وكلامه وحركاته.

ومن الملاحظ أنَّ الحنفية جعلوا علّة الكراهة التحريمية أو التنزيهية على حسب الحال للعديد من الأحكام في مشابهة كلِّ واحدٍ منهما للآخر، أو يقولون: «للتخنُّث»، أو «للتزيُّن»؛ لأنَّهما من الهيئات الخاصّة بالنِّساء، كما فعلوا ذلك في منع الرَّجل من العلك ولبس الأصفر وخضاب اليد والرَّجل والتَّزيُّن بدهن الشَّارب والحاجب وأخذ الشَّعر من الحاجب والخدين.

However, the legal ruling regarding imitating females usually varies, depending on the extent to which the act has been actualised in form, and whether one had the intent to imitate. Thus, imitating the actions of a female in form only is offensive, that is, one's actions are permissible but contradict the more appropriate [*khilāf al-awlā*]. However, if one imitates a female with intent, then his action is considered to be severely offensive. Although, it is worth noting that the imitation of a female by a male in form could be considered as being severely offensive—*even* if performed without intent—if it is considered to detract from one's social integrity.

Below is a detailed discussion of the aforementioned examples [and their legal rulings] according to the Ḥanafī school:

1. Imitating females by chewing gum

Gum is a substitute for the *siwāk* for females due to their gums being considered delicate, and therefore it is regarded as a female specific act. Al-Marghīnānī states, 'Upon what we have mentioned, it (chewing gum) is considered offensive for men if done without excuse. However, it has also been said that it is not recommended [for a male to chew gum] due to it being considered from the imitation of females.'[1] Ibn al-Humām comments, 'That is, it is not offensive; it is permissible, except for females, as it is their *siwāk* and therefore recommended for them.'[2]

The obvious import of the discussion is that chewing gum for men is considered permissible but seems to contradict the more appropriate. However, to prevent men and women from being in imitation of each other, chewing gum is not recommended for men the way it is for females.

---

[1] *Al-Hidāya* (1:123)
[2] *Fatḥ al-Qadīr* (1:207)

ويتفاوت الحكم بالتَّشبُّه بالنِّساء بحسب تحقّق صورة الفعل ووجود القصد بالتَّشبُّه، فمَن شابه صورة فعل النِّساء كره له تنزيهاً: أي كان فعله مباحاً، ولكنَّه خلاف الأولى، ومَن قصد التَّشبُّه بالنِّساء كان فعلُه مكروهاً تحريماً، ويُمكن لمشابهة الرَّجل للمرأة في صورة الفعل أن تكره تحريماً وإن لم يقصد التشبه إن دخلت في خوارم المروءة.

وتفصيل الأمثلة السَّابقة عند الحنفية:

١.التشبه بالمرأة في استعمال العلك:

فإنَّه مختصٌّ بالمرأة؛ لكونه يقوم مقام السِّواك في حقِّها لرقّة لثتها، قال المرغيناني[1]: «يكره للرِّجال على ما قيل إذا لم يكن من علّة، وقيل: لا يستحبُّ لما فيه من التشبه بالنِّساء»، قال ابن الهمام[2]: «أي ولا يكره، فهو مباح بخلاف النِّساء، فإنَّه يستحب لهن؛ لأنَّه سواكهن».

فظاهر الكلام يدلُّ على أنَّ السِّواك في حقِّ الرَّجل مباحٌ وخلافُ الأولى وليس مستحباً كما هو في حقّ المرأة؛ لئلا تكون مشابهة بينهم.

---

(١) ينظر: الهداية 1: 123.

(٢) ينظر: فتح القدير 1: 207.

Ibn 'Ābidīn states, 'It is offensive for those not fasting, as the proof for imitating women requires that the dislike with regards to males is devoid of any opposition [*fatḥ*],[1] and the apparent import of it is that it is severely offensive [*ṭā'*][2] but, it has been said: it is permissible, and that is the opinion of Fakhr al-Islām where he states, "There is an indication in the discussion of Muḥammad [b. Ḥasan al-Shaybānī] that it is not offensive for someone who is not fasting, but it is recommended for men to not do it, except due to a valid excuse like halitosis."'[3]

2. Red, yellow and safflower coloured clothing

It is mentioned in *al-Muḥīṭ* that it is offensive for one to wear a red shirt or one dyed with safflower, as it is considered from the clothing of females and imitating them is offensive.[4] On the authority of 'Alī ﷺ who said, 'The Messenger of Allah ﷺ forbade me from reciting whilst bowing, and from wearing gold and safflower,'[5] meaning clothes dyed with safflower. However, it also includes that which has been dyed with saffron and *memecylon tinctorium* [*wars*], which is the colour yellow. This prohibition is specific for males.[6]

---

[1] [*Fatḥ al-Qadīr*]
[2] [*Ḥāshiya al-Ṭaḥṭāwī 'alā al-Durr al-Mukhtār*]
[3] *Radd al-Muḥtār* (2:417)
[4] *Al-'Uqūd al-Durriyya* (2:323)
[5] *Ṣaḥīḥ Muslim* (3:1648) & *Sunan al-Tirmidhī* (4:226)
[6] *Al-Tabyīn* (6:230) & *al-Baḥr al-Rā'iq* (8:216)

3.4 حكم التَّشبُّه بالنِّساء عند الحنفية

قال ابن عابدين[1]: «وكره للمفطرين؛ لأنَّ الدليل ـ أعني التشبه بالنساء ـ يقتضي الكراهة في حقهم خالياً عن المعارض،«فتح»، وظاهره أنَّها تحريمية «ط»، وقيل: يباح، هو قول فخر الإسلام حيث قال: وفي كلام محمد إشارة إلى أنَّه لا يكره لغير الصائم، ولكن يُستحبُّ للرِّجال تركه إلا لعذر مثل أن يكون في فمه بخر».

2. لون اللباس كالحمرة والصفرة والمعصفر:

وفي «المحيط»: ويُكره لبس الثَّوب الأحمر والمعصفر...؛ لأنَّها كسوة النساء، ويكره التشبه بهنّ[2]، فعن علي ﷺ، قال: (نهاني النبيّ ﷺ عن القراءة وأنا راكع، وعن لبس الذهب والمعصفر)[3]: أي الثوب المصبوغ بالعصفر. وكذلك المصبوغ بالزعفران وأيضاً المصبوغ بالورس، وهو الأصفر، وهذا النهي خاص بالرِّجال[4].

---

(1) ينظر: رد المحتار 2: 417.

(2) ينظر: العقود الدرية 2: 323.

(3) ينظر: صحيح مسلم 3: 1648، وسنن الترمذي 4: 226.

(4) ينظر: التبيين 6: 230، والبحر الرائق 8: 216.

3. Beautifying oneself by dyeing one's hands and feet

It is permissible for females but offensive for males, as they are prohibited from this type of beautification except for medicinal purposes. It is also offensive because it is from adornment which is only permissible for females and not for males, and also because it is from the imitation of females.[1]

4. Beautifying oneself by oiling the moustache and eyebrows with the intent of beautification

Beautification is essentially something particular to females, and thus regardless of how much a female exaggerates in it for the sake of her husband, it is regarded as good and admirable, as long as she does not display it in front of others. Males, on the other hand, should make an effort to be appealing and presentable by having concern over oneself, with the condition that it does not reach a stage where it would be considered from the beautification of females and that one still remains protective over one's social integrity. Paying attention to one's outward appearance in a way that does not detract from one's social integrity is regarded as a good and desirable objective, as it is from making yourself handsome and presentable and not considered to be from beautifying.

Al-Marghīnānī states, 'It is not an issue for men to use *kohl* if used for medicinal purposes and not for beautification; and it is considered good to oil the moustache if one did not intend beautification, as it does the same thing as dyeing.'[2]

---

[1] *Minḥa al-Sulūk* (3:19), *al-Baḥr al-Rā'iq* (8:208) & *Radd al-Muḥtār* (6:422)
[2] *Al-Hidāya* (2:347)

3.4 حكم التَّشبُّه بالنِّساء عند الحنفية

3. التزين بالخضاب لليد والرِّجل:

فهو مباح للمرأة مكروه للرَّجل؛ لأنَّهم ممنوعون عن مثل هذه الزينة، إلا لأجل التداوي، ولأنَّ ذلك تزيّن، وهو مباح للنساء دون الرِّجال، ولأنَّه تشبه بالنِّساء[1].

4. التزين بدهن الشارب والحاجب بقصد الزينة:

لأنَّ التَّزين خاصٌّ بالنِّساء، فهي مهما بالغت بالاهتمام بنفسها لزوجها فهو حسن ما لم تظهر به أمام الأجانب، بخلاف الرِّجال فيكون في حقّه التَّجمل، وهو العناية بنفسه ما لم يصل إلى درجة التزين كالنساء ويبقى محافظاً على مروءته، فعنايته بمظهره الذي لا يعدّ خارماً للمروءة يعتبر من التجمّل لا التزين وهو حسن.

قال المرغيناني[2]: «ولا بأس بالاكتحال للرِّجال إذا قصد به التداوي دون الزينة، ويستحسن دهن الشارب إذا لم يكن من قصده الزينة؛ لأنَّه يعمل عمل الخضاب».

---

(1) ينظر: منحة السلوك 3: 19، والبحر الرائق 8: 208، ورد المحتار 6: 422.

(2) ينظر: الهداية 2: 347.

Ibn al-Humām[1] states, 'It is mentioned in *al-Kāfī*, "It is preferable to oil one's facial hair if one did not intend beautification, as there are traditions related with regards to it. It has been stipulated for one to have no intent, as—Allah ﷻ knows best—it is regarded from beautifying oneself. Ibn Mas'ūd ؓ narrates, "The Messenger of Allah ﷺ used to dislike ten traits, and from them he mentioned beautifying oneself inappropriately."[2]

'And on the authority of Yaḥyā b. Sa'īd who said, 'Abū Qatāda al-Anṣārī ؓ asked the Messenger of Allah ﷺ, "I have plentiful hair, shall I comb it?" To which the Messenger of Allah ﷺ replied, "Yes, and honour it." Abū Qatāda would thus oil his hair sometimes twice in one day, due to the Messenger of Allah ﷺ saying to him, "Honour it."[3]

'Oiling and combing his hair twice a day was no doubt an exaggerated response from Abū Qatada ؓ as he wished to follow the instruction of the Messenger of Allah ﷺ and it was not done to fulfil lower desires which invites one to outward beautification and vanity. We know this because an aspired level of being presentable can be achieved by doing less than what he did, and there is a difference between being presentable and [blameworthy] beautification. The former allows one to uphold oneself in a dignified manner, displaying blessings with gratitude rather than arrogance.

---

[1] *Fatḥ al-Qadīr* (2:347)
[2] *Sunan Abū Dāwūd* (2:489), *al-Mujtabā* (8:141), *Musnad Aḥmad* (1:380), *Ṣaḥīḥ Ibn Ḥibbān* (12:496) & *al-Mustadrak* (4:216)
[3] *Al-Muwaṭṭa'* (2:949)

وقال ابن الهمام[1]: «في «الكافي»: يستحب دهن شعر الوجه إذا لم يكن من قصده الزينة، به وردت السنة، فقيد بانتفاء هذا القصد فكأنَّه والله أعلم؛ لأنَّه تبرج بالزينة، فعن ابن مسعود ﷺ: (كان النبي ﷺ يكره عشر خصال وذكر منها التبرج بالزينة لغير محلها)[2].

وعن يحيى بن سعيد أنَّ أبا قتادة الأنصاري ﷺ قال لرسول الله ﷺ: (إنَّ لي جَمَّةً أفأرجِّلُها؟ فقال رسول الله ﷺ: نعم وأكرمها، فكان أبو قتادة ربَّما دهنها في اليوم مرَّتين لما قال له رسول الله ﷺ: وأكرمها)[3].

فإنَّما هو مبالغة من أبي قتادة ﷺ في قصد الامتثال لأمر رسول الله ﷺ لا لحظ النفس الطالبة للزينة الظاهرة، وذلك لأنَّ الجمال والإكرام المطلوب يتحقق مع دون هذا المقدار...، هذا ولا تلازم بين قصد الجمال وقصد الزينة، فالقصدُ الأوَّل لدفع الشين وإقامة ما به من الوقار وإظهار النعمة شكراً لا فخراً.

---

[1] ينظر: فتح القدير 2: 347.

[2] سنن أبي داود 2: 489، والمجتبى 8: 141، ومسند أحمد 1: 380، وصحيح ابن حبان 12: 496، والمستدرك 4: 216، وصححه.

[3] ينظر: الموطأ 2: 949.

This behaviour ultimately stems from a refined and sagacious self [*nafs*], while the second stems from weakness of the self. Some have said that dyeing is an affirmed sunna but was not intended for beautification, however, if through it one achieves beautification, then there is no harm, as long as he does not give it any worth.'

5. For a male to pluck his cheeks and eyebrows

To pluck to the extent that it is imitative of effeminate men is considered offensive, but whatever does not reach that level is permissible. There is no difference between plucking and shaving with regards to the legal ruling. It is mentioned in *al-Muḍmarāt*, 'There is no issue in plucking the eyebrows and facial hair as long as it is not imitative of effeminate men;' a similar opinion has been mentioned in *al-Mujtabā*. And al-Ṭaḥṭāwī[1] states, 'It is fine for one to pluck the eyebrows and facial hair as long as it is not imitative of effeminate men. Such similar statements have also been made in *al-Yanābī* and *al-Muḍmarāt*; the intended meaning therein being mutilation, due to the tradition, "Allah ﷻ curses the female who plucks her eyebrows and the female who plucks the eyebrows of others."'[2]

In conclusion, these examples make clear the distinguishing qualities between the male and female. Beautification is seen to be a quality specific for females, and if a male was to copy her in that then he would be seen to be an imitator. Similarly, 'effeminacy,' because it is seen as imitating a female in her behaviour and manner, which is the type of imitation a male is prohibited from. Ultimately, all these examples fall under the category of the unlawful form of imitation between the genders.

---

[1] *Ḥāshiya al-Ṭaḥṭāwī ʿalā al-Marāqī* (2:512), *al-Fatāwā al-Hindiyya* (5:359) & *Barīqa Maḥmūdiyya* (4:174, 4:83)
[2] *Al-Muwaṭṭaʾ* (2:949)

3.4 حكم التَّشبُّه بالنِّساء عند الحنفية

وهو أثر أدب النفس وشهامتها، والثاني أثر ضعفها، وقالوا: بالخضاب وردت السُّنة، ولم يكن لقصد الزينة ثم بعد ذلك إن حصلت زينة فقد حصلت في ضمن قصده المطلوب، فلا يضرُّه إذا لم يكن ملتفتاً إليه».

5.أخذ الرَّجل لشعر خديه أو حاجبيه:

فيكره منه ما يكون تشبهاً بالمخنثين، وما لم يصل إلى هذا الحدّ فهو مباح، ولا يوجد فرق بين النتف والحلق في الحكم، ففي «المضمرات»: ولا بأس بأخذ الحاجبين وشعر وجهه ما لم يشبه المخنث. اهـ، ومثله في «المجتبى»، وقال الطحطاوي[1]: «ولا بأس بأن يأخذ شعر الحاجبين وشعر وجهه ما لم يتشبه بالمخنثين، ومثله في «الينابيع» و«المضمرات»، والمراد ما يكون مشوهاً؛ لخبر: «لعن الله النامصة والمتنمصة»[2] ».

فهذه الأمثلة توضح وجود علامات فارقة بين الرَّجل والمرأة، مثل التزين فهو خاص بالمرأة، فإن فعله الرَّجل كان متشبهاً، وكذلك التخنيث؛ لأنَّه مشابهة المرأة في سلوكها، فهو من التشبه فيمنع منه، وكل هذا يندرج تحت أصل التشبه الممنوع بين الجنسين.

---

(1) ينظر: حاشية الطحطاوي على المراقي 2: 512. وينظر: الفتاوى الهندية 5: 359، وبريقة محمودية 4: 174، 4: 83.

(2) ينظر: الموطأ 2: 949.

Chapter Four
The Relationship between Imitating Females and Shaving the Beard

As long as we have decided that imitating females is part of culture, and it is culture that distinguishes for us whether a certain type of behaviour is specific to men or women, then it is possible for us to refer to culture to help us determine the issue of the beard.

Thus, if according to culture in a particular society, shaving the beard was considered imitative of females, then it would have the same ruling as imitation and considered to be slightly offensive due to imitating the outward form; but, if it was done with intent then it would be severely offensive. However, if shaving the beard was considered to detract from one's social integrity, then it would be deemed as severely offensive [whether it was done with intent or not].

There is no doubt that the application of this foundation [*aṣl*] varies from one community to another. It appears, however, that many present-day communities do not consider shaving the beard to be from imitating females and are therefore not affected by the rulings applied to imitating females. Though, if we were to find a community that considered shaving the beard to be from imitating females, the aforementioned rulings regarding it would be applied. And Allah knows best.

املطلب الرابع

علاقة التشبه بالنِّساء بحلق اللحية

طالما أنَّه تقرَّر أنَّ التشبه بالنساء هو جزء من العرف، وهو الذي يُميِّز لنا هل هذا السُّلوك خاصٌّ بالمرأة أو الرَّجل، فيمكننا أن نرجع للعرف لتحديد مسألة اللحية.

فإن كان في العرف أنَّ حالق لحيته متشبهاً بالنِّساء في نظر المجتمع فيلحق بالتَّشبه بالنساء، ويكون عليه حكم التشبه من الكراهة التنزيهة في مشابهة الفعل أو الكراهة التحريمة إن وجد القصد منه، ما لم يصل التشبه بالنساء في حلق اللحية إلى كونه خارم للمروءة، فحينئذ يكون مكروهاً تحريماً.

ولا شك أنَّ تطبيق مثل هذا الأصل يتفاوت من مجتمع لآخر، والظاهر أنَّ عامة المجتمعات في هذا العصر لم يعد الحلق للحية تشبهاً بالنساء فيها، وبالتالي لا يتأثر بأحكام التَّشبُّه بالنساء، وإن وجدنا مجتمعاً يعدّ الحلق من التشبه بالنساء فينطبق عليه حكمه السابق، والله أعلم.

SECTION FIVE
GENERAL NECESSITY [*ʿUMŪM AL-BALWĀ*]

Initially the reader may fail to understand the relationship between general necessity and the beard owing to his belief that general necessity is specifically only used in the presence of necessity [*ḍarūra*], thus asking himself what necessity is there in shaving or shortening the beard? However, in reality, general necessity is not only used when there is a necessity, but it relates to anything that is widespread and common regardless of necessity. General necessity not only allows one to take advantage of exemptions, but also allows one to benefit from other scholarly opinions from within and outside of the school. In the following chapters, we will try to elaborate on the intended meaning of general necessity, the legal ruling of the beard in the Shāfiʿī and Mālikī schools, and any textual references with regards to shaving and shortening the beard mentioned in the Ḥanafī school.

المبحث الخامس

من جهة عموم البلوى

يخفى في البدء على القارئ علاقة عموم البلوى باللحية؛ لاعتقاده أنّ عموم البلوى خاصّة بالضرورة فقط، وبالتالي أي ضرورة في حلق أو قص اللحية، وفي الحقيقة عموم البلوى ليست متعلقة بالضرورة فحسب، بل تطلق على كلِّ ما يشيع وينتشر وإن لم يكن فيه ضرورة، ويكون في عموم البلوى رخصة في الاستفادة من الأقوال الأخرى للمجتهدين سواء داخل المذهب أو خارجه؛ لذلك نعرض هنا المقصود من عموم البلوى، وحكم اللحية عند الشافعية والمالكية، وحلق اللحية وقصّها في عبارات الحنفية في المطالب الآتية:

Chapter One

THE INTENDED MEANING OF GENERAL NECESSITY

General necessity is an extensive and diverse subject due to its extremely important role in the application of legal rulings. It is considered from one of the principles of the guidelines of a Mufti [*rasm al-muftī*], ultimately being derived from the major foundation of 'necessity'. It is also well-known that necessity has the potential to change and modify a legal ruling, in contrast to culture which simply clarifies and specifies a ruling, as has been mentioned previously in the section of social integrity.

This modification of a legal ruling in the presence of necessity is what has been mentioned in the Qur'an when Allah ﷻ says, ❨*...except when forced by hunger.*❩[1] Due to the presence of necessity, the legal ruling was modified, thus making the consumption of carrion, swine and alcohol permissible.

The meaning of necessity is evident in general necessity and therefore assumes the same legal ruling [as necessity]. An example is the issue of the cat, as a result of general necessity and the prevalence of cats found wandering in and around people's homes and drinking from their water, the legal ruling changes from the leftover water of a cat being considered impure to it being considered pure as a way of alleviating difficulty; on the authority of Abū Qatāda ﷺ who said, 'The Messenger of Allah ﷺ said, "It is not impure, but rather it is from those that live in your midst."'[2]

---

[1] [*The Qur'an, A new translation by M. A. S. Abdel Haleem*, Livestock, 6:119 (p. 89)]

[2] *Ṣaḥīḥ Ibn Khuzayma* (1:55), *Ṣaḥīḥ Ibn Ḥibbān* (4:115) & *Sunan al-Tirmidhī* (1:151), who has authenticated it.

المطلب الأول

المقصود بعموم البلوى

إنَّ الكلام عن عموم البلوى متشعب وطويل؛ لما له من أهمية كبيرة في تطبيق الأحكام الشرعية، فأحد قواعد علم رسم المفتي هو عموم البلوى، وهو متفرِّع تحت الأصل الكبير، وهو الضرورة، ومعلومٌ أنَّ الضرورة مغيرة للأحكام بخلاف العرف فإنَّه معرف للأحكام، كما سبق في مبحث المروءة.

وتغيير الضرورة للأحكام كما في قوله تعالى: ﴿إلا ما اضطررتم إليه﴾، فعندما حصلت ضرورة تغير الحكم فجاز أكل الميتة والخنزير وشرب الخمر.

وعموم البلوى يظهر فيها معنى الضَّرورة فتأخذ حكمها، كما هو الحال في الهرة فبسبب عموم البلوى فيها، وأنها تكثر في البيوت وتشرب من مائها، تغيَّر حكمها من نجسة لطاهرة؛ رفعاً للحرج، فعن أبي قتادة ﷺ قال ﷺ: «إنها ليست بنجس إنها من الطوافين عليكم أو الطوافات»[1].

---

(1) ينظر: صحيح ابن خزيمة 1: 55، وصحيح ابن حبان 4: 115، وسنن الترمذي 1: 151، وصححه.

Issues that are regarded as general necessity are those which both the common and select from society are in need of, or that which has an element of need in the majority of circumstances, or that which is not possible to guard oneself against, or that which is difficult to avoid.[1]

However, it is more fitting to define it as: *The effect of a prevalent thing that is contradictory to a foundation in the Sacred Law which is made permissible if placed under another foundation of the Sacred Law.*

The following are examples of the application of this definition in Islamic jurisprudence [*fiqh*]:

The cat

Since, the cat is [from those animals] which are commonly found in and around people's homes, the ruling [of its leftover water] was modified from being considered impure (as it is an animal whose meat is unlawful to consume) to being considered pure, due to the element of necessity in this.

Animal droppings

Due to the difficulty in trying to prevent one's shoes or leather socks [*khuff*] from stepping on animal droppings found on pathways, the ruling was similarly modified from being considered impure to it being excused. The necessity [that warrants this type of change in a ruling] has materialised through it being so prevalent and widespread. This contrasts with chicken droppings and human dung; as both of them are rarely found on pathways and thus stepping on it is not considered to be from general necessity. Another example that does not fall under general necessity is the urine of animals whose meat is lawful to consume; this is because the ground normally absorbs urine and dries it out and hence stepping on it with one's shoes or leather socks is not a frequent occurrence.[2]

---

[1] *Tarwīḥ al-Jinān* (p. 31)
[2] *Badā'i' al-Ṣanā'i'* (1:81)

والأمرُ الذي تعمّ به البلوى: هو ما يحتاج إليه الخاصّ والعامّ، أو ما تمسّ به الحاجة في الأحوال الأكثرية، أو ما لا يُمكن الاحتراز عنه، أو ما عسر الاجتناب عنه[1].

والأَوْلى في تعريفه: **تأثير شيوع ما هو مخالفٌ لأصل شرعيّ إنْ ألحق بأصل شرعيّ آخر يجوِّزه.**

وتطبيق هذا التعريف في الفقه:

ففي مسألة الهرة بسبب انتشارها في البيوت انتقلت من النَّجاسة؛ لأنها غير مأكولة اللحم إلى إلى الطهارة؛ لوجود الضرورة.

وفي مسألة الأرواث في الطُّرقات انتقلت من النَّجاسة إلى العفو فيها؛ لتعذّر صيانة الخفاف والنعال عنها، فتحقَّقت فيها الضَّرورة لعموم البلوى بها، بخلاف خرء الدجاج والعذرة؛ لأن ذلك قلما يكون في الطرق، فلا تعم البلوى بإصابته، وبخلاف بول ما يؤكل لحمه؛ لأن ذلك تنشفه الأرض ويجف بها فلا تكثر إصابته الخفاف والنعال[2].

---

[1] ينظر: ترويح الجنان ص31.

[2] ينظر: بدائع الصنائع 1: 81.

It has been related from Muḥammad [b. Ḥasan al-Shaybānī] ﷺ that, when he entered Rayy and saw the necessity, he issued a legal verdict stating that even a large amount of impurity is excused; they compared the soil of Bukhara to it. It has been reported that it was at that moment when he rescinded his opinion regarding leather socks.[1]

Water flowing over an impurity

Water can be considered pure despite it flowing over an impurity. For example, when snow water flows over dung and dirt found along its path, if the impurity disappears and mixes [with the water] to the extent that its effects can no longer be perceived, then in these instances it becomes permissible to make *wuḍū'* using that water, even if the whole of the river bed was impure. Note that this is with the condition that the water was initially regarded as a large amount such that one could not see to the bottom of it. If one could see to the bottom, it would be regarded as impure. In *al-Multaqaṭ* some of the scholars have mentioned, 'The water is pure even if it was small in amount but was flowing.' Al-ʿImādī states, 'These rulings are referred to and drawn upon due to general necessity in our countries where water commonly flows over animal dung.'[2]

All three Imams, Abū Ḥanīfa, Abū Yūsuf and Muḥammad agree that general necessity is a cause for lightening the legal ruling. This verifies and confirms the truthfulness of the well-known matter, 'Whatever becomes a general necessity, its ruling is lightened [*mā ʿammat baliyyatuhu khaffat qaḍiyyatuhu*].'[3]

Wearing silk

The relied upon opinion is that it is impermissible for men to wear silk regardless of whether it is touching the skin directly, or whether there is a barrier between it and the skin.

---

[1] *Al-Hidāya* (1:206)
[2] *Minḥa al-Khāliq* (1:89)
[3] *Al-Baḥr* (1:241) & *al-Durr al-Mukhtār* (1:316)

1.5 المقصود بعموم البلوى

فعن محمد ﷺ: أنه لما دخل الري ورأى البلوى أفتى بأن الكثير الفاحش لا يمنع أيضاً، وقاسوا عليه طين بخارى، وعند ذلك رجوعه في الخف يروى[١].

وفي مسألة طهارة الماء رغم مروره على نجاسة، كماء الثلج إذا جرى على طريق فيه سرقين ونجاسة إن تغيبت النجاسة واختلطت حتى لا يرى أثرها يتوضأ منه ولو كان جميع بطن النهر نجسا، فإن كان الماء كثيراً لا يرى ما تحته فهو طاهر، وإن كان يرى فهو نجس، وفي «الملتقط» قال بعض المشايخ: الماء طاهر، وإن قلَّ إذا كان جارياً، قال العمادي: وهذه المسائل يستأنس بها لما عمت به البلوى في بلادنا من اعتيادهم إجراء الماء بسرقين الدواب[٢].

واتفاق الأئمة الثلاثة أبو حنيفة وأبو يوسف ومحمّد على أنَّعموم البلويسبب للتخفيف في الأحكام الشرعية، فيقع الاتفاق على صدق القضية المشهورة، وهي أنَّ ما عمت بليته خفت قضيته[٣].

وفي مسألةِ لبس الحرير فالمعتمد حرمةلبسها للرَّجل سواءٌ كانت ملتصقةً على الجسم أو يوجد حائل بينها وبين الجسم.

---

(١) ينظر: الهداية ١: ٢٠٦.

(٢) ينظر: منحة الخالق ١: ٨٩.

(٣) ينظر: البحر ١: ٢٤١، والدر المختار ١: ٣١٦.

Yet, in a narration from Abū Ḥanīfa he states, 'It is impermissible only if it touches the skin;' and it has been mentioned in *al-Qunya*, 'That is a huge concession when faced in a scenario where there is general necessity,[1] and therefore it would not be offensive to wear silk if there was no actual contact with one's skin. Thus, if it was worn above a shirt made from gazelle or something similar, it would not be regarded as offensive.[2]

Liquid impurities

Shoes or leather socks sullied by liquid impurities are not purified except by washing them. However, according to Abū Yūsuf, if one was to wipe it against some earth such that no trace of the impurity was left, then it would be considered pure due to the general necessity in this issue.[3]

Selling fruits remaining on the tree
with the condition to leave them remaining on it

If the fruits [on the tree] were not fully ripe and still growing then the sale is regarded as invalid [*fāsid*] according to all of them. However, if they had finished growing then it is invalid only according to Abū Ḥanīfa and Abū Yūsuf—this being in accordance with 'deductive analogy' [*qiyās*]. Muḥammad, however, believes it to be permissible by way of 'exception' [*istiḥsān*], and this is the opinion al-Ṭaḥāwī preferred due to the general necessity therein.[4]

Making a vow [nadhr]
with the condition one does not desire to manifest

When making a vow, if the condition is fulfilled then it is obligatory upon one to fulfil the vow, even if someone stipulated a condition that he did not desire to manifest.

---

[1] *Radd al-Muḥtār* (1:351)
[2] *Lisān al-Ḥukkām* (1:378)
[3] *Al-Hidāya* (1:36)
[4] *Fatḥ al-Qadīr* (6:287)

5.1 المقصود بعموم البلوى

وعن أبي حنيفة: إنَّما يحرم إذا مست الجلد. قال في «القنية»: وهي رخصةٌ عظيمةٌ في موضع عَمَّت به البلوى[1]، فلا يكره لبس الحرير إذا لم يتصل بجلده حتى لو لبسه فوق قميص من غزل أو نحوه لا يكره[2].

وفي النجاسة الرطبة التي تصيب الخفّ فلا تطهر إلا بالغسل، وعند أبي يوسف إذا مسحه بالأرض حتى لم يبق أثر النجاسة يطهر؛ لعموم البلوى[3].

وفي مسألة بيع الثمر على الشجر بشرط الترك فإن لم يكن تناهى عظمه فالبيع فاسد عند الكلّ، وإن كان قد تناهى عظمه فهو فاسد عند أبي حنيفة وأبي يوسف، وهو القياس، ويجوز عند محمد استحساناً، واختاره الطحاوي؛ لعموم البلوى[4].

وفي مسألة النذر بشرط ووجد الشرط وفّى بالمنذور وإن علَّقه بشرط لا يريد كونه:

---

[1] ينظر: رد المحتار 1: 351.

[2] ينظر: لسان الحكام 1: 378.

[3] ينظر: الهداية 1: 36.

[4] ينظر: فتح القدير 6: 287.

For example, if one was to say, 'If I drink alcohol then upon me is a thousand dinars.' According to Abū Ḥanīfa he has the choice between either fulfilling the vow or taking the expiation [*kaffāra*]. This is because the meaning of the oath [*yamīn*] is included in it, which is to prohibit oneself, and its apparent meaning is that it still remains a vow. Due to this, he can choose between the two options and is free to incline towards whichever one he wants.

This differs to someone who stipulated a condition but desired its manifestation, for example if one said, 'If Allah ﷻ cures me from my illness...' due to the non-existence of the meaning of an oath therein. It is mentioned in *al-Hidāya* that this explanation is the correct one, and it is also the opinion Ismāʿīl al-Zāhid would use when issuing legal verdicts, as is mentioned in *al-Ẓahīriyya*. Al-Walwāljī has stated that the scholars of Balkh and Bukhara give their legal verdicts based upon this [view] and it is also what Shams al-Aʾimma [al-Sarakhsī] preferred due to overwhelming necessity present in the current age.[1]

Making a mistake when reciting the Qurʾan

The later scholars like Ibn Muqātil, Ibn Salām, Ismāʿīl al-Zāhid, Abū Bakr al-Balkhī, al-Hindawānī and al-Ḥalwānī have all allowed much more room for manoeuvre in this matter, as opposed to earlier scholars like Abū Ḥanīfa, Abū Yūsuf and Muḥammad. They (later scholars) state, 'A grammatical mistake does not outright invalidate the prayer, even if believing that is considered disbelief, as the majority of people do not have the ability to distinguish between the various grammatical states.'

Qāḍī Khān states, 'The opinion of the later scholars has greater scope, whereas the opinion of the earlier scholars is safer. If the mistake was replacing a letter with another letter and it was considered possible to easily differentiate between the two [letters] without difficulty, for example, between the letters *ṣād* and *ṭāʾ*, such that one recited *ṭālihāt* instead of *ṣālihāt*, then there is agreement that in this instance it is considered invalid.'

---

[1] *Al-Baḥr al-Rāʾiq* (4:320)

كإن شربت الخمر فعليّ ألف دينار، وعن أبي حنيفة: أنّه مخيّر بين الوفاء أو الكفّارة؛ لأنَّ فيه معنى اليمين، وهو المنع، وهو بظاهره نذرٌ، فيتخيّر ويميل إلى أي الجهتين شاء بخلاف ما إذا كان شرطاً يريد كونه كقوله إن شفى الله مريضي لانعدام معنى اليمين فيه، قال في «الهداية» وهذا التفصيل هو الصحيح وبه كان يفتي إسماعيل الزاهد كما في «الظهيرية»، وقال الولوالجي: مشايخ بلخ وبخارى يفتون بهذا، وهو اختيار شمس الأئمة؛ لكثرة البلوى في هذا الزمان[1].

وفي مسائل زلة القارئ توسع المتأخرون: كابن مقاتل وابن سلام وإسماعيل الزاهد وأبي بكر البلخي والهندواني وابن الفضل والحلواني، بخلاف المتقدمين: كأبي حنيفة وأبو يوسف ومحمد، فقالوا: إنَّ الخطأ في الإعراب لا يفسد مطلقاً ولو اعتقاده كفراً؛ لأنَّ أكثر النَّاس لا يميزون بين وجوه الإعراب. قال قاضي خان: وما قال المتأخرون أوسع، وما قاله المتقدمون أحوط؛ وإن كان الخطأ بإبدال حرف بحرف، فإن أمكن الفصل بينهما بلا كلفة كالصاد مع الطاء كأن قرأ الطالحات مكان الصالحات فاتفقوا على أنَّه مفسد.

'However if it was something that was not distinguishable except with an element of hardship and difficulty, like between the letters *ẓā'* and *ḍād*, or *ṣād* and *sīn*; then the majority of scholars hold that this is not invalidating due to the presence of general necessity.'[1]

Renting a waterway with the water

This is permissible due to general necessity, even though, in reality, it should be impermissible because the rental contract is based upon the use of a specific commodity. This is the case unless one leased the land instead, in which case the water would also be included in it (the contract) by way of association and in this instance it would be considered permissible from the onset.[2]

Crop sharing [muzāra'a] and irrigation [musāqa]

With regards to these matters, the opinions of Abū Yūsuf and Muḥammad are usually used when forming legal opinions due to the need and necessity therein.[3]

In all these various issues we find that according to one opinion or understanding, the issue is regarded impermissible, whereas according to another opinion or understanding the issue is rendered permissible. Thus, we can ascertain that general necessity or *'umūm al-balwā* has had an influence in the decision to choose the opinion of permissibility and preferring it over other opinions, regardless of whether one of the opinions was based upon deductive analogy [*qiyās*] or upon exception [*istiḥsān*], or even if one of the opinions was the opinion of a *mujtahid* scholar and the other an opinion of another *mujtahid* scholar.

---

[1] *Radd al-Muḥtār* (1:631) From the principles of the early scholars [*al-mutaqaddimūn*] is that, 'The relied upon position is it not being considered invalid when the meaning has not changed drastically and there being a similar example in the Qur'an according to Abū Yūsuf; and when there is congruence in meaning according to the other two.'
[2] *Al-Durr al-Mukhtār* (6:36)
[3] *Al-Tabyīn* (5:125)

1.5 المقصود بعموم البلوى

وإن لم يمكن إلا بمشقة كالظاء مع الضاد والصاد مع السِّين فأكثرهم على عدم الفساد؛ لعموم البلوى[1].

وفي مسألة إجارة القناة مع الماء يفتى بالجواز؛ لعموم البلوى، والأصلُ عدم الجواز؛ لوقوع الإجارة على استهلاك العين مقصوداً إلا إذا آجر الأرض، فحينئذٍ يدخل الماء تبعاً فيجوز[2].

وفي المزارعة والمساقاة يفتى بقول أبي يوسف ومحمد؛ لمكان الضرورة والبلوى[3].

ففي هذه المسائل على اختلافها كانت المسألة من وجه أو قول لا تجوز، ومن وجه آخر أو قول آخر تجوز، فأثر عموم البلوى في اختيار الجواز وتقديمه على غيره، سواء كانت إحداهما قياس والأخرى استحسان، أو إحداهما قول لمجتهدٍ والأخرى قول لمجتهد آخر.

---

(1) ينظر: رد المحتار 1: 631. ومن قواعد المتقدمين: أنَّ المعتبر عدم الفساد عند عدم تغيّر المعنى كثيراً وجود المثل في القرآن عند أبي يوسف، والموافقة في المعنى عندهما.

(2) ينظر: الدر المختار 6: 36.

(3) ينظر: التبيين 5: 125.

One could say that general necessity should be restricted to the chapters of purity and impurity, because they are from the repeated daily actions in the life of a Muslim and they are also repeated multiple times each single day. Al-Laknawī states, 'General necessity has an effect in the chapters of purity and impurity but not in the chapters of the lawful and unlawful as has been clearly stated by a group of scholars. If we agree that it is fine to use in that (the chapters of the lawful and unlawful) then we would be making permissible the impermissible simply because they are considered to be from general necessity, like backbiting, usury, listening to musical instruments and other unlawful matters.'[1]

However, this is open for discussion, as the examples that have preceded in terms of general necessity were from a wide range of chapters in *fiqh*, such as the chapter of oaths, transactions, renting, crop-sharing, irrigation, prayer, and clothing, which negates the limiting of general necessity to just the chapters of purity and impurity. It does not by extension make all things unlawful lawful, as the condition for permissibility in general necessity is the presence of an opinion from a *mujtahid* scholar in that issue, or the presence of another well-considered legal foundation we can build our ruling of permissibility upon due to general necessity. Backbiting, usury and musical instruments have no evidence whatsoever to being considered in this discussion, due to the overwhelming harm and evil in them, but also due to the strength of the evidence of its unlawfulness. And Allah ﷻ knows best.

---

[1] *Tarwīḥ al-Jinān* (p. 31)

وأما قصر تأثير البلوى على أبواب الطهارة والنجاسة؛ لأنَّها من الأعمال المتكررة في حياة المسلم ويحتاج إليها يومياً مع تكرارها في اليوم الواحد، كما قال اللكنوي[1]: «إنَّ عموم البلوى، إنَّما يؤثر في باب الطهارة والنجاسة، لا في باب الحرمة والإباحة، صرَّح به الجماعة... ، ولو فرض صحة ذلك للزم إباحة المنكرات التي عمّت به البلوى: كالغيبة، وأكل الربا، واستماع الملاهي، وغير ذلك من الأمور المنهية».

وهذا محلُّ نظر؛ لأنَّ ما سبق ذكره لشمول عموم البلوى لعامة أبواب الفقه من اليمين والبيوع والإجارة والمزارعة والمساقاة والصَّلاة واللباس ينفي هذا التخصيص بأبواب الطهارة والنجاسة، ولا تحصل بذلك إباحة جميع المنكرات؛ لأنَّ شرط الجواز بعموم البلوى وجود قول مجتهد فيها أو أصل فقهيّ معتبر يبنى عليه الحكم بالجواز لعموم البلوى، والغيبة والربا والملاهي لا وجه لاعتبارها؛ لكثرة فسادها وضررها، وقوة أدلة حرمتها، والله أعلم.

---

[1] ينظر: ترويح الجنان ص31.

CHAPTER TWO
THE LEGAL RULING OF THE BEARD
ACCORDING TO THE SHĀFI'Ī AND MĀLIKĪ SCHOOLS

It has been acknowledged in previous discussions that general necessity is present in anything that has become common and prevalent amongst people, even if there was no actual necessity therein, as was in the case of wearing silk. It is, however, important to understand that if we can find another legal foundation to build the ruling upon, we should do so, or if there is another respected legal opinion that we can benefit from, then we should use it. This is, no doubt, better and more appropriate than pushing people towards committing prohibited, destructive and sinful actions.

In the following discussion, we will try to establish that the relied upon position regarding the beard in the *Shāfi'ī* school is of it being sunna and not necessary. Thus, it is not forbidden to shave or trim the beard and someone who does so is not considered sinful. With regards to the *Mālikīs*, they have a strong opinion that does not forbid trimming the beard if it is not seen as disfigurement [*muthla*].

The likes of these opinions issued by recognised and respected schools, enters the beard into the realm of disagreement [*khilāf*], such that it is impermissible to reprimand someone who may differ with one's own opinion. In addition, it also opens the door for one to use these opinions in the application of general necessity, since the act of shaving and trimming [the beard] has become prevalent amongst the general Muslim populace. This means that in this matter we should not aspire to push people towards the unlawful and sinful as long as there is a respected legal verdict from one of the recognised schools of law, since it is an issue that has ultimately become common and widespread between the Muslims.

المطلب الثاني

حكم اللحية عند الشافعية والمالكية

سبق تقرير أنَّ عموم البلوى في أمر ـ وهو انتشاره وشيوعه بين الناس ـ وإن لم يكن فيه ضرورة كما في مسألة لبس الحرير، إن أمكن أن نجد أصلاً فقهياً نحمله أو قول لفقيه معتبر نأخذ، فهو أولى من أن نوقع الناس في المهالك والحرمة والإثم.

وهنا نثبت أنَّ المعتمد عن الشافعية هو سنية اللحية لا وجوبها، وبالتَّالي لا يحرم حلقها أو قصّها، ولا يكون آثماً فاعل ذلك، وعند المالكيّة في قول قويّ لا يحرم تقصير اللحية ما لم يكن فيه مثلة.

ومثل هذه الأقوال من هذه المذاهب المعتبرة تدخل مسألة اللَّحية في دائرة الخلاف التي لا يجوز الإنكار فيها على مَن خالفنا، وتفتح باباً بأن يعمل بهذه الأقوال تطبيقاً لقاعدة عموم البلوى بعد انتشار هذا الفعل من الحلق أو القص عند عامة المسلمين، فلا نسعى فيه إلى إيقاع الناس في الإثم والحرمة طالما أنَّه صدر اجتهاد معتبر من مذاهب معتبرة في مسألة شاعت وانتشرت بين المسلمين.

The Shāfiʿī School

Dr Amjad Rashid, a Shāfiʿī scholar, states, 'In conclusion, the relied upon position in our school, which is what we find the two Shaykhs, al-Nawawī and al-Rāfiʿī, upon, and what many of the later Imams relied upon when issuing legal verdicts, is that: leaving the beard for males is an emphasised sunna but is not deemed necessary. Whoever shaves or shortens it without an excuse is not regarded sinful but has committed an offensive act due to his divergence from the encouragement that has been related in various traditions, but also due to his divergence from the actual action of the Messenger of Allah ﷺ. According to us (the Shāfiʿīs), the one who performs an offensive act, like leaving a sunna, is not blameworthy and not deserving of punishment, as you have read in the statements of Qāḍī al-Bayḍāwī mentioned previously, however, such a person has been deprived of plentiful reward.

'As for shaving or shortening the beard due to a valid excuse like an illness, or out of fear of a tyrant that threatens him if he lengthens his beard, then there is no blame upon him; just as Allah ﷻ says, ⟨*He has placed no hardship in your religion.*⟩[1] And Allah ﷻ is Omniscient and the Most Wise.

'This is what the two Shaykhs, the emendators of our school, Imam Abū al-Qāsim al-Rāfiʿī and Abū Zakariyyā al-Nawawī supported and confirmed in concordance with the opinion of the proof of Islam, al-Ghazālī. They believed that to lengthen the beard is recommended [*mandūb*] but not necessary, and therefore it is not considered unlawful to shave or shorten it without an excuse. However, it is because of one's contravention of the command and guidance of the Prophet ﷺ—through both his speech and action—to leave it.

---

[1] [*The Qur'an, A new translation by M. A. S. Abdel Haleem*, The Pilgrimage, 22:78 (p. 89)]

أولاً: مذهب الشافعية :

قال الدكتور أمجد رشيد الشافعي:«والحاصلُ أنَّ مذهبَنا المعتمدَ الذي عليه الشيخان النووي والرافعي واعتمده أئمةُ الفتوى من المتأخرين: أنَّ إعفاءَ اللحية للرِّجال سنةٌ مؤكَّدةٌ وليست واجبة، فمَن حلقها أو قصَّرها من غير عذرٍ لم يأثم ولكنَّه ارتكب مكروهاً؛ لمخالفته ما ثبت الحثُّ عليه في صحيح الأخبار وما فَعَله النبيُّ ﷺ، وفاعلُ المكروه كتاركِ السُّنة لا يذمُّ عندنا بمعنى أنَّه: لا يَسْتحقُّ العقابَ على ذلك، كما علمتَ من كلام القاضي البيضاوي آنفاً، ولكن يفوتُ صاحبَهما الثوابُ الجزيلُ.

أما مَن حلق لحيتَه أو قصَّرها لعُذر كمرضٍ أو خوفٍ من ظالمٍ يتهدَّدُه لأجل إعفائها فلا شيءَ عليه، كما قال الله تعالى:﴿وما جعل عليكم في الدين من حرج﴾ والله تعالى أعلم وأحكم.

حيث... اعتمدَه الشيخان الإمامان محرِّراً مذهبنا الإمام أبو القاسم الرافعي والإمام أبو زكريا النووي تبعاً للإمام حجة الإسلام الغزالي: إنَّ إعفاءَ اللحية مندوبٌ وليس بواجب؛ فلا يحرم حلقُها ولا تقصيرُها من غير عذر، لكنه مكروهٌ لمخالفته الأمرَ والهديَ النبويَّ بإعفائها قولاً وفعلاً

'This is the relied upon position in the school and the settled upon legal verdict due to the well-known principle among the later scholars which states that, the relied upon position in the school is whatever the two Shaykhs have declared and emendated. However, if they differ, then the opinion of Nawawī is given precedent, and we do not look at who has disagreed with them even if he is someone of greater rank. In this issue we see that both have agreed upon the offensiveness of shaving or shortening the beard, and this is the opinion that many of the later Imams of the school have also supported in accordance with them. Therefore, it is incumbent for you to take their evident words which establish that the relied upon position in the school of shaving and shortening the beard is of it being offensive. The opinion which states that shaving the beard is unlawful is deemed a weak opinion.

'Imam al-Ḥāfiẓ b. al-Mulaqqin cites the opinion of Imam al-Ḥalīmī in his Minhāj, "It is impermissible for anyone to shave their beard or eyebrows," but then comments upon it saying, "What has been mentioned previously with regards to shaving the beard is good, even if it is well-known in the school that it is offensive." In *al-Rawḍ* by Ibn al-Muqrī the Yemeni and its commentary by Shaykh al-Islām Zakariyyā [al-Anṣārī] he states (in the chapter of the *'aqīqa*[1]), "Plucking of the beard is offensive when it first starts growing, due to the preference of social integrity and a pleasant physical appearance." The annotator, Imam al-Shihāb Aḥmad al-Ramlī, the Imam of his time in Egypt states, "His statement, 'Plucking of the beard is offensive (till the end)' and to shave it is similar to it, means that the statement of al-Ḥalīmī in his *Minhāj*, 'It is impermissible for anyone to shave their beard or eyebrows' is considered weak."

---

[1] [The Islamic tradition of the sacrifice of an animal on the occasion of a child's birth]

وهذا القولُ هو معتمدُ المذهب وعليه الفتوى؛ لِما هو معلومٌ من قاعدة المذهب عند المتأخرين: أنَّ ما قاله الشيخان وحرَّراه هو معتمدُ المذهب، فإن اختلفا فالترجيحُ لقول النووي، وأنه لا ينظر إلى مَن خالفهما وإن جلَّت مرتبتُه، وقد رأيتَ اتفاقَهما هنا على القول بكراهة حلق اللحية أو تقصيرها، وهذا القولُ هو ما اعتمده كثيرٌ من أئمة المذهب من المتأخرين تبعاً للشيخين، وإليك كلامَهم المبيِّنَ لمعتمد المذهب من كراهة حلق وتقصير اللحية، وأنَّ القولَ بحرمة حلقها قولٌ ضعيف عندنا:

ذكر الإمامُ الحافظُ ابنُ الملقِّن قولَ الإمام الحَلِيمي في «منهاجه»: «لا يحلُّ لأحدٍ أن يحلق لحيته ولا حاجبيه» ثمّ قال معلقاً عليه: «وما ذكره في حقِّ اللحية حسنٌ وإن كان المعروفُ في المذهب الكراهة». اهـ وفي «الروض» للإمام ابن المقري اليمني و«شرحه» لشيخ الإسلام زكريا (في باب العقيقة) ما نصه: «(و) يكره (نتفُها) أي: اللحية أول طلوعها إيثاراً للمُرُودةِ وحُسْنِ الصورة». اهـ قال المحشي إمامُ أهل عصره بمصرَ الإمامُ الشهابُ أحمد الرملي:«(قوله ويكره نتفُها أي: اللحية إلخ) ومثلُه حلقُها، فقولُ الحَلِيمِي في«منهاجه»: (لا يحلُّ لأحدٍ أن يحلقَ لحيته ولا حاجبيه) ضعيفٌ». اهـ.

'He has also clearly expressed that in his legal verdicts—that is Shihāb al-Ramlī—that he was once asked (as is mentioned in the chapter of the *'aqīqa*), "Is it unlawful to shave or pluck the hair of the cheek?" To which he replied, "For a male to shave or pluck the beard is offensive, but not unlawful, and the statement of al-Ḥalīmī in his *Minhāj* that, 'It is unlawful for anyone to shave their beard or eyebrows,' is regarded as being weak." His son, Imam Shams al-Din al-Ramlī, whose legal verdicts are the most reliable from the people of the school in Egypt, states in al-Nihāya in the chapter of the *'aqīqa* that, "It is recommended to part the hair, to comb it and to release the beard; however, it is offensive to pluck or shave it."

'Shaykh al-Islām Shihāb b. Ḥajar al-Haytamī has also clearly expressed that to shave the beard is offensive, and the opinion that declares it to be unlawful is considered weak. His legal verdicts are relied upon by those of our school in most countries. He writes in *al-Tuḥfa* (in the chapter of the *'aqīqa*), "They have mentioned here with regards to the beard and the like a disliked quality, from it: to pluck or shave it, and likewise the eyebrows. The statement of al-Ḥalīmī, 'it is unlawful' does not negate this understanding, as we can interpret the statement to mean to negate it being in the middle between both permissibility and impermissibility, and the text[1] is in agreement with that[2] opinion if the statement, 'it is not lawful [*lā yaḥill*]' is interpreted as that. However, to interpret is as being 'unlawful' [*yaḥrum*] would be contradictory to the relied upon opinion.'"[3]

---

[1] He means the text of Imam al-Shāfiʿī which indicates the unlawfulness of shaving the beard.

[2] That is, what agrees with the opinion of al-Ḥalīmī.

[3] *Qaṭʿ al-Mariyya fī Bayān Madhhab al-Shāfiʿiyya fī Ḥalq wa-Taqṣīr al-Liḥya*

وصرَّح بذلك أيضاً في «فتاويه» ـ أعني الشهاب الرملي ـ فقد سئل كما في (باب العقيقة): «هل يحرم حلقُ الذقن ونتفُها أو لا؟ فأجاب: بأن حلقَ لحية الرجل ونتفَها مكروهٌ لا حرامٌ وقولُ الحَلِيمي في «منهاجه»:(لا يحل لأحد أن يحلق لحيتَه ولا حاجبيه) ضعيفٌ».

وقال ولدُه ـمعتَمَدُ الفتوى عند المصريين من أهل مذهبنا ـ الإمامُ شمسُ الدين الرملي في «النهاية» (باب العقيقة): «ويندب فرقُ الشعر وترجيلُه، وتسريحُ اللحية ويكره نتفُها وحلقُها».

وبكراهةِ حلق اللحية وضعفِ القول بتحريمه صرَّح شيخُ الإسلام الشهاب ابن حجر الهيتمي ـوهو معتمدُ الفتوى في أكثر الأقاليم عند أهل مذهبنا ـ ونصُّه في «التحفة» (باب العقيقة): «(فرع) ذكروا هنا في اللحية ونحوها خصالاً مكروهةً؛ منها: نتفُها وحلقُها، وكذا الحاجبان، ولا ينافيه قولُ الحليمي: «لا يحل ذلك» لإمكان حمله على أن المرادَ نفيُ الحلِّ المستوي الطرفين، والنصُّ[1] على ما يوافقه[2] إن كان بلفظ: «لا يحل» يحملُ على ذلك، أو «يحرم»[3] كان خلافَ المعتمد»[4].

---

(1) يريد نصَّ الإمام الشافعي المفيد لحرمة حلق اللحية.

(2) أي: على ما يوافق قول الحليمي.

(3) عطف على قوله (بلفظ يحل) يعني: أو كان نصُّ الشافعي بلفظ (يحرم).

(4) ينظر: قطع المرية في بيان مذهب الشافعية في حلق وتقصير اللحية

The Mālikī School

The legal ruling of shaving the beard differs from the ruling of shortening the beard in the Mālikī school. They openly express that it is unlawful to shave the beard but differ with regards to shortening it into two main opinions:

First, to not trim the beard to less than a fist-length.

Second, to trim the beard according to the culture ['urf] of the people, with the condition that it is not considered disfigurement—this condition has been mentioned by al-Nafrāwī and al-'Adawī.

Al-Nafrāwī states, 'It is unlawful for males to shave it. As for shortening it, if it is not long then it is likewise [unlawful]. If however, it has become very long and profuse, then he has indicated his verdict with his statement, "Mālik said, It is fine to trim from its length if it became excessively long" such that it exceeds the norm of most people. In this instance, one can trim the excess to stop it from making one's appearance unpleasant. The ruling with regards to trimming is recommended, and it is fine [to do so] here as it is better than the other [option]. It is well-known that there is no limit to how much one can trim, but it is recommended for one to trim to the point where one's appearance becomes pleasant. Al-Bājī states one should trim that which exceeds a fist-length, as indicated by the actions of 'Umar and Abū Hurayra as both would trim from their beard anything that exceeded a fist-length. The intended meaning of 'its length' is the length of the hair, and therefore includes the hair on the sides and thus making it fine to trim that area as well.'[1]

Al-'Adawī states, 'Some of the commentators interpreted the term 'profuse' to mean that which exceeds the normal amount for the majority of people; in this instance, it is recommended for one to trim the excess, as by not trimming it would makes one's appearance unpleasant.

---

[1] *Al-Fawākih al-Dawānī* (al-Nafrāwī) (2:307)

ثانياً: مذهب المالكية:

اختلف حكم الحلق عن حكم القص عند المالكية، فصرحوا في الحلق بالحرمة، وأما القص فاختلفوا على قولين:

الأول: عدم تقصير اللحية أقل من قبضة.

والثاني: يقصر من اللحية على عرف المجتمع، وبشرط أن لا يكون مثلة، وهذا التفصيل ذكره النفراوي والعدوي.

قال النفراوي[1]: «يحرم حلقها إذا كانت لرجل، وأما قصها فإن لم تكن طالت فكذلك، وأما لو طالت كثيرا فأشار إلى حكمه بقوله: قال مالك: ولا بأس بالأخذ من طولها إذا طالت طولاً كثيراً. بحيث خرجت عن المعتاد لغالب الناس فيقص الزائد؛ لأنَّ بقاءه يقبح به المنظر، وحكم الأخذ الندب فلا بأس هنا لما هو خير من غيره، والمعروف لا حد للمأخوذ، وينبغي الاقتصار على ما تحسن به الهيئة، وقال الباجي: يقص ما زاد على القبضة، ويدل عليه فعل عمر وأبي هريرة فإنَّهما كانا يأخذان من لحيتهما ما زاد على القبضة، والمراد بطولها طول شعرها فيشمل جوانبها فلا بأس بالأخذ منها أيضاً».

وقال العدوي: «وفسر بعض الشراح الكثرة بأن خرجت عن المعتاد لغالب الناس: أي فيندب له أن يقص الزائد؛ لأنَّ بقاءه يقبح به المنظر.

---

[1] ينظر: الفواكه الدواني 2: 307.

'If one asks, what is the ruling of shortening the beard when the beard is not extremely profuse or is slightly profuse? I say, Some of the commentators have clearly expressed that it is unlawful to shorten the beard if it is not profuse, like shaving. It is apparent that the basis of it being unlawful—as has been explained before—is if, by it, one reaches the stage of disfigurement, which becomes apparent when one oversteps the bounds whilst trimming when it (the beard) is not profuse or is only slightly profuse.

'However, if the beard was only slightly profuse and shortening it would not result in disfigurement, then the obvious is that it is considered as 'leaving the more appropriate' [*khilāf al-awlā*], and this [opinion] has been rendered accurate.

'It is well known that there is no limit to how much one can trim, that is if it has become extremely profuse. We say it is fine to shorten it. The issue differs according to the two opinions, the more well-known opinion being that there is no limit to how much one can trim, meaning that one should limit himself to what would make one's appearance pleasant. The opposite to the well-known, is what al-Bājī said, that one should trim only that which has exceeded a fist-length.'[1]

---

[1] *Ḥāshiya al-'Adawī 'alā Kifāya al-Ṭālib al-Rabbānī* (2:445)

فإن قلت: وما حكم القص عند عدم الطول أو الطول القليل؟

قلت: صرح بعض الشراح بأنه يحرم القص إن لم تكن طالت كالحلق، والظاهر أنَّ محل الحرمة كما أفدناك سابقاً إذا كان يحصل بالقص مثلة، وهو ظاهر عند عدم الطول أو الطول القليل وتجاوز في القص.

وأما إذا طالت قليلاً وكان القص لا يحصل به مثلة، فالظاهر أنه خلاف الأولى وحرر.

والمعروف لا حد للأخذ منها: أي أنَّها إذا طالت كثيراً، وقلنا: لا بأس بالأخذ منها فاختلف على قولين المعروف منهما أنَّه لا حدّ للأخذ: أي فيقتصر على ما تحسن به الهيئة، ومقابل المعروف ما قاله الباجي: إنَّه يقصّ ما زاد على القبضة»[1].

---

(1) ينظر: حاشية العدوي على كفاية الطالب الرباني 2: 445.

Despite the fact that the beard is not an unknown or rare issue, and is something that is part of a man's life from puberty till death, we find that the manuals of law in the Ḥanafī school do not address the issue in a lucid manner. Thus, there is no mention of it in the books of *Ẓāhir al-Riwāya*, which form the basis of the school, the concise manuals [*mutūn*] or in any of the well-known commentaries.

This is extremely odd, how can a school with such vastness *not* concern itself with addressing such a common issue? However, what helps us understand this is if we approach the issue in the same way we approach customary acts, rather than acts of worship. This is because the former ultimately varies from one culture to another, hence the jurists did not see the need to determine any specific details with regards to it. Similarly, this is also the case with clothing; the jurists do not specify a certain way of dressing, even though dress is of utmost importance. This is because this matter returns to culture, and so they merely defined the limits of what is considered obligatory to cover; and there are other similar examples.

Al-Rāzī states, 'There are three levels of dress:
[I] Compulsory—this is what covers the private areas of one's body and protects him from the harm of heat and cold, being a medium-sized dress made from cotton or linen, and in my opinion cotton is better.
[II] Recommended—this is to wear fine clothes for the purpose of beautifying, making oneself look pleasant and to manifest the blessings of Allah ﷻ upon oneself.
[III] Unlawful—this is to wear clothes for the purpose of arrogance and conceit.'[1]

---

[1] *Tuḥfa al-Mulūk* (p. 320)

المطلب الثالث

حلق اللحية وقصُّها في كتب الحنفية

رغم أنَّ مسألة اللحية ليست من المسائل الخفية أو النادرة الوقوع، بل هي ملازمة للرجال من بلوغهم إلى وفاتهم، إلا أننا نجد أن كتب الحنفية لم تطرح المسألة بصورة واضحة، فلم تذكر في كتب ظاهر الرِّواية التي هي أساس المذهب ولا في المتون ولا في الشروح المشهورة.

وهذا في غايةِ الغرابةِ، كيف لمذهب بهذه السعة لا يعتني بذكر مثل هذه المسألة المشهورة، ويدفع مثل هذا الاستغراب عن المذهب بتعامله مع المسألة تعامل العادات لا العبادات، وهذا متفاوت من عرف إلى عرف، فلم يذكروا تفصيلاً متعلقاً بها؛ لاختلاف الأعراف في ذلك، كما هو الواقع في لبس الثياب، فلا يتكلَّمون عن هيئة خاصّة به مع كثرة أهميته؛ لكونه راجعاً للعرف، وإنَّما يُبيِّنون حدود العورة، وأمثاله من الأحكام العامة.

قال الرازي[1]: «واللبسُ على ثلاث مراتب :فرضٌ: وهو ما يسترُ بدنه، ويدفع عنه ضررَ الحرِّ والبرد من وسطِ ثياب القطن أو الكتان، والقطنُ عندي أفضل. ومستحبٌّ: وهو لبس الثياب الجميلة للتجمّل والتزيّن وإظهار نعمة الله ﷻ. وحرامٌ: وهو لبسُها للتكبّر والخيلاء».

---

(١) ينظر: تحفة الملوك ص320

Due to the beard being regarded from those things related to one's outward appearance and culture, similar to dress, any details relating to it have ultimately been left unmentioned. This is what we previously acknowledged in the explicit statement of al-ʿImādī in which he states, 'If shaving the beard detracts from one's social integrity then it [his testimony] is unaccepted. If, however, it does not [detract from one's social integrity] then it is accepted.'[1] Ibn ʿĀbidīn commentates upon this [statement] saying, 'Based upon this, if he was from those amongst whom shaving is considered the norm and do not deem it to be something despicable between them, then there is no detraction from his social integrity and his testimony is accepted.'[2]

The following examples help to illustrate and affirm that this issue falls under the rubric of custom:

1. In most of the manuals of the Ḥanafī school, the great jurists confine themselves to only mentioning the sunna length of the beard, just as they do with regards to dress, where they simply outline the preferred. Al-Rāzī states, 'The best of clothes are white,'[3] due to what has been related from the Messenger of Allah ﷺ, 'Wear white clothes, as it is considered the best from your clothes, and bury your dead in them.'[4]

Some explicit statements that affirm the sunna being a fist-length are:

Al-Marghīnānī said, 'He should not do it—that is, dyeing to lengthen the beard—if the beard is already the sunna-length of a fist.'[5]

---

[1] *Tanqīḥ al-Fatāwā al-ʿImādiyya* (1:429)
[2] Ibid. (1:429)
[3] *Tuḥfa al-Mulūk* (p. 321)
[4] *Ṣaḥīḥ Ibn Ḥibbān* (12:242), *Sunan al-Tirmidhī* (3:319) who considered it sound & *Sunan Abū Dāwūd* (4:8)
[5] *Al-Hidāya (with Fatḥ al-Qadīr)* (2:347) & *Minḥa al-Sulūk* (1:268)

3.5 حلق اللحية وقصُّها في كتب الحنفية

ولمّا كان حال اللحية من الهيئات والعادات كاللباس سُكِت عن التَّفاصيل المتعلِّقة بها، وهذا ما مرّ معنا صريحاً في عبارة العمادي[1]: «فإن كان حلق اللحية يُخل بالمروءة يمنع القبول ـ أي الشهادة ـ وإلا فلا»، وشرحها ابن عابدين فقال[2]: «فعلى هذا فإن كان ممن يعتادون الحلق ولا يعدونه رذيلة بينهم لا يُخل بمروءته فتقبل شهادته... ».

ومما يؤكد هذا الفهم للمسألة في كونها من العادات ما يأتي:

1. إنَّ أكابر الفقهاء في عامة كتب الحنفية يقتصرون بالتَّصريح في اللحية على القدر المسنون كما اهتموا بذلك في اللِّباس في بيان المستحبّ، قال الرَّازيّ[3]: «وأفضل الثياب البيض»؛ لما روي أنَّ رسول الله ﷺ قال: (البسوا من ثيابكم البياض، فإنَّها من خير ثيابكم وكفنوا فيها موتاكم)[4].

ومن العبارات المصرحة بسنيّة القبضة:

قال المرغينانيّ[5]: «ولا يفعل ـ أي الخضاب ـ لتطويل اللحية إذا كانت بالقدر المسنون وهي القبضة».

---

[1] ينظر: تنقيح الفتاوى العمادية 1: 429.

[2] ينظر: المصدر السابق

[3] في تحفة الملوك ص321، الفاروق.

[4] في صحيح ابن حبان 12: 242، وسنن الترمذي 3: 319، وصححه، وسنن أبي داود 4: 8.

[5] في الهداية 2: 347، مع الفتح، وينظر: منحة السلوك 1: 268.

Raḍī al-Dīn al-Sarakhsī said, 'The sunna-length is a fist-length; that being when a man clenches a fist from his beard and cuts whatever exceeds that. This is what Muḥammad has narrated in *Kitāb al-Āthār* from the Imam [Abū Ḥanīfa]. He said, "...and that is what he was upon."'[1]

Al-Zaylaʿī said, "If the beard is the sunna-length, which is a fist-length, then, whatever exceeds that should be trimmed."[2]

Ibn Nujaym said, 'Leaving the beard [*iʿfāʾ al-liḥya*] means to leave it until it becomes dense and profuse; the sunna is a fist-length—whatever exceeds that should be trimmed.'[3]

Al-Sannāmī said, 'Do not trim it less than the sunna-length, which is a fist-length.'[4]

2. The Ḥanafī jurists have expressed that lengthening the beard is from the beautification [*zīna*] which is desired for males. Muḥammad states, relating from Abū Ḥanīfa, 'to leave it until it becomes dense and profuse; and trimming whatever exceeds a fist-length is sunna, as it is from beautification, and making it profuse is from perfecting that beauty, whereas to keep it excessively long contradicts beauty.'[5]

---

[1] *Radd al-Muḥtār* (6:407)
[2] *Tabyīn al-Ḥaqāʾiq* (1:331)
[3] *Al-Baḥr al-Rāʾiq* (3:12)
[4] *Niṣāb al-Iḥtisāb* (1:122)
[5] *Durar al-Ḥukkām* (1:322) & *al-Ikhtiyār* (4:167)

3.5 حلق اللحية وقصُّها في كتب الحنفية

وقال رضي الدِّين السَّرَخْسيّ: «والسُّنّة فيها القبضة: وهو أن يقبض الرَّجل لحيته فما زاد منها على قبضة قطعه كذا ذكره محمد في «كتاب الآثار» عن الإمام، قال: وبه أخذ»[1].

وقال الزَّيلعيّ[2]: «اللحية إذا كانت بقدر المسنون وهي القبضة وما زاد على ذلك يقص».

وقال ابنُ نُجيم[3]: «وإعفاء اللحية تركها حتى تكث وتكثر، والسنة قدر القبضة فما زاد قطعه».

وقال السنّامي[4]: «ولا تنقصوها من القدر المسنون وهو القبضة».

2.1.إنَّ فقهاء الحنفية نصّوا على أنَّ إطالة اللحية من الزِّينة المطلوبة للرَّجل، قال محمد عن أبي حنيفة: تركها حتى تكث وتكثر، والتقصير منها سنة فيما زاد على القبضة؛ لأنَّها زينة وكثرتها من كمال الزِّينة وطولها الفاحش خلاف الزينة[5].

____

[1] ينظر: رد المحتار 6: 407.

[2] ينظر: تبيين الحقائق 1: 331.

[3] ينظر: البحر الرائق 3: 12.

[4] ينظر: نصاب الاحتساب 1: 122.

[5] ينظر: درر الحكام 1: 322، والاختيار 4: 167.

By placing [the beard] under the rubric of beautification, it teaches us that it is from the varying customary practices of a people, as the understanding of what is acceptable beautification for a male differs from place to place.

3. The jurists have given serious importance to preventing one from lengthening the beard more than a fist-length. Their clear expression in affirming the sunna to be a fist-length is a way in urging people not to lengthen more than that, and thus not contradict the sunna appearance. This is because their outward appearance will not be in line with the teachings of Islam, and so they said, 'It is left until it becomes dense and profuse; trimming it is from the sunna and so whatever exceeds a fist length is trimmed.'[1]

Rather, al-Saghnāqī explicitly states in *al-Nihāya* that it is actually necessary to trim anything in excess of a fist-length, 'It is necessary to trim whatever exceeds a fist-length.'[2] Al-Ḥaṣkafī states, 'Leaving it results in sin,'[3] meaning that it is sinful to not trim that which has exceeded a fist-length.

4. Some of the jurists have clearly expressed that to lengthen the beard is sunna and recommended. Shams al-A'imma al-Sarakhsī said, 'The sunna is to trim the moustache and to lengthen the beard.'[4]

Al-'Aynī said, 'Lengthening the beard: [that is,] extending it and making it profuse, as it was from the semblance of some non-Arabs to trim the beard and lengthen the moustache, and so the Messenger of Allah ﷺ encouraged his nation to differ from their ways.'[5]

---

[1] *Al-Bināya* (4:73)
[2] *Fatḥ al-Qadīr* (2:347)
[3] *Al-Durr al-Mukhtār* (2:417)
[4] *Al-Mabsūṭ* (4:74)
[5] *Sharḥ Sunan Abī Dāwūd* (1:163)

3.5 حلق اللحية وقصُّها في كتب الحنفية

وكونها من الزينة يفيد أنَّها من العادات المتفاوتة في هذا الاعتبار للزينة الحسنة للرجل من مجتمع إلى مجتمع.

3.1.الاهتمامُ الشَّديدُ من الفقهاء في المنع من الزيادة على قدر القبضة، ففي تصريحهم القبضة المسنونة يرغبون الناس بعدم الزيادة عليها فيخالفوا الهيئة المسنونة؛ لأنَّ صورتهم لن تكون ملائمة لهدي الإسلام، فقالوا: يتركها حتى تكثف وتكبر، والقصُّ سُنّة فما زاد على قبضة قطعها[1].

بل صرَّح السغناقي بوجوب قطع ما يزيد عن القبضة، ففي «النهاية»: وما وراء ذلك يجب قطعه[2]. قال الحصكفي[3]: «ومقتضاه الإثم بتركه»: أي الإثم بترك قصّ ما زاد على القبضة.

4. التصريح من بعض الفقهاء بأنَّ الأعفاء سنة ومندوب، قال شمس الأئمة السَّرَخْسيّ[4]: «السُّنَّةُ قَصُّ الشَّارب وإعفاء اللحى».

وقال العَينيّ[5]: «إعفاء اللِّحية: إرسالها وتوفيرها؛ لأنَّ بعض الأعاجم كان من زيهم قص اللحى، وتوفير الشوارب، فنَدَبَ ﷺ أُمَّتَه إلى مخالفتهم».

---

[1] ينظر: البناية 4: 73.

[2] ينظر: فتح القدير 2: 347.

[3] ينظر: الدر المختار 2: 417.

[4] ينظر: المبسوط 4: 74.

[5] ينظر: شرح سنن أبي داود 1: 163.

5. The great Imam, Ibrāhīm al-Nakha'ī—who is regarded as one of the most influential personalities in the Ḥanafī school, the teacher of Abū Ḥanīfa and the teacher of his teacher Ḥammād b. Abī Sulaymān—explicitly declares that it is permissible to shorten the beard indefinitely, as long as it is not imitating of the people of the book. Abū Ḥanīfa states, relating from Ḥammād who relates from Ibrāhīm that, 'There is no issue for a man to shorten his beard as long as it does not imitate non-Muslims.'[1]

The fact that the issue of imitating non-believers is a matter that returns to culture has been discussed previously. If a particular outward appearance is widespread in society then it is not considered to be from blameworthy imitation.

6. The jurists have mentioned that the causal factor behind lengthening the beard is to prevent the imitation of non-Muslims, as is touched upon in some of the traditions related to the beard, where it becomes evident that the motive for lengthening one's beard is to differ from non-Muslims. On the authority of Ibn 'Umar ﷺ who said, 'The Messenger of Allah ﷺ said, "Differ from the disbelievers; shorten your moustaches and lengthen your beards."'[2]

And on the authority of Abū Hurayra ﷺ who said, 'The Messenger of Allah ﷺ said, "Shorten your moustaches and let your beards grow freely; differ from the Magians."'[3]

---

[1] *Kitāb al-Āthār* (1:234)
[2] *Ṣaḥīḥ Muslim* (1:222)
[3] Ibid.

5.3 حلق اللحية وقصُّها في كتب الحنفية

5. تصريح الإمام الكبير إبراهيم النَّخعيّ، الذي يُعَدُّ من أكثر الأشخاص تأثيراً في المذهب الحنفي، وهو أُستاذ لأبي حنيفة، وأُستاذ أستاذه حماد بن أبي سليمان بجواز الأخذ من اللحية مطلقاً ما لم يكن متشبهاً بأهل الكتاب، فعن أبي حنيفة عن حماد عن إبراهيم أنَّه قال: «لا بأس أن يأخذ الرَّجل من لحيته ما لم يتشبه بأهل الشرك»[1].

وسبق تحرير أنَّ مسألةَ التَّشبُّه بغير المسلمين راجعةٌ للعرف، فإن كانت هيئة معينة منتشرة في المجتمع لم تعدَّ من التَّشبُّه المذموم.

6. ذكر الفقهاء أنَّ العلَّة من إعفاء اللحى هو منع التشبه بغير المسلمين، كما ورد في بعض روايات أحاديث اللحية، حيث بينت أنَّ السبب في إعفاء اللحية، هو مخالفة المشركين، فعن ابن عمر ﷺ قال ﷺ: (خالفوا المشركين أحفوا الشوارب وأوفوا اللحى)[2]، وعن أبي هريرة ﷺ، قال ﷺ: (جزوا الشوارب وأرخوا اللحى خالفوا المجوس)[3].

---

[1] ينظر: كتاب الآثار 1: 234.

[2] ينظر: صحيح مسلم 1: 222.

[3] ينظر: المصدر السابق

Ibn al-Humām states: 'This sentence is situated as the causal factor,[1] that is the sentence: "differ from the disbelievers" or "differ from the Magians."' Al-Kāsānī says, 'Because it is from imitating the Christians, it is offensive.'[2]

It is thus textually explicitly stated that the causal factor for lengthening the beard is in order to differ from the disbelievers, whether they are from the polytheists, Magians or people of the book. This particular causal factor of differing [from them] can bring sin upon someone if shaving the beard was considered from their rites, if one intended to imitate them, and if one was from the very first people to do so, that is, [at a time] where it had not yet become general custom in society. These conditions are, more or less, non-existent. Shaving the beard is not seen as a rite for the disbelievers, rather the devout from them are actually well-known for lengthening their beards, therefore differing [from them] would require not lengthening one's beard. One does not intend to imitate the disbelievers when shaving, as shaving and trimming has essentially become a general custom in society. Therefore, the legal ruling that stems from this causal factor no longer remains as it was; and Allah ﷻ knows best.

7. There are explicit statements from the jurists that the prohibition in shaving the beard is due to it being seen as disfigurement [*muthla*], meaning that it is something ugly, repulsive, and antithetical to the concept of beauty, and therefore not appropriate for a male to perform such an act. However, it is well-known that the issue of disfigurement returns to culture, and therefore culture would be the factor that decides whether the beard is regarded as disfigurement or not. Hence, if shortening the beard is not regarded as disfigurement then the offense is no longer present.

---

[1] *Fatḥ al-Qadīr* (2:348)
[2] *Al-Badā'i' al-Ṣanā'i'* (2:141)

قال ابن الهمام[1]: «فهذه الجملة واقعة موقع التعليل»: أي جملة: «خالفوا المشركين»، أو «خالفوا المجوس»، وقال الكاساني[2]: «ولأنَّ ذلك تشبه بالنصارى فيكره».

وهذا صريحٌ في النَّصِّ بأنَّ علَّةَ الإعفاء هي المخالفةُ لغير المسلمين على اختلاف أصنافهم من مشركين أو مجوس أو أهل كتاب، وهذه العلَّة في المخالفة تفيد الإثم إن كان حلق اللحية شعاراً لهم ويقصد التشبه بهم ويفعله ابتداءً وليس عرفاً عاماً في المجتمع، ولم يبق شيءٌ من هذه الضوابط عموماً، فلم يعد الحلق شعاراً لغير المسلمين، بل إنَّ رجال الدِّين عندهم مشهورون بإطالة اللحى فأصبحت المخالفة تقضتي عدم الإطالة، ولا يُقصد التشبه بغير المسلمين في الحلق، وصار الحلق والتقصير عرفاً عاماً في المجتمع، فلم يبق الحكم لهذه العلة كما كان، والله أعلم.

7.تصريح الفقهاء أنَّ المنع من حلق اللحية بسبب كونه مثلة: أي بشع وشنيع ومناف للزينة فلا يليق بالمرء فعله، ومعلومٌ أنَّ مسألة المثلة عرفية، فيكون هو الضابط في تحديد أنَّها مثلة أم لا، فإن لم يكن الأخذ منها من المثلة لم تعد الكراهة موجودة.

---

(1) ينظر: فتح القدير 2: 348.

(2) ينظر: بدائع الصنائع 2: 141.

Al-Kāsānī says—in rebuttal of the opinion of al-Shāfi'ī that it is recommended to trim the beard when leaving the state of *iḥrām* [*taḥallul*], 'This is not credible, as the necessary—as proven by the aforementioned text—is to shave the head; shaving the beard is regarded as disfigurement; Allah ﷻ has beautified males with their beards and women with their locks.'[1]

8. There is an explicit statement by Ibn al-Humām that to shorten less than a fist-length is not permissible if this action was specific for effeminate men, that is, those that imitate females in their outward appearance. He states, 'As for shortening it and it is less than that—just as some western and effeminate men do—then, no one has permitted it.'[2]

This reminds us of the mistake that has become widespread in some books, with regards to understanding the statements of Ibn al-Humām. They understand the statement, 'no one has permitted it' to mean an inference of consensus by Ibn al-Humām, meaning that there is scholarly agreement upon the necessity of keeping a beard. This understanding is indeed distant, as the fist-length—as we have noted previously—is not necessary according to the relied upon position in the Shāfi'ī school, and likewise according to one of the two opinions in the Mālikī school. It is also contradictory to what has been mentioned in the books of the Ḥanafī school which clearly state that to keep a fist-length beard is actually sunna and not necessary. As a result, based on this interpretation [of Ibn al-Humām's statement], the fist-length became necessary and any disagreement between the jurists was discarded; and this understanding is unacceptable.

---

[1] *Al-Badā'i' al-Ṣanā'i'* (2:141)
[2] *Fatḥ al-Qadīr* (2:348)

3.5 حلق اللحية وقصُّها في كتب الحنفية

قال الكاسانيّ[1] في رد قول الشافعي باستحباب الأخذ من اللحية عند التحلل: «وهذا ليس بشيء؛ لأنَّ الواجب حلق الرأس بالنَّص الذي تلونا، ولأنَّ حلق اللحية من باب المثلة ؛ لأنَّ الله تعالى زين الرجال باللحى، والنِّساء بالذَّوائب».

8. تصريح ابن الهمام أنَّ الأخذ بما دون القبضة ليس مباحاً إن كان هذا الفعل خاصّاً بالمخنَّثة: أي مَن يتشبَّهون بالنِّساء في هيئاتهم، فقال[2]: «وأما الأخذ منها وهي دون ذلك كما يفعله بعض المغاربة ومخنثة الرجال فلم يبحه أحد».

وهذا ينبهنا إلى الخطأ الذي شاع في بعض الكتب في فهم عبارة ابن الهمام، حيث فهم من جملة: «فلم يبحه أحد»، نقل الإجماع من ابن الهمام على اتفاق العلماء على وجوب اللحية، وهذا الفهم بعيدٌ جداً؛ لأنَّ المعتمد عند الشافعية عدم وجوب القبضة، وكذلك في أحد القولين عند المالكية، ويُعارض ما اشتهر في كتب الحنفية من قولهم القبضة المسنونة، وليس القبضة الواجبة، فعلى هذا الفهم صارت القبضة واجبة وانتفى خلاف الفقهاء، فلم يكن هذا الفهم مقبولاً.

---

(1) ينظر: بدائع الصنائع 2: 141.

(2) ينظر: فتح القدير 2: 348.

What supports this is what he states a few sentences before, in explanation of the words of the author of *al-Hidāya* regarding the pronoun ['it' in the sentence], 'and *it* is a fist', 'that is, the sunna-length for a beard.'[1] This is an explicit expression by Ibn al-Humām which clarifies that the fist-length is in reality considered sunna and not necessary. He does not then contradict himself after a few sentences by saying that a fist-length is necessary; and Allah ﷻ knows best.

Likewise, this is what al-Shurunbulālī,[2] Ibn ʿĀbidīn,[3] al-Ḥaṣkafī[4] and al-Shalabī[5] did, where they initially elaborated that the sunna-length of the beard is a fist, but later on, they go on to mention the expression of Ibn al-Humām verbatim, which talks about it (shortening) being impermissible if seen as disfigurement, imitating females, or from the actions of effeminate males.

Thus, a type of negligence has occurred when declaring the beard to be necessary and to shave it as being unlawful, by relying solely on the explicit statements of Ibn al-Humām and the books of legal verdicts.

---

[1] *Fatḥ al-Qadīr* (2:348)
[2] *Al-Shurunbulāliyya* (1:208)
[3] *Minḥa al-Khāliq* (2:302) & *Radd al-Mukhtār* (2:418)
[4] *Al-Durr al-Mukhtār* (2:417)
[5] *Ḥāshiya al-Shalabī ʿalā Tabyīn al-Ḥaqāʾiq* (1:331)

ويؤيد هذا أنَّ ابن الهمام قال قبلها بأسطر [1] في شرح كلام صاحب «الهداية» لضمير: «وهو القبضة»: «أي القدر المسنون من اللحية»، فهذا صريح من ابن الهمام أنَّ قدرَ القبضة مسنون وليس واجباً، فلا يعارض نفسه بعدها بأسطر، ويقول: بوجوب القبضة، والله أعلم.

وكذلك ما فعله الشُّرُنْبلاليُّ [2] وابنُ عابدين [3] والحَصْكَفيُّ [4] والشلبي [5] حيث تكلَّموا في البداية عن القدر المسنون للحية وهو القبضة، ثمَّ بعدها ذكروا عبارة ابن الهمام كما هي، مما يدلُّ على عدم الإباحة إن كان مثلة وتشبهاً بالنِّساء من فعل المخنثين.

وحصل نوع تساهل في إطلاق الوجوب على اللحية والحرمة للحلق اعتماداً على ظاهر عبارة ابن الهمام وكتب الفتاوى:

---

(1) ينظر: فتح القدير 2: 348.

(2) ينظر: الشرنبلالية 1: 208.

(3) ينظر: منحة الخالق 2: 302، ورد المحتار 2: 418.

(4) ينظر: الدر المختار 2: 417.

(5) ينظر: حاشية الشلبي على تبيين الحقائق 1: 331.

It has also been mentioned in *al-Nawāzil* in the chapter of marriage that, 'Abū Bakr[1] was asked about a woman who cut her hair, to which he replied, "She should seek forgiveness from Allah ﷻ, repent and not do it again." He was then asked, "But what if she did it with the permission of her husband?" To which he replied, "There is no obedience to the creation of Allah ﷻ when it is in disobedience to the Creator." It was then said to him, "Why is it not allowed for her to do it?" He replied, "Because she has imitated the acts of men and the Messenger of Allah ﷺ has stated, "Allah ﷻ has cursed those men who imitate women, and those women who imitate men."[2] in addition to the fact that the hair of a woman is equivalent to a man's beard and therefore, just as it is unlawful for a man to cut his beard it is unlawful for a female to cut her hair.'[3]

Al-Ḥaṣkafī states, "...and it is mentioned in *al-Mujtabā*, 'If she cuts the hair from her head she is regarded as sinful and is cursed.' In *al-Bazzāziyya* the author adds, 'even if it is done with the permission of the husband,' since, there is no obedience to creation when it is in disobedience to the Creator; this is why it is unlawful for a male to cut his beard. Thus, the causal factor [with regards to the unlawfulness of a female cutting her hair] is the imitation of males."[4]

---

[1] Muḥammad b. al-Faḍl al-Kamārī al-Bukhārī, Abu Bakr al-Faḍlī. Al-Kafawī states, 'He was a great Imam and a revered teacher, depended upon in transmission [*riwāya*] and followed with regards to its comprehension [*dirāya*]. Imams from all around travelled to meet him and many of the famous books of legal verdicts are full of his verdicts and transmissions. (*Al-Jawāhir al-Muḍiyya* (3:300/302), *Ṭabaqāt Ibn al-Ḥannā'ī* (p. 62), *al-Fawā'id al-Bahiyya* (p. 303-304) & *Muqaddima ʿUmda al-Riʿāya* (1:16))

[2] *Ṣaḥīḥ al-Bukhārī* (7:159) & *Sunan Abū Dāwūd* (4:60)

[3] *Niṣāb al-Iḥtisāb* (1:122)

[4] *Al-Durr al-Mukhtār* (6:407)

فذكر في «النَّوازل» في كتاب النكاح: سُئِل أبو بكر[1] عن امرأة قطعت شعرها قال: عليها أن تستغفر الله تعالى وتتوب ولا تعود إلى مثله، قيل: فإن فعلت ذلك بإذن زوجها، قال: لا طاعة لمخلوق في معصية الخالق، قيل له: لِمَ لا يجوز ذلك لها: قال: لأنَّها شبهت نفسها بالرجال، وقد قال النَّبيّ ﷺ: (لعن اللهُ تعالى المتشبهين من الرِّجال بالنِّساء، والمتشبهات من النِّساء بالرِّجال)[2]، ولأنَّ الشَّعر للمرأة بمنزلة اللحية للرَّجل، فكما لا يحلّ للرَّجل أن يقطع لحيته لا يحلُّ للمرأة أن تقطع شعرها)[3].

وقال الحصكفيّ[4]: وفي «المجتبى»: «قطعت شعر رأسها أثمت ولعنت، زاد في «البزازية» وإن بإذن الزوج؛ لأنَّه لا طاعة لمخلوق في معصية الخالق، ولذا يحرم على الرَّجل قطع لحيته، والمعنى المؤثر التَّشبُّه بالرِّجال».

---

(1) وهو محمد بن الفضل الكَمَاريّ البُخَاريّ، أبو بكر الفَضْلِيّ، قال الكفوي: كان إماماً كبيراً وشيخاً جليلاً، معتمداً في الرواية مقلداً في الدراية رحل إليه أئمة البلاد، ومشاهير كتب الفتاوى مشحونة بفتاواه ورواياته، (ت371هـ). ينظر: الجواهر المضية3: 300–302، وطبقات ابن الحنائي ص62، والفوائد البهية ص303– 304، ومقدمة العمدة1: 16.

(2) ينظر: صحيح البخاري7: 159، وسنن أبي داود4: 60.

(3) ينظر: نصاب الاحتساب ص143.

(4) ينظر: الدر المختار6: 407.

Ibn ʿĀbidīn, after quoting the statement of al-ʿImādī regarding the beard, which establishes that the beard is ultimately referred back to social integrity, says, 'However, it may be said that, persisting upon minor sins is sinful.'

He then continues by quoting the statements of al-Ḥaṣkafī and Ibn al-Humām, commentating after them with his statement, 'Persisting upon an unlawful act is sinful even if was by performed by someone who did not intend to belittle it (the sinful act), or it was not regarded from that which detracts from one's honesty and social integrity. Hence, the statement of the author, al-ʿImādī, is not verified, so ponder this.'[1]

And ʿAbd al-ʿAlī al-Laknawī states, '[The term] lengthening the beard [*iʿfāʾ al-liḥya*] is an indication for its generality, because to lengthen the beard is necessary [*wājib*].'[2]

In the following paragraphs, we will attempt to discuss and evaluate the aforementioned statements:

A. The statements that forbid a female from shaving [their heads]—which is the sunna for men—should be understood in the context of Hajj; Allah ﷻ says, ❨*...with a shaved head or with cropped hair.*❩[3] Ibn ʿUmar ☀ narrates, 'The Messenger of Allah ﷺ said, "O Allah! Have mercy upon the shavers!" They proclaimed, "And the ones who crop, Messenger of Allah." He ﷺ repeated, "O Allah, have mercy upon the shavers!" They asked once again, "And the ones who crop, Messenger of Allah." He ﷺ then said, "And the ones who crop."'[4]

---

[1] *Tanqīḥ al-Fatāwā al-ʿImādiyya* (1:429)
[2] *Rasāʾil al-Arkān* (p. 20)
[3] [*The Qurʾan, A new translation by M. A. S. Abdel Haleem,* Triumph, 48:27 (p. 336)]
[4] *Ṣaḥīḥ Muslim* (2:945) & *Ṣaḥīḥ al-Bukhārī* (2:616)

5.3 حلق اللحية وقصُّها في كتب الحنفية

وقال ابن عابدين[1] بعد نقل كلام العمادي في اللحية بأنَّها ترجع للمروءة: «لكن قد يقال: إن الإدمان على الصغيرة مفسق...» ثم نقل كلام الحصكفي وابن الهمام وعقب عليه بقوله: «فحيث أدمن على فعل هذا المحرَّم يفسق وإن لم يكن ممن يستخفونه ولا يعدونه قادحاً للعدالة والمروءة فكلام المؤلَّف ـ أي العمادي ـ غير محرَّر فتدبَّر».

وقال عبد العلي اللكنوي[2]: «إعفاء اللحية قرينة على العموم؛ لأنَّ إعفاء اللحية واجب».

ويُمكن مناقشة هذه النُّصوص بما يلي:

أ.إنَّ هذه النصوص في منع المرأة من الحلق في الحجّ كما هو السُّنَّة للرَّجل، قال تعالى: {مُحَلِّقِينَ رُءُوسَكُمْ وَمُقَصِّرِينَ} [الفتح: 27]، وعن ابن عمر ﵄: (إنَّ رسول الله ﷺ قال: اللهم ارحم المحلقين، قالوا: والمقصرين يا رسول الله، قال: اللهم ارحم المحلقين، قالوا: والمقصرين يا رسول الله، قال: والمقصرين)[3].

---

(1) ينظر: تنقيح الفتاوى العمادية1: 429.

(2) ينظر: رسائل الأركان ص20.

(3) ينظر: صحيح مسلم 2: 945، وصحيح البخاري 2: 616.

It has also been narrated from 'Alī ﷺ that, 'The Messenger of Allah ﷺ forbade women from shaving their heads.'[1] Therefore, it is not necessary for a woman to shave her head when wanting to release herself from the state of sanctity [*iḥrām*]—contrary to males—as her hair is a source of beauty for her, and she has not been ordered to remove her beauty to exit the state of *iḥrām*. Similarly, the beard, which is seen as a source of beauty in a man, has also not been ordered to be removed in order to exit the state of *iḥrām*. Shaving the head with regards to a female is considered as disfigurement. Al-Marghīnānī states, 'And because shaving the hair with regards to her is seen as disfigurement, like shaving the beard is with regards to males.'[2]

B. A man is forbidden to shave [his beard] and a female is forbidden to shave [her head] due to the ugliness and repulsiveness in that resulting in both losing their beauty and attractiveness. This is because a female normally acquires beauty through her hair, and a male through his beard. Al-Sarakhsī states, 'Shaving with regards to her is considered as disfigurement, and disfigurement is unlawful. Her hair is a source of beauty for her just as the beard is for males, and thus similarly to a male who does not shave his beard when exiting the state of *iḥrām*, she should not shave her head.'[3] And al-Qārī states, 'That is because the locks of a female are equivalent to a man's beard in appearance and beauty.'[4]

---

[1] *Sunan al-Tirmidhī* (3:248), *Sunan al-Nasāʾī al-Kubrā* (8:312) & *Musnad al-Bazzār* (2:92). Al-Haythamī states in *al-Majmaʿ* (3:263), 'On the authority of ʿUthmān who said, "The Messenger of Allah ﷺ forbade the woman from shaving her head." (Related by al-Bazzār; Rūḥ b. ʿAṭāʾ is in the chain and he is considered weak). On the authority of ʿĀʾisha who said, "The Messenger of Allah ﷺ forbade the woman from shaving her head." (Related by al-Bazzār. Muʿallā b. ʿAbd al-Raḥmān is in the chain who is known for fabrication; Ibn ʿAdī said, "I have hope that he is acceptable.")'

[2] *Al-Hidāya* (with *al-Bināya*) (4:274)

[3] *Al-Mabsūṭ* (4:33)

[4] *Mirqāt al-Mafātīḥ* (7:2845)

3.5 حلق اللحية وقصُّها في كتب الحنفية

كما ورد عن عليّ ﷺ قال: «نهى رسول الله ﷺ أن تحلق المرأة رأسها»[1]، فليس على المرأة للتَّحلُّل أن تحلقَ شعر رأسها، كما هو الحال للرَّجل؛ لأنَّ شعرَ رأسها زينة لها، ولم تؤمر بإزالة زينتها للتَّحلل، كما أنَّ اللحية للرَّجل زينة له فلم يؤمر عند التَّحلل بحلقها، فكان حلق شعر رأسها من المثلة لها، قال المَرغينانيُّ[2]: «ولأنَّ حلق الشَّعر في حقِّها مثلة، كحلق اللحية في حق الرِّجال».

ب. إنَّ الحلقَ ممنوعٌ للمرأة والرَّجل لما فيه الشناعة والبشاعة، فيذهب جمالهما وزينتهما؛ لأنَّ زينة المرأة بشعر رأسها والرَّجل بلحيته، قال السَّرَخْسيّ[3]: «ولأنَّ الحلق في حقها مثلة، والمثلة حرام، وشعر الرأس زينة لها كاللحية للرَّجل فكما لا يحلق الرَّجل لحيته عند الخروج من الإحرام لا تحلق هي رأسها». وقال القاري[4]: «وذلك لأنَّ الذوائب للنساء كاللحى للرِّجال في الهيئة والجمال».

---

(1) ينظر: سنن الترمذي 3: 248، وسنن النسائي الكبرى 8: 312، ومسند البزار 2: 92، قال الهيثمي في المجمع 3: 263: «عن عثمان قال: «نهى رسول الله ﷺ أن تحلق المرأة رأسها». رواه البزار، وفيه روح بن عطاء، وهو ضعيف. وعن عائشة «أنَّ النبي ﷺ نهى أن تحلق المرأة رأسها». رواه البزار، وفيه معلى بن عبد الرحمن، وقد اعترف بالوضع، وقال ابن عدي: أرجو أنه لا بأس به».

(2) ينظر: الهداية 4: 274، مع البناية.

(3) ينظر: المبسوط 4: 33.

(4) ينظر: مرقاة المفاتيح 7: 2845.

This shows us that the prohibition which forbids both males and females from shaving, is so that it does not lead to the loss of beauty, as well as it being seen to be a form of disfigurement. Therefore, if these meanings are not present—for example, when a female shortens her hair or a male his beard—then it is not forbidden but can actually be commendable.

C. The use of the phrase, 'there is no obedience to creation...' and 'Allah ﷻ has cursed those males that imitate...' as evidence by the jurists, implies that the female, in shaving her hair completely or cutting it in a male fashion, has imitated men through this, as she has lost her beauty, making the act sinful. However, if she shortened her hair in a manner that increased her beauty in the eyes of her husband, then she will not fall into this prohibition.

And likewise, the male, if shaving the beard in his culture is regarded to be imitative of females or of non-Muslims, then it is prohibited. However, if it is not considered so, then it is not prohibited, as has been discussed previously in the sections on imitating females and imitating non-Muslims.

D. The jurists have also clearly expressed that the effectual causal factor which brings about sin, is the 'imitation of males by females,' through shaving or shortening in a way that is imitative of males. Ibn ʿĀbidīn states, 'The effectual causal factor which makes her sinful is the imitation of males, as that is impermissible similar to the imitation of females [by males].'[1] Thus, when a female shortens her hair and there is no imitation, the sin in this is negated.

This is unequivocal in proving that the prohibiting factor is 'imitation', that is, when both the male and female imitate each other. Though, if imitation is no longer present in these acts, such that they become part of the common culture of a society, then these acts are no longer considered legally forbidden.

---

[1] *Radd al-Muḥtār* (6:407)

وهذا يبيّن لنا أنَّ المنع من الحلق لكل من الرَّجل والمرأة كيلا يؤدي إلى إزالة الزينة لهما، ويعتبر من التَّمثيل بهما، فإن لم يكن هذا متحقق فيها كالتقصير لشعر المرأة أو لحية الرجل فلا يمنع، بل يكون مستحنّ.

ج.إن استدلال الفقهاء بـ: لا طاعة لمخلوق... ولعن الله تعالى المتشبهين... يدلُّ على أنَّها شابهت الرَّجل بأن حلقت تماماً أو قصّرت مثل الرَّجل وأزالت جمالها، فكان ما تفعله معصية، بخلاف ما لو قصّرت شعرها بما يزيد جمالها في نظر زوجها، فلن تكون واقعة تحت هذا النهي.

وكذلك الحال للرَّجل إن كان يعدّ حلقه للحيته تشبهاً بالمرأة عرفاً أو بغير المسلمين فيكون منهياً عنه، وإلا فلا، كما سبق في مبحث التشبه بالمرأة ومبحث التشبه بغير المسلمين.

دـ.صرَّح الفقهاء أنَّ العلة المؤثرة في تحقيق الإثم هو تشبه المرأة بالرَّجل، وهذا يكون بالحلق والتَّقصير بما يشبه الرِّجال، قال ابن عابدين[1]: «العلة المؤثرة في إثمها التَّشبُّه بالرِّجال، فإنَّه لا يجوز كالتَّشبه بالنِّساء»، وانتفاء التشبه في تقصيرها ينفي الإثم.

وهذا صريحٌ بأنَّ المانع هو التَّشبُّه من كلِّ من الرَّجل والمرأةِ بالآخر، فإن انتفى التشبه بينهما بهذه الأفعال، وصارت عرفاً شائعاً في المجتمع لم يعد ممنوعاً شرعاً.

---

[1] ينظر: رد المحتار 6: 407.

E. The beard is customary ['āda], and differing customs in different societies affect the legal ruling. This means that they help establish whether shortening or shaving the beard is considered to detract from one's social integrity, or whether it is imitative of non-Muslims, or whether it is seen as being imitative of females. Therefore, it may be, that those jurists who forbade it did so based on the custom that was prevalent in their time.

'Abd al-'Azīz al-Ghumārī states, 'Those from the jurists who held that to keep a beard is necessary and to shave it is forbidden, did so—as we have mentioned previously—based on the culture that they were raised on, grew up in, and became accustomed to in their social life. This was also the case with us before shaving the beard became widespread here in Morocco. We used to deem shaving the beard as an enormous evil and the greatest of sins, as it opposed the state of our bearded society. This is also supported by the fact that the jurists did not make unlawful everything whose prohibition was based on imitation.'[1]

As long as the general culture in Muslim society is no longer accustomed to lengthening the beard, then it is fitting that the legal ruling changes, adjusting itself to the change in culture; and Allah﷾ knows best.

F. The books, whether *al-Nawāzil* or *al-Bazzāziyya*, that mention these opinions, are essentially books of legal verdicts [*fatāwā*], and it is well known that not everything that is mentioned in them is accepted if we fail to locate a juristic foundation to build the ruling upon. Ibn 'Ābidīn states, 'This is why our scholars have declared that not everything found in the books of legal verdicts is used if it contradicts what is found in the manuals and commentaries.'

---

[1] *Ifāda Dhawī Afhām anna Ḥalq al-Liḥya Makrūh wa-Laysa bi-Ḥarām* (p. 26-27)

فـ.إنَّ اللحية من العادات، واختلاف عادات المجتمعات فيها يؤثر على الحكم بحيث يكون قصها أو حلقها خارماً للمروءة أو تشبهاً بغير المسلمين أو تشبهاً بالنساء، فلعلَّ من حرم إلى الفقهاء استند إلى عرفهم في ذلك.

قال عبد العزيز الغماري[1]: «ومن قال من الفقهاء بوجوب اللحية وتحريم حلقها، إنَّما حكم بذلك كما قلنا لأجل العادة، التي تربّى فيها، ونشأ عليها، وألفها في حياته الاجتماعية، كما كان الحال عندنا في المغرب قبل انتشار حلق اللحية، كنا نرى حلقها السوءة الكبرى، والموبقة العظمى؛ لكون ذلك مخالفاً لحالة مجتمعنا الملتحي، والدليل على هذا أنَّ الفقهاء لم يقولوا بتحريم كل ما ورد النهي عنه لأجل التشبه».

وطالما أنَّ العرف العام بين المسلمين لم يعد على إطلاق اللحية، فينبغي للحكم أن يختلف معه على حسب اختلاف العرف، والله أعلم.

هـ.إنَّ الكتب التي ذكرت هذا سواء «النوازل» أو «البزازية» فإنَّها من كتب الفتاوى، ومعلوم أنَّه لا يؤخذ بكلِّ ما فيها ما لم نجد لها أصلاً فقهياً نبني الحكم عليه، قال ابن عابدين: «ولهذا صرَّح علماؤنا بأنَّه لا يُفتى بما في كتب الفتاوى إذا خالف ما في المتون والشروح.

---

[1] ينظر: إفادة ذوي الأفهام ص26-27.

Imam Qāḍī al-Quḍāt Shams al-Dīn al-Ḥarīrī, one of the commentators of *al-Hidāya*, mentions in his book *Īḍāḥ al-Istidlāl ʿalā Ibṭāl al-Istibdāl*, narrating from al-Imam Ṣadr al-Dīn Sulaymān that, 'These legal verdicts are the preferences of the scholars, and thus, do not contradict the manuals of the school.' He further said, 'And similarly this was the opinion of others in our school, and this is what I am upon too.'[1] Al-Laknawī states, 'The Mufti should strive to refer to the relied upon books, and should not rely upon just any book, especially the books of legal verdicts, which are like the desert when one does not know the rank and status of the author.'[2]

All in all, we have not found an acceptable legal foundation that allows us to build upon it the ruling of the impermissibility of shaving the beard, neither from the perspective of the 'derivation principles', 'imitating non-Muslims', 'social integrity' or 'imitating females'. However, if these meanings were present, then shaving the beard would be legally prohibited; but if they are not present then there is, in reality, no basis for this ruling; and Allah ﷻ knows best.

G. These rulings have been cited from books like *al-Mujtabā* and *al-Durr al-Mukhtār* by al-Ḥaṣkafī, whose rulings are essentially unverified and unrevised. Al-Laknawī states, 'I have examined *al-Qunya* and *al-Mujtabā* and found them both to include some strange rulings, but they sufficiently discuss various benefits in detail. However, Ibn Wahbān and others have declared that, "He is *Muʿtazilī* in belief, Ḥanafī in law, and his books are not reliable as long as they are not congruent with others, as it contains both the brilliant and the not so brilliant."'[3]

---

[1] *Tanbīh al-Wulāt* (1:366)
[2] *Al-Nāfiʿ al-Kabīr* (p. 26)
[3] *Al-Fawāʾid al-Bahiyya* (p. 349)

3.5 حلق اللحية وقصُّها في كتب الحنفية

وقد ذكر الإمام قاضي القضاة شمس الدّين الحريريّ أحد شرّاح «الهداية» في كتابه «إيضاح الاستدلال على إبطال الاستبدال» نقلاً عن الإمام صدر الدين سليمان: أنَّ هذه الفتاوى اختيارات المشايخ، فلا تُعارض كتب المذهب، قال: وكذا كان يقول غيره من مشايخنا، وبه أقول أيضاً»[1]. وقال اللكنويّ: 'ينبغي للمفتي أن يجتهد في الرجوع إلى الكتب المعتمدة، ولا يعتمد على كلِّ كتاب، لا سيما الفتاوى التي هي كالصحاري ما لم يعلم حال مؤلفه وجلالة قدره»[2].

ولم نجد أصلاً فقهياً معتبراً نبني عليه حرمة قطع الرَّجل للحيته لا من جهة أصول الاستنباط أو التشبه بغير المسلمين أو المروءة أو التشبه بالنساء، إلا إذا كانت هذه المعاني متحققة حينئذ، فيمنع شرعاً، وإن لم تكن متحقِّقة فلا وجه لهذا الحكم، والله أعلم.

و.إنَّ هذا المسألة نقلت في الكتب غير المحققة والمنقحة مسائلها مثل: «المجتبى» و«الدر المختار» للحصكفي، قال اللكنوي: 'طالعت 'القنية' و'المجتبى' فوجدتهما على المسائل الغريبة حاويين، ولتفصيل الفوائد كافيين، إلا أنَّه صرَّح ابن وهبان وغيره: أنَّه معتزلي الاعتقاد، حنفي الفروع، وتصانيفه غير معتبرة ما لم يوجد مطابقتها لغيرها؛ لكونها جامعة للرطب واليابس»[3].

<hr>

[1] ينظر: تنبيه الولاة 1: 366.

[2] ينظر: النافع الكبير ص26.

[3] ينظر: الفوائد البهية ص349.

Ibn ʿĀbidīn states that, 'Because of the extreme brevity and succinctness in *al-Durr al-Mukhtār*, *al-Ashbāh wal-Naẓāʾir*, and other such similar books, they could be considered riddles. In addition to this, various citations are dropped in numerous places, and that which is contradictory is chosen over the preferred opinion. Moreover, sometimes opinions from another school are preferred in matters where no-one from the school has commented upon them.'[1]

Despite the caveat that Ibn ʿĀbidīn has provided upon the status of *al-Durr al-Mukhtār*, we find that in the issue at hand (the beard), he has not verified the matter, and has relied upon the apparent text, without revising or reviewing it in the books of the Ḥanafī school, which he would normally do. His ruling is based upon its apparent meaning, and the apparent meaning of the statement of Ibn al-Humām. He also states that the statement of al-ʿImādī is unverified and encourages the reader to ponder.

However, this is deserving of a substantial amount of attention and contemplation, as we have come to know after pondering and verifying many rulings in tens of pages that the statement of al-ʿImādī is verified and is actually in agreement with: firstly, the very foundations found within the school, and secondly, the statements of some of the major jurists of the school. What Ibn ʿĀbidīn has mentioned precedes his thought relating to the matter, and he fails to verify the issue; and that is all.

As for the statement of ʿAbd al-ʿAlī al-Laknawī that declares it is necessary to keep a beard, perhaps he has used the 'command' [*amr*] transmitted in various traditions as a basis. Although he is following the way of the Hadith jurists [*muḥaddithī al-fuqahāʾ*] in this, this way is not acceptable when attempting to distinguish between varying opinions. We have also previously mentioned in the first section how the 'command' does not necessarily imply necessity in the issue of the beard; and Allahﷻ knows best.

---

[1] *Sharḥ ʿUqūd Rasm al-Muftī* (1:13)

وقال ابن عابدين: "الدر المختار"، و'الأشباه والنظائر' ونحوها فإنَّها لشدة الاختصار والإيجاز كادت تلحق بالألغاز مع ما اشتملت عليه من السقط في النقل في مواضع كثيرة وترجيح ما هو خلاف الرَّاجح، بل ترجيح ما هو مذهب الغير مما لم يقل به أحد من أهل المذهب"[1].

ورغم تنبيه ابن عابدين على حال «الدر المختار»، إلا أنَّه في مسألتنا هذه لم يحررها واعتمد على ظاهر عبارته بدون مراجعة وتنقيح للمسألة من كتب الحنفية كما هي عادته، فكان حكمه مبنياً على ظاهرها مع ظاهر عبارة ابن الهمام فحسب، وجعل كلام ابن العمادي غير محرر، وأمر القارئ بالتدبر.

وهذا محلُّ نظر كبير؛ لأننا بعد التَّدبر والاستفاضة في تحرير المسألة في عشرات الصفحات، وجدنا أنّ كلامَ العماديّ محرَّرٌ ومتوافقٌ مع أُصول المذهب وعبارات أكابر فقهائه، وما ذكره ابنُ عابدين سبق فكر منه؛ لأنّه لم يُحرِّر المسألة فحسب.

وأمّا كلام عبد العلي اللكنوي بالوجوب فلعله اعتمد فيه على الأمر الوارد في الأحاديث، وهو في ذلك يسلك مسلك محدثي الفقهاء، وهذا المسلك ليس بمعتبر في الترجيح بين الأقول، وسبق في المبحث الأول بيان عدم دلالة الأمر على ذلك في مسألة اللحية، والله أعلم.

---

[1] ينظر: شرح عقود رسم المفتي 1: 13.

Through the previous discussion, it becomes evident to us that the clear explicit statements of the Ḥanafīs in most of the books, with regards to the beard, imply that it is a sunna. They also indicate that the opinion that forbids shaving is an opinion that some of the books of legal verdicts and unreliable books have mentioned incongruously, and therefore it is unsuitable for one to rely upon them.

However, even if these statements—in the books of legal verdicts and those books considered unreliable which imply that shaving the beard is unlawful—were accepted, then we could, in application of the principle of general necessity, and in the presence of various other legal foundations that make it lawful, and multiple explicit statements which indicate that the beard is sunna, prevent ourselves from throwing Muslims into the impermissible, pushing them towards sin and reprimanding them with regards to this matter. In reality, we wish to allow people to be able to follow the Messenger of Allah ﷺ, whether that is through outward appearance or through responding to the call of Islam. Therefore, how can one accept this opinion [of necessity in the beard] when one knows that what has been discussed in the books of the Ḥanafī school is due to what resembles a fault in understanding, and thus not an opinion in the school? *Even if*, we accept that it is an opinion in the school, then it should be regarded as a weak opinion and of no consideration; and Allah ﷻ knows best.

ومن خلال النظر السابق يظهر لنا أنَّ عبارات الحنفية الصريحة الظاهر في عامة الكتب فيما يتعلق باللحية تدل على السنية، وأنَّ القول بالتحريم في حلق اللحية شذَّت به بعض العبارات في كتب الفتاوى والكتب غير المعتبر، فلا ينبغي التعويل عليها.

ولو سُلِّم بها في كتب الفتاوى وغير المعتبر من تحريم حلق اللحية، فعملاً بقاعدة عموم البلوى من وجود أصول فقهية متعددة في عدم حرمة ذلك، وصريح عبارات عديدة بأنَّ اللحية سنة يمتنع إيقاع المسلمين في الحرمة والتأثيم والإنكار عليهم في هذه المسألة، وإنَّما يسعى فيها للترغيب لتحقيق هدي النبي ﷺ سواء بالمظهر أو طريق الدعوى للإسلام، كيف وقد عرف أنَّ ما حصل في كتب الحنفية أشبه بخطأ في الفهم، وليس قولاً في المذهب، ولو سُلِّم بأنَّه قول في المذهب، فيكون قولاً ضعيفاً لا عبرة به، والله أعلم.

From what has preceded, it is evident that the issue of the beard has numerous legal foundations upon from which the ruling can potentially be derived, and therefore the ruling would differ depending on which foundation we decide to use. This is a frequent occurrence with regards to legal rulings. Ibn Ḥajar al-ʿAsqalānī states, whilst discussing the matter of wearing red garments that, 'The verified opinion with regards to this issue is that if the prohibition present in wearing red is because it is considered to be from the clothing of non-Muslims, then therein lies a religious requirement; however, it [wearing red] should be regarded to be from one of their religious rites [in order to be prohibited]. If it is from their clothing but is no longer considered to be from their religious rites, then the meaning likewise no longer remains, thus removing the offense. If the prohibition is due it being considered to be from the clothing of females, then the matter is referred back to the prohibition in imitating females, and thus the prohibition is as a result of it (imitation) and not as a result wearing red itself. If, however, it (the prohibition) is because of vanity or detracting from one's social integrity, then it is forbidden.'[1]

In the following conclusion, we shall mention the legal ruling derived from these legal foundations.

---

[1] *Fatḥ al-Bārī* (10:306)

وممّا سبق تبين أنَّ لمسألة اللحية أصولاً متعدِّدة يمكن لنا أن نبنيها عليها، وبالتالي يختلف حكمها على حسب كل أصل منها، وهذا شائع في المسائل الفقهية، قال ابن حجر عن مسألة لبس الأحمر[1]: « والتحقيق في هذا المقام أنَّ النهي عن لبس الأحمر إن كان من أجل أنَّه لبس الكفار ـ فهو لمصلحة دينية لكن كان ذلك شعارهم حينئذٍ، وهم كفار ثمّ لمّا لم يصر الآن يختصّ بشعارهم زال ذلك المعنى فتزول الكراهة ـ، وإن كان من أجل أنَّه زي النساء فهو راجع إلى الزجر عن التشبه بالنساء فيكون النهي عنه لا لذاته، وإن كان من أجل الشهرة أو خرم المروءة فيمنع حيث يقع ذلك».

وسنذكر حكم اللحية على حسب هذه الأصول في الخاتمة.

---

[1] ينظر: فتح الباري 10: 306.

CONCLUSION

I would like to mention here the most significant results which I have arrived at in this treatise:

1. The derivation principles [*uṣūl istinbāṭ*] according to the Ḥanafīs do not imply the necessity of keeping a beard, but rather they enter it into the arena of sunna and recommendation.

2. According to the Ḥanafīs the beard is considered from the additional sunna [*sunan al-zawā'id*], and thus, based on this foundation, it would be recommended, as it is from one's customary practices and not worship.

3. Primordiality [*fiṭra*] means the sunna in the statements of most of the Ḥanafīs. Therefore, those traditions that mention the beard being from primordiality actually imply—based upon their understanding—that to keep a beard is sunna and not necessary.

4. According to the Ḥanafīs the beard is not regarded to be from blameworthy imitation, as long as: the one shaving or shortening it does not purposefully intend to imitate, it is not from the religious rites [*sha'ā'ir*] of non-Muslims, and it has become common custom in Muslim society. However, if one shaved it or shortened it out of belittlement or in mockery of the Sunna or Islam, then one fears for that person disbelief. To this person the aforementioned principle cannot be applied, and his action would be considered to be from blameworthy imitation.

5. Social integrity is the praiseworthy culture or customs in a society, and thus if shaving or shortening the beard was considered by the culture to be blameworthy, and detracting from one's social integrity, then shaving and shortening the beard is offensive. However, if shaving and shortening is widespread in society, and is no longer regarded as a deficiency, in one's social integrity, then shaving and shortening is no longer offensive.

الخاتمة

أذكر فيها أبرز النتائج التي توصلت إليها في البحث:

1.إنَّ أصول الاستنباط عند الحنفية لا يستفاد منها وجوب اللحية، وإنَّما تجعلها في دائرة السنية والاستحباب.

2.تعتبر اللحية من سنن الزوائد عند الحنفية فتأخذ حكم الاستحباب على هذا الأصل؛ لأنَّها من العادات لا العبادات.

3.الفطرة معناها السنة في عبارة عامة الحنفية، فالأحاديث التي ذكرت اللحية من الفطرة تفيد على قولهم: أنَّها سنة لا واجبة.

4.لا تعدُّ اللحية من التشبه المذموم عند الحنفية ما لم يقصد حالقها أو قاصها التشبه أو تكون شعاراً لغير المسلمين أو يكون فعل الحلق أو القص ليس عرفاً شائعاً في المجتمع المسلم، لكن إن قصها أو حلقها مستخفاً أو مستهزئاً بسنة الإسلام فيخشى عليه الكفر، وفي هذا لا تنطبع هذه الضوابط على اللحية بحيث يكون حلقها أو قصها من التشبه المذموم.

5.إنَّ المروءة هي العرف الممدوح في المجتمع، فإن كانت حلقُ اللحية أو قصُّها في عرف مجتمع مذموماً وخارماً للمروءة كان حلق اللحية أو قصُّها مكروهاً، وإن كان الحلقُ والقصُّ هو الشائع في المجتمع ولا يعتبر معيباً فلا يكون الحلق أو القص مذموماً، ولا يعتبر من خوارم المروءة.

This is the state of most Muslim societies today, where to shave or shorten the beard is not regarded to be from those things that detract from one's social integrity, and thus upon this foundation shaving the beard is not offensive. This, however, does not prevent from encouraging people to follow the sunna of the Messenger of Allah ﷺ in this.

6. The issue of imitating women is an issue that ultimately returns back to culture ['urf], which is the factor that decides whether a certain action or appearance is particular for males or females. Every act that is considered in a culture to be imitative of women is blameworthy and offensive. However, shaving the beard is not considered in Muslim societies to be from the imitation of women, and the one who shaves does not desire to imitate females. Therefore, upon this foundation, shaving is not deemed to be from imitation of females, and hence is not offensive, when looked at from this point of view.

7. General necessity ['umūm al-balwā] is considered from the constituents of necessity [ḍarūra], even though it is different from it, in that it includes anything that is widespread and prevalent in society *even if* there is no necessity therein. Thus, if we find a foundation or another legal opinion from a respected *mujtahid* (author jurist) which lifts the sin from people, then we make use of it in application of the understanding of general necessity.

In the issue of the beard we find the Shāfi'īs declare the beard to be sunna, and likewise there is a strong opinion in the Mālikī school which permits shortening it as long as it is not seen as disfigurement. The majority of the books in the Ḥanafī school indicate that the beard is also sunna. Therefore, there is no need for us to consider or hold on to some of the confusing statements in the school that make it unlawful, in application of this foundation.

وهذا هو الحال في المجتمعات المسلمة الآن أن الحلق أو التقصير ليس من خوارم المروءة، فعلى هذا الأصل تكون مكروة، وهذا لا يمنع الترغيب فيها اتباعاً لسنة النبي ﷺ.

6.إنَّ التشبه بالنِّساء مسألة عرفية، فالذي يحدد هذا التصرف والمظهر خاص بالرَّجل أو المرأة هو العرف، فكل تصرف في العرف يعدّ تشبهاً بالنساء يكون مذموماً ومكروهاً، وحلق اللحية لا يعتبر في المجتمعات المسلمة من التشبه بالنساء، ولا يظنّ من يفعل بذلك أنَّه يرغب التشبه بالنساء، وبناء على ذلك يعتبر الحلق من التشبه بالنساء، فلا يكره من هذا الوجه.

7.تعتبر عموم البلوى من أفراد الضرورة وإن كانت مختلفة عنها بحيث تشمل كلَّ ما يشيع وينتشر في المجتمع وإن لم يكن فيه ضرورة، فإن وجدنا أصلاً أو قولاً لمجتهدٍ معتبر في رفع الإثم عن النَّاس فعلنا تحقيقاً لمفهوم عموم البلوى، وفي مسألةِ اللحية وجدنا الشَّافعية قالوا: بسُنيّة اللَّحية، وفي قول قويٌّ عند المالكية بجواز التَّقصير مالم يكن مثلةً، وعامّة كتب الحنفيّة تدلُّ على سنيّة اللحيّة، فلا حاجة لنا حينئذٍ للالتفات لبعض العبارات الموهمة عند الحنفيةِ للحرمةِ والتَّمسُّك بها عملاً بهذا الأصل.

We hope that the readers of this treatise will expand their hearts for others, and that they do not reprimand them in a legal issue that is essentially disputed and differed upon. It is not from those issues of a Muslim that needs his or her full concern. The call is to desirously follow the Messenger of Allah ﷺ in his outward appearance, in an attempt to achieve the optimal human state. We should continue to encourage all Muslims and make beloved to them the beard to fully emulate the example of the Messenger of Allah ﷺ, but not simply to avoid falling into the unlawful, as it is ultimately a disputed issue.

وما نرجوه من القارئين لهذا البحث أن يتسع صدرهم لغيرهم، فلا ينكرون عليهم في مسألة فقهية خلافية، فأمر اللحية متسع، وليست هي قضية المسلمين التي تحتاج منا أن نوجه كل اهتمامنا لها، وأنَّ الدَّعوى إلى الاقتداءِ بحضرة النَّبيّ ﷺ في هيئتِه مرغوب فيه؛ لتحقيق الكمال البشري، وليبقى تعاملنا فيما يتعلَّق باللحية على ترغيبِ المسلمين وتحبيبهم بها تأسياً بالنبي ﷺ، لا أنه من إنكار المنكر؛ لأنها مختلف فيها.

BIBLIOGRAPHY

'Abbāsī, Muḥammad al-, *al-Fatāwā al-Mahdiyya fīl-Waqāʾiʿ al-Miṣriyya*. Cairo, Egypt: al-Maṭbaʿa al-Azhariyya al-Miṣriyya, 1301 AH

'Abd al-Barr, Yūsuf b. 'Abdullah b., *Al-Istidhkār*, ed. 'Abd al-Muṭī Qalʿatjī. Dār al-Waʿī & Dār Qutayba, 1413 AH.

Abī Shayba, by 'Abdullah b. Muḥammad b., *Al-Muṣannaf fīl-Aḥādīth wal-Āthār*, ed. Kamāl al-Ḥūt. Riyadh: Maktaba al-Rushd, 1409 AH.

'Adawī, 'Alī al-Ṣaʿīdī al-, *Ḥāshiya al-ʿAdawī ʿalā Kifāya al-Ṭālib al-Rabbānī*, ed. Yūsuf al-Biqāʿī. Beirut, Lebanon: Dār al-Fikr.

Anṣārī, 'Abd al-ʿAlī Muḥammad b. Niẓām al-Dīn al-, *Fawātiḥ al-Raḥamūt bi-Sharḥ Musallam al-Thubūt*. Beirut, Lebanon: Dār al-ʿUlūm al-Ḥadīthiyya.

Anṣārī, Abū Yūsuf Yaʿqūb b. Ibrāhīm al-, *Āthār Abī Yūsuf*, ed. Abū al-Wafā. Beirut, Lebanon: Dār al-Kutub al-ʿIlmiyya, 1355 AH.

Aṣbahānī, Abū Nuʿaym Aḥmad b. 'Abdullah al-, *Ḥilya al-Awliyāʾ wa-Ṭabaqāt al-Aṣfiyāʾ*. Beirut, Lebanon: Dār al-Kutub al-ʿIlmiyya, 1403 AH.

Aṣbaḥī, Mālik b. Anas al-, *Muwaṭṭaʾ Mālik*, ed. Muḥammad Fuʾād 'Abd al-Bāqī. Beirut, Lebanon: Dār Iḥyāʾ al-Turāth al-ʿArabī.

'Asqalānī, Abū al-Faḍl Aḥmad b. 'Alī b. Ḥajar al-, *Fatḥ al-Bārī Sharḥ Ṣaḥīḥ al-Bukhārī*, eds. Muḥammad Fuʾād 'Abd al-Bāqī and Muḥibb al-Dīn al-Khaṭīb. Beirut, Lebanon: Dār al-Maʿrifa, 1379 AH.

Awzjandī, Ḥasan b. Manṣūr b. Maḥmūd al-, *Al-Fatāwā al-Khāniyya (Fatāwā Qāḍī Khān)* (published in the marginalia of *al-Fatāwā al-Hindiyya*) Egypt: al-Maṭbaʿa al-Amīriyya Būlāq, 1310 AH.

'Aynī, Abū Muḥammad Maḥmūd b. Aḥmad Badr al-Dīn al-, *Al-Bināya fī Sharḥ al-Hidāya*. Dār al-Fikr, 1980.

'Aynī, Abū Muḥammad Maḥmūd b. Aḥmad Badr al-Dīn al-, *Minḥa al-Sulūk fī Sharḥ Tuḥfa al-Mulūk*, ed. Muḥammad Fārūq al-Badrī (under the supervision of Muḥyī Hilāl al-Sarḥān) Master's Thesis, University of Baghdad, Iraq, 1421 AH.

'Aynī, Abū Muḥammad Maḥmūd b. Aḥmad Badr al-Dīn al-, *'Umda al-Qārī Sharḥ Ṣaḥīḥ al-Bukhārī*. Beirut, Lebanon: Dār Iḥyāʾ al-Turāth al-ʿArabī (photocopied from the *al-Munīriyya* print).

'Aynī, Badr al-Dīn Maḥmūd b. Aḥmad Badr al-Dīn al-, *Sharḥ Sunan Abī Dāwūd*, ed. Abū al-Mundhir Khālid b. Ibrāhīm al-Miṣrī. Riyadh, Saudi Arabia: Maktaba al-Rushd, 1420 AH/1999.

Bābartī, Akmal al-Dīn Muḥammad b. Muḥammad al-Rūmī al-, *al-'Ināya 'alā al-Hidāya* (printed in the marginalia of *Fatḥ al-Qadīr lil-'Ājiz al-Faqīr*). Beirut, Lebanon: Dār Iḥyā' al-Turāth al-'Arabī.

Balūshī, 'Abd al-Laṭīf al-, *al-Ḥilya fī I'fā' al-Liḥya*. Al-Maktaba al-Shāmila.

Mujaddidī al-Barkatī, Muḥammad 'Amīm al-Iḥsān al-, *Qawā'id al-Fiqh*. Karachi, Pakistan: 1407 AH/1986.

Bayhaqī, Abū Bakr Aḥmad b. al-Ḥasan al-, *Shu'b al-Īmān*, ed. Muḥammad Basyūnī Zaghlūl. Beirut, Lebanon: Dār al-Kutub al-'Ilmiyya, 1410 AH

Bazzār, Abū Bakr Aḥmad b. 'Amr al-, *Musnad al-Bazzār* (*al-Baḥr al-Zakhkhār*, ed. Maḥfūẓ al-Raḥmān. Beirut, Lebanon: Mu'assasa 'Ulūm al-Qur'ān & Maktaba al-'Ulūm wal-Ḥikam, 1409 AH

Bukhārī, Abū 'Abdullah Muḥammad b. Ismā'īl al-Ju'fī al-, *Ṣaḥīḥ al-Bukhārī*, ed. Muṣṭafā al-Bughā. Beirut, Lebanon: Dār Ibn Kathīr & Dār al-Yamāma, 3rd ed., 1407 AH

Bukhārī, Muḥammad Amīn b. Maḥmūd al-, (also known as, Amīr Bādshāh al-Ḥanafī), *Taysīr al-Taḥrīr*. Beirut, Lebanon: Dār al-Fikr.

Burhānfūrī, Niẓām al-Dīn al-, & Jawnfūrī, Qāḍī Muḥammad Ḥusayn al-, & Ḥusaynī, 'Alī Akbar al-, and Jawnfūrī, Ḥāmid b. Abī al-, et al, *al-Fatāwā al-Hindiyya*. Egypt: al-Maṭba'a al-Amīriyya Būlāq, 1310 AH

Dāraquṭnī, Abū al-Ḥusn 'Alī b. 'Umar al-, *Sunan al-Dāraquṭnī*, ed. al-Sayyid 'Abdullah Hāshim. Beirut, Lebanon: Dār al Ma'rifa, 1386 AH.

Ghumārī, 'Abd al-'Azīz al-, *Ifāda Dhawī Afhām anna Ḥalq al-Liḥya Makrūh wa-Laysa bi-Ḥarām*. Palestine: Āl al-Bayt, I'dād al-Markaz al-Waṭanī lil-Buḥūth wal-Dirāsāt, 2015.

Ḥaddādī [and later al-Munāwī], 'Abd al-Ra'ūf b. Tāj al-'Ārifīn b. 'Alī b. Zayn al-'Ābidīn al-, *Al-Taysīr bi-Sharḥ al-Jāmi' al-Ṣaghīr*. Riyadh, Saudi Arabia: Maktaba Imām al-Shāfi'ī, 3rd ed., 1408 AH/1988.

Ḥākim, Muḥammad b. 'Abdullah al-, *al-Mustadrak 'alā al-Ṣaḥīḥayn*, ed. Muṣṭafā 'Abd al-Qādir. Beirut, Lebanon: Dār al-Kutub al-'Ilmiyya.

Ḥalabī, Ibrāhīm b. Muḥammad b. Ibrāhīm al-, *Multaqā al-Abḥur*. Maṭbaʿa ʿAlī Bek, 1291 AH, and ed. Wahbī Sulaymān Ghāwjī al-Albānī. Beirut, Lebanon: Muʾassasa al-Risāla, 1409 AH.

Haleem, M.A.S. Abdel, The Qurʾān a new translation. Oxford: OUP, 2004

Ḥamīd, ʿAbd al-Karīm al-, *Ishʿār al-Ḥarīṣ ʿalā ʿAdam Jawāz al-Taqṣīṣ min al-Liḥya li-Mūkhālafatihi al-Tanṣīṣ*. Riyadh: 1420 AH

Ḥamīd, Muḥammad al-, *Ḥukm al-Liḥya fīl-Islām*. Jordan, Zarqa: Maktaba al-Manār, 3rd ed., 1403 AH) [included in the tracts of Shaykh Muḥammad al-Ḥamīd]

Ḥamīd, Muḥyī al-Dīn ʿAbd al-, *Ārāʾ al-ʿUlamāʾ fī Ḥalq wa-Taqṣīr al-Liḥya*. Beirut, Lebanon: Muʾassasa al-Kutub al-Waqfiyya, 2002.

Ḥanafī, Abū al-ʿAbbās Aḥmad b. Yūnus b. Muḥammad al-, (Ibn al-Shilbī), *Ḥāshiya al-Shilbī ʿalā Tabyīn al-Ḥaqāʾiq*. Egypt: Al-Maṭbaʿa al-Amīriyya Būlāq, 1313 AH

Ḥanafī, Muḥammad b. Farāmūz b. ʿAlī al-, (Mullā Khusrū), *Durar al-Ḥukkām Sharḥ Ghurar al-Aḥkām*. Al-Sharika al-Ṣaḥafiyya al-ʿUthmāniyya, 1310 AH

Ḥanbal, Aḥmad b., *Musnad Aḥmad b. Ḥanbal*. Egypt: Muʾassasa Qurṭuba.

Harawī, Abū al-Ḥasan ʿAlī b. Sulṭān Muḥammad al-Qārī al-, *Mirqāt al-Mafātīḥ Sharḥ Mishkāt al-Maṣābīḥ*. Al-Maktab al-Islāmī.

Ḥaṣkafī al-Ḥanafī, Muḥammad b. ʿAlī b. Muḥammad al-, *Al-Durr al-Mukhtār Sharḥ Tanwīr al-Abṣār*. Beirut, Lebanon: Dār Iḥyāʾ al-Turāth al-ʿArabī.

Ḥassūna, Muḥammad, *al-Liḥya fīl-Kitāb wal-Sunna wa-Aqwāl Salaf al-Umma*. Egypt: Dār al-Kutub wal-Sunna, 2007.

Haythamī, ʿAlī b. Abī Bakr al-, *Majmaʿ al-Zawāʾid wa-Manbaʿ al-Fawāʾid*. Dār al-Rayyān lil-Turāth, 1407 AH, & Beirut: Dār al-Kuttāb al-ʿArabī.

Ḥibbān, Muḥammad b., *Ṣaḥīḥ Ibn Ḥibbān bi-Tartīb Ibn Bulbān*, ed. Shuʿayb al-Arnāʾūṭ. Beirut, Lebanon: Muʾassasa al-Risāla, 2nd ed., 1414 AH.

al-Ḥusaynī, ʿAlāʾ al-Dīn Muḥammad b. Muḥammad Amīn (Ibn ʿĀbidīn) b. ʿUmar b. ʿAbd al-ʿAzīz ʿĀbidīn al-, *Qurra ʿAyn al-Akhyār li-Takmila Radd al-Muḥtār ʿalā al-Durr al-Mukhtār Sharḥ Tanwīr al-Abṣār*. Beirut, Lebanon: Dār al-Fikr.

Ḥusaynī, 'Alā' al-Dīn Muḥammad b. Muḥammad Amīn (Ibn 'Ābidīn) b. 'Umar b. 'Abd al-'Azīz 'Ābidīn al-, *al-Hadiyya al-'Alā'iyya*, ed. Muḥammad Sa'īd al-Burhānī, 5th ed., 1416 AH.

Ḥaṣkafī, Muḥammad 'Alā' al-Dīn al-Ḥiṣnī al-, *Ifāḍa al-Anwār 'alā Matn Uṣūl al-Manār*. Egypt: al-Maṭba'a Muṣṭafā al-Bābī al-Ḥalabī, 2nd ed., 1399 AH.

Ibn 'Ābidīn al-Ḥanafī, Muḥammad Amīn b. 'Umar, *Al-'Uqūd al-Duriyya fī Tanqīḥ al-Fatāwā al-Ḥāmidiyya*. Egypt: Al-Maṭba'a al-Amīriyya Būlāq, 1300 AH.

Ibn 'Ābidīn al-Ḥanafī, Muḥammad Amīn b. 'Umar, *Minḥa al-Khāliq 'alā al-Baḥr al-Rā'iq*. Dār al-Ma'rifa, 2nd ed.

Ibn 'Ābidīn al-Ḥanafī, Muḥammad Amīn b. 'Umar, *Nashr al-'Urf fī Binā Ba'ḍ al-Aḥkām 'alā al-'Urf*, ed. Ṣalāḥ Abū al-Ḥājj (commentary and notes upon an old copy published by Dār al-Fikr).

Ibn 'Ābidīn al-Ḥanafī, Muḥammad Amīn b. 'Umar, *Radd al-Muḥtār 'alā al-Durr al-Mukhtār*. Beirut, Lebanon: Dār Iḥyā' al-Turāth al-'Arabī.

Ibn 'Ābidīn al-Ḥanafī, Muḥammad Amīn b. 'Umar, *Sharḥ 'Uqūd Rasm al-Muftī*, Beirut, Lebanon: Dār Iḥyā' al-Turāth al-'Arabī.

Ibn 'Ābidīn al-Ḥanafī, Muḥammad Amīn b. 'Umar, *Tanbīḥ al-Wulāt wal-Ḥukkām 'alā Aḥkām Shātim Khayr al-Anām aw-Aḥad Aṣḥābihi al-Kirām*, ed. Ṣalāḥ Abū al-Ḥājj. Amman, Jordan: Markaz Anwār al-'Ulamā' al-Duwalī lil-Dirāsāt.

Ibn Dāwūd, Sulaymān, *Musnad Abī Dāwūd al-Ṭayālisī*. Beirut, Lebanon: Dār al-Ma'rifa.

Ibn Māza al-Bukhārī al-Ḥanafī, Abū al-Ma'ālī Burhān al-Dīn Maḥmūd b. Aḥmad b. 'Abd al-'Azīz b. 'Umar, *al-Muḥīṭ al-Burhānī fil-Fiqh al-Nu'mānī fiqh al-Imām Abī Ḥanīfa*, ed. 'Abd al-Karīm Sāmī al-Jundī. Beirut, Lebanon: Dār al-Kutub al-'Ilmiyya, 1424 AH/2004.

Jārūd, 'Abdullah b. 'Alī b. al-, *Al-Multaqā min al-Sunan al-Musnada*. Beirut, Lebanon: Mu'assasa al-Kitāb al-Thaqāfiyya, 1408 AH.

Jaṣṣāṣ, Abū Bakr al-, *Sharḥ Mukhtaṣar al-Ṭaḥāwī*, ed. Sā'id Bakdāsh, et al. Beirut, Lebanon: Dār al-Bashā'ir, 2010.

Jurjānī, Al-Sayyid al-Sharīf 'Alī b. Muḥammad b. 'Alī al-Zayn al-Ḥusaynī al-, *Al-Ta'rīfāt*. Egypt: al-Maṭba'a Muṣṭafā al-Bābī al-Ḥalabī, 1938

Juwaynī, Abū al-Maʿālī Rukn al-Dīn al-, (Imam al-Ḥaramayn), *Nihāya al-Maṭlab fī Dirāya al-Madhhab*, ed. ʿAbd al-ʿAẓīm Maḥmūd al-Dīb. Dār al-Minhāj.

Kalābādhī al-Bukhārī, Abū Bakr Muḥammad b. Abū Isḥāq Ibrāhīm b. Baḥr Yaʿqūb al-, *al-Fawāʾid al-Mashhūr bi-Maʿānī al-Akhbār*, eds. Muḥammad Ḥasan Ismāʿīl & Aḥmad Farīd al-Mazīdī. Beirut, Lebanon: Dār al-Kutub al-ʿIlmiyya, 1420 AH/1999.

Ibn al-Humām, Kamāl al-Dīn Muḥammad b. ʿAbd al-Wāḥid, *Fatḥ al-Qadīr*. Beirut, Lebanon: Dār Iḥyāʾ al-Turāth al-ʿArabī & Dār al-Fikr.

Kāsānī, Abū Bakr b. Masʿūd al-, *Badāʾiʿ al-Ṣanāʾiʿ fī Tartīb al-Sharāʾiʿ*. Beirut, Lebanon: Dār al-Kutub al-ʿArabī, 2ⁿᵈ ed., 1402 AH & Dār al-Kutub al-ʿIlmiyya.

Khādimī, Abū Saʿīd al-, *Barīqa Maḥmūdiyya fī Sharḥ Ṭarīqa Muḥammadiyya*. Dār Iḥyāʾ al-Kutub al-ʿArabiyya.

Kāndahlawī, Muḥammad Zakariyyā al-, *Wujūb Iʿfāʾ al-Liḥya*, ed. Ibn Bāz.

Khuzayma al-Sulamī, Muḥammad b. Isḥāq b., *Ṣaḥīḥ Ibn Khuzayma*, ed. Muḥammad Muṣṭafā al-Aʿẓamī. Beirut, Lebanon: al-Maktab al-Islāmī, 1390 AH.

Ibn Malak, ʿAbd al-Laṭīf b. ʿAbd al-ʿAzīz al-Kirmānī, *Sharḥ al-Manār*. Al-Maṭbaʿa al-ʿUthmāniyya fī Dār al-Khilāfa, 1316 AH.

Laknawī, ʿAbd al-ʿAlī Muḥammad al-, *Rasāʾil al-Arkān*. Lucknow, India: al-Maṭbaʿ al-ʿAlawī, 1309 AH.

Laknawī, ʿAbd al-Ḥayy al-, *al-Fawāʾid al-Bahiyya fī Tarājim al-Ḥanafiyya*, ed. Aḥmad al-Zuʿbī. Beirut, Lebanon: Dār al-Arqam, 1998.

Laknawī, ʿAbd al-Ḥayy al-, *Muqaddima ʿUmda al-Riʿāya Ḥāshiya Sharḥ al-Wiqāya*. Delhi, India: al-Maṭbaʿ al-Mujtbāʾī, 1340 AH.

Laknawī, ʿAbd al-Ḥayy al-, *Tarwīḥ al-Jinān bi-Ḥukm Shurb al-Dukhān*. Lucknow: al-Maṭbaʿ al-Muṣṭafāʾī, 1300 AH.

Laknawī, ʿAbd al-Ḥayy al-, *ʿUmda al-Riʿāya Ḥāshiya Sharḥ al-Wiqāya*, ed. Ṣalāḥ Abū al-Ḥājj. Beirut, Lebanon: Dār al-Kutub al-ʿIlmiyya, 2009.

Laknawī, ʿAbd al-Ḥayy, *al-Nāfiʿ al-Kabīr li-man Yuṭāliʿ al-Jāmiʿ al-Ṣaghīr*. ʿĀlam al-Kutub, 1406 AH.

Laknawī, 'Abd al-Ḥayy, *Naf' al-Muftī wal-Sā'il bi-Jam' Mutafarriqāt al-Masā'il*, ed. Ṣalāḥ Abū al-Ḥājj. Beirut, Lebanon: Dār Ibn Ḥazm, 2001 AH.

Maḥbūbī Ṣadr al-Sharī'a, 'Ubaydullah b. Mas'ūd al-, *Al-Tawḍīḥ Sharḥ al-Tanqīḥ*. Dār al-Kutub al-'Arabiyya al-Kubrā, 1327 AH.

Maḥrūs, Muḥammad, *Al-Īḍāḥ wal-Bayān al-Ẓuhūrī* (a commentary upon, al-Tashīl al-Ḍarūrī li-Masā'il al-Qudūrī by Muḥammad 'Āshiq Ilāhī al-Burnī). Al-Maktaba al-Shāmila, 1420 AH.

Marghīnānī, Abū al-Ḥasan 'Alī b. Abī Bakr al-, *al-Hidāya Sharḥ Bidāya al-Mubtadī*. Egypt: al-Maṭba'a Muṣṭafā al-Bābī al-Ḥalabī, Final ed.

Marzubān, Muḥammad b. Khalaf b. al-, *al-Murū'a*, ed. Muḥammad Khayr. Beirut, Lebanon: Dār Ibn Ḥazm, 1420 AH.

Mawṣilī al-Ḥanafī, 'Abdullah b. Maḥmūd al-, *al-Mukhtār*, ed. Zuhayr 'Uthmān. Dār al-Arqam.

Mawṣilī, 'Abdullah b. Maḥmūd al-, *Al-Ikhtiyār li-Ta'līl al-Mukhtār*, ed. Zuhayr 'Uthmān. Dār al-Arqam.

Mullā Jiyūn, Aḥmad b. Abī Sa'īd al-Ṣiddīqī al-Mīhawī, also known as, *Nūr al-Anwār Sharḥ al-Manār*. Egypt: Al-Maṭba'a al-Amīriyya Būlāq, 1316 AH.

Ibn Manẓūr, Abū Faḍl Muḥammad b. Mukrim al-Ifrīqī al-Miṣrī, *Lisān al-'Arab*, eds. 'Abdullah al-Kabīr, Muḥammad Ḥasbullah, Hāshim al-Shādhilī. Beirut, Lebanon: Dār al-Ma'ārif.

Ibn Nujaym, Zayn al-Dīn b. Ibrāhīm b. Muḥammad al-Miṣrī, *Al-Baḥr al-Rā'iq Sharḥ Kanz al-Daqā'iq*. Beirut, Lebanon: Dār al-Ma'rifa.

Ibn Nujaym, Zayn al-Dīn b. Ibrāhīm b. Muḥammad al-Miṣrī, *Fatḥ al-Ghaffār bi-Sharḥ al-Manār*. Egypt: al-Maṭba'a Muṣṭafā al-Bābī al-Ḥalabī, 1355 AH.

Ibn al-Mulaqqin al-Shāfi'ī, 'Umar b. 'Alī, *Al-I'lām bi-Fawā'id 'Umda al-Aḥkām*, ed. 'Abd al-'Azīz al-Mashīqah. Saudi Arabia: Dār al-'Āṣima, 1417 AH.

Munāwī, 'Abd al-Ra'ūf al-, *Fayḍ al-Qadīr Sharḥ al-Jāmi' al-Ṣaghīr*. Egypt: al-Maktaba al-Tijāriyya al-Kubrā, 1356 AH.

Muqaddam, Muḥammad al-, *Adilla Taḥrīm Ḥalq al-Liḥya*. 4th ed., 1985.

Muṭarrizī, Nāṣir b. 'Abd al-Sayyid al-, *al-Mughrib fī Tartīb al-Mu'rab*. Dār al-Kuttāb al-'Arabī.

Nasafī, Abū al-Barakāt ʿAbdullāh b. Aḥmad Ḥāfiẓ al-Dīn al-, *Kanz al-Daqāʾiq*, ed. Ibrāhīm al-Ḥanafī al-Azharī. Egypt: Al-Maṭbaʿa al-Ḥamīdiyya al-Miṣriyya, 1328 AH.

Nasāʾī, Aḥmad b. Shuʿayb al-, *Al-Mujtabā min al-Sunan*, ed. ʿAbd al-Fattāḥ Abū Ghudda. Aleppo, Syria: Maktab al-Maṭbūʿāt al-Islāmiyya, 2nd ed., 1406 AH.

Nasāʾī, Aḥmad b. Shuʿayb al-, *Sunan al-Nasāʾī al-Kubrā*, eds. ʿAbd al-Ghaffār al-Bandāwī & Sayyid Kusruwī Ḥasan. Beirut, Lebanon: Dār al-Kutub al-ʿIlmiyya, 1411 AH.

Naysābūrī, Muslim b. al-Ḥajjāj al-Qushayrī al-, *Ṣaḥīḥ Muslim*, ed. Muḥammad Fuʾād ʿAbd al-Bāqī. Beirut, Lebanon: Dār Iḥyāʾ al-Turāth al-ʿArabī.

Nafrāwī al-Mālikī, Aḥmad b. Ghunaym al-, *al-Fawākih al-Dawānī ʿalā Risāla Ibn Abī Zayd al-Qayrawānī*. Beirut, Lebanon: Dār al-Fikr.

Qasṭallānī, Abū ʿAbbās Aḥmad b. Muḥammad al-, *Irshād al-Sārī li-Sharḥ Ṣaḥīḥ al-Bukhārī*. Egypt: al-Maṭbaʿa al-Amīriyya Būlāq, 7th ed., 1323 AH.

Ibn Abī al-Dunyā, Abū Bakr ʿAbdullāh b. Muḥammad b. ʿUbayd b. Sufyān b. Qays al-Baghdādī al-Umawī al-Qurashī, *Iṣlāḥ al-Māl*, ed. Muḥammad ʿAbd al-Qādir ʿAṭā. Beirut, Lebanon: Muʾassasa Kutub al-Thaqāfiyya, 1414 AH/1993.

Qazwīnī, Muḥammad b. Yazīd b. Mājah al-, *Sunan Ibn Mājah*, ed. Muḥammad Fuʾād ʿAbd al-Bāqī. Beirut, Lebanon: Dār al-Fikr.

Quḍāʾī, Abū ʿAbdullāh Muḥammad b. Salāma al-, *Musnad al-Shihāb*, ed. Ḥamdī al-Salafī. Beirut, Lebanon: Muʾassasa al-Risāla, 2nd ed., 1407 AH.

Qudūrī, Aḥmad b. Muḥammad al-, *Mukhtaṣar al-Qudūrī*. Egypt: al-Maṭbaʿa Muṣṭafā al-Bābī al-Ḥalabī, 3rd ed., 1377 AH.

Quṭlūbghā al-Ḥanafī, Qāsim b., *Khulāṣa al-Afkār Sharḥ Mukhtaṣar al-Manār*, ed. Ṣalāḥ Abū al-Ḥajj. Amman, Jordan: Markaz Anwār al-ʿUlamāʾ al-Duwalī lil-Dirāsāt.

Rashīd, Amjad. *Qaṭʿ al-Mariyya fī Bayān Madhhab al-Shāfiʿiyya fī Ḥalq wa-Taqṣīr al-Liḥya*. Unpublished manuscript.

Rāzī, al-, *Khulāṣa al-Dalāʾil Sharḥ al-Qudūrī*, ed. Ṣalāḥ Abū al-Ḥājj. Amman, Jordan: Markaz Anwār al-ʿUlamāʾ al-Duwalī lil-Dirāsāt.

Rāzī, Muḥammad b. Abī Bakr b. ʿAbd al-Qādir al-, *Mukhtār al-Ṣiḥāḥ*, ed. Ḥamza Fatḥ-Allāh. Beirut, Lebanon: Muʾassasa al-Risāla, 1417 AH.

Rāzī, Muḥammad b. Abū Bakr al-, *Tuḥfa al-Mulūk*, ed. Ṣalāḥ Abū al-Ḥājj. Amman, Jordan: Dār al-Fārūq, 2006.

Rāzikhī, ʿAlī al-, *Al-Jāmiʿ fī Aḥkām al-Liḥya*. Yemen: Dār al-Āthār, 2005.

Riṣāʿ al-Mālikī, Muḥammad b. Qāsim al-, *Sharḥ Ḥudūd Ibn ʿArafa*. Al-Maktaba al-ʿIlmiyya.

Rūmī, ʿAbd al-Raḥmān b. Muḥammad al-, (Shaykh Zādeh), *Majmaʿ al-Anhur Sharḥ Multaqā al-Abhur*. Dār al-Ṭibāʿa al-ʿĀmira, 1316 AH.

Ṣadr al-Sharīʿa, ʿUbaydullah b. Masʿūd, *al-Niqāya* (published with *Fatḥ Bāb al-ʿInāya Sharḥ al-Niqāya*, by Mullā ʿAlī al-Qārī), eds. Muḥammad Nizār & Haytham Nizār. Dār al-Arqam, 1418 AH.

Ṣāḥib, Ismāʿīl b. ʿAbbād al-, *al-Muḥīṭ fīl-Lugha*, ed. Muḥammad Ḥasan Āl Yāsīn. Baghdad, Iraq: Maṭbaʿa al-Maʿārif, 1395 AH.

Ṣāliḥī, Muḥammad b. Yūsuf al-, *ʿAqd al-Jumān fī Manāqib al-Imām al-Aʿẓam Abī Ḥanīfa al-Nuʿmān*. Medina al-Munawwara: Maktaba al-Īmān.

Samarqandī, ʿAlāʾ al-Dīn Muḥammad b. Aḥmad al-, *Tuḥfa al-Fuqahāʾ*. Beirut, Lebanon: Dār al-Kutub al-ʿIlmiyya.

Sannāmī al-Ḥanafī, ʿUmar b. Muḥammad b. ʿIwaḍ al-, *Niṣāb al-Iḥtisāb*. Al-Maktaba al-Shāmila.

Sanʿānī, ʿAbd al-Razzāq b. Humām al-, *al-Muṣannaf*, ed. Ḥabīb al-Raḥmān al-Aʿẓamī. Beirut, Lebanon: Al-Maktab al-Islāmī, 2nd ed., 1403 AH.

Sarakhsī, Abū Bakr Muḥammad b. Abī Sahl al-, *al-Mabsūṭ*. Beirut, Lebanon: Dār al-Maʿrifa, 1406 AH.

Shurunbulālī, Ḥasan b. ʿAmmār b. ʿAlī al-, *Ghunya Dhawī al-Aḥkām fī Bughya Durar al-Ḥukkām*. Durr Saʿādāt, 1308 AH, & al-Sharika al-Ṣaḥafiyya al-ʿUthmāniyya, 1310 AH.

Sijistānī, Sulaymān b. Ashʿath al-, *Sunan Abū Dāwūd*, ed. Muḥammad Muḥyī al-Dīn ʿAbd al-Ḥamīd. Beirut, Lebanon: Dār al-Fikr.

Ṭabarānī, Abū al-Qāsim Sulaymān b. Aḥmad al-, *Al-Muʿjam al-Awsaṭ*, ed. Ṭāriq b. ʿIwaḍullah. Egypt: Dār al-Ḥaramayn, 1415 AH.

Ṭabarānī, Abū al-Qāsim Sulaymān b. Aḥmad al-, *al-Muʿjam al-Kabīr*, ed. Ḥamdī al-Salafī. Mosul, Iraq: Maktaba al-ʿUlūm wal-Ḥikam, 2nd ed., 1404 AH.

Ṭaḥāwī, Aḥmad b. Muḥammad b. Salāma al-, *Sharḥ Ma'ānī al-Āthār*, ed. Muḥammad Zuhrī al-Najjār. Beirut, Lebanon: Dār al-Kutub al-'Ilmiyya, 1399 AH.

Ṭaḥṭāwī al-Ḥanafī, Aḥmad b. Muḥammad al-, *Ḥāshiya al-Ṭaḥṭāwī 'alā Marāqī al-Falāḥ*, ed. Muḥammad 'Abd al-'Azīz al-Khālidī. Beirut, Lebanon: Dār al-Kutub al-'Ilmiyya, 1418 AH.

Tirmidhī, Muḥammad b. 'Īsā al-, *Sunan al-Tirmidhī*, ed. Aḥmad Shākir et al. Beirut, Lebanon: Dār Iḥyā' al-Turāth al-'Arabī.

Tumurtāshī al-Ghazzī, Muḥammad b. 'Abdullah al-Khaṭīb al-, *Tanwīr al-Abṣār wa-Jāmi' al-Biḥār*. Maṭba'a al-Taraqqī bi-Ḥāra al-Kaffāra, 1332 AH.

Tuwayjirī, Maḥmūd al-, *Al-Radd 'alā man Ajāza Tahdhīb al-Liḥya*. Riyadh: Maktaba al-Ma'ārif, 1985.

'Uthmānī, Muḥammad Taqī al-, *Takmila Fatḥ al-Mulhim bi-Sharḥ Ṣaḥīḥ al-Imām Muslim*. Karachi: Maktaba Dār al-'Ulūm, 1422 AH.

Wafā al-Qurashī, 'Abd al-Qādir b. Muḥammad b. Abī al-, *Al-Jawāhir al-Muḍiyya fī Ṭabaqāt al-Ḥanafiyya*, ed. 'Abd al-Fattāḥ al-Ḥilū. Beirut: Mu'assasa al-Risāla, 2nd ed., 1413 AH.

Wehr, Hans, A Dictionary of Modern Written Arabic (Arabic-English), ed. by J Milton Cowan. Wiesbaden: Harrosowitz, 1979.

Ibn al-Ḥannā'ī, 'Alī b. Amrullah Qanālī Zādeh, *Ṭabaqāt al-Ḥanafiyya*. Mosul, Iraq: Maṭba'a al-Zahrā' al-Ḥadīthiyya, 2nd ed., 1380 AH.

Zayla'ī, 'Uthmān b. 'Alī al-, *Tabyīn al-Ḥaqā'iq Sharḥ Kanz al-Daqā'iq*. Egypt, Būlāq: al-Maṭba'a al-Amīriyya, 1313 AH.

Zurqānī, Muḥammad b. 'Abd al-Bāqī al-, *Sharḥ al-Zurqānī 'alā Muwaṭṭa' Mālik*. Beirut, Lebanon: Dār al-Ma'rifa, 1398 AH.

المراجع

1. آثار أبي يوسف: لأبي يوسف يعقوب بن إبراهيم الأنصاري (ت182هـ)، ت: أبو الوفا، دار الكتب العلمية، بيروت، 1355هـ.

2. الاختيار لتعليل المختار: لعبد الله بن محمود الموصلي (ت683هـ)، ت: زهير عثمان، دار الأرقم، بدون تاريخ طبع.

3. أدلة تحريم حلق اللحية: لمحمد المقدم، ط4، 1985.

4. آراء العلماء في حلق وتقصير اللحية: لمحيي الدِّين عبد الحميد، مؤسسة الكتب الوقفية، بيروت، ط1، 2002م.

5. إرشاد الساري لشرح صحيح البخاري: لأبي العباس أحمد بن محمد القسطلاني (ت923هـ)، المطبعة الأميرية ببولاق مصر، ط7، 1323هـ، وأيضاً: طباعة أوفست دار الكتاب العربي، بيروت.

6. الاستذكار: للإمام يوسف بن عبد الله ابن عبد البر (ت463)، تحقيق: الدكتور عبد المعطي قلعه جي، دار قتيبة ودار الوعي، ط1، 1413هـ.

7. إشعار الحريص على عدم جواز التقصيص من اللحية لمخالفته التنصيص: لعبد الكريم الحميد، الرياض، ط1، 1420هـ.

8. إصلاح المال: لأبي بكر عبد الله بن محمد بن عبيد بن سفيان بن قيس البغدادي الأموي القرشي المعروف بابن أبي الدنيا (ت: 281هـ)، ت: محمد عبد القادر عطا، مؤسسة الكتب الثقافية – بيروت، ط1، 1414هـ – 1993م.

9. الاعلام بفوائد عمدة الاحكام لعمر بن علي ابن الملقن الشافعي، (ت804هـ)، ت: عبد العزيز المشيقح، دار العاصمة، السعودية، ط1، 1417هـ.

10. إفادة ذوي الأفهام أنَّ حلق اللحية مكروه وليس بحرام: لعبد العزيز الغماري، إعداد المركز الوطني للبحوث والدراسات، آل البيت، فلسطين، 2015م.

11. إفاضة الأنوار على متن أصول المنار:لمحمد علاء الدين الحصني (ت1088هـ)، مطبعة مصطفى البابي الحلبي، مصر، ط2، 1399هـ.

12. الإيضاح والبيان الظهوري: للدكتور محمد محروس على التسهيل الضروري لمسائل القدوري: لمحمد عاشق إلهي البرني، بغداد، 1420هـ.

13. البحر الرائق شرح كَنْز الدقائق: لإبراهيم ابن نجيم المصري زين الدين (ت970هـ)، دار المعرفة، بيروت، بدون تاريخ طبع.

المراجع

14. بحر الفوائد المشهور بمعاني الأخبار: لأبي بكر محمد بن أبي إسحاق إبراهيم بن يعقوب الكلاباذي البخاري، ت: محمد حسن محمد حسن إسماعيل – أحمد فريد المزيدي، دار الكتب العلمية – بيروت، ط1، 1420هـ – 1999م.

15. بدائع الصنائع في ترتيب الشرائع:لأبي بكر بن مسعود الكاساني (ت587هـ)، دار الكتاب العربي، بيروت. ط2، 1402هـ، وأيضاً: طبعة دار الكتب العلمية.

16. بريقة محمودية في شرح طريقة محمدية: لأبي سعيد الخادمي، دار إحياء الكتب العربية.

17. البناية في شرح الهداية:لأبي محمد محمود بن أحمد العَيْني بدر الدين (762–855هـ)، دار الفكر، ط1، 1980مـ.

18. تبيين الحقائق شرح كَنْز الدقائق:لعثمان بن علي الزيلعي فخر الدين (ت743هـ)، المطبعة الأميرية، مصر، ط1، 1313هـ.

19. تحفة الفقهاء: لعلاء الدين محمد بن أحمد السَّمَرْقَنْدِي (ت539هـ)، دار الكتب العلمية، بيروت، بدون تاريخ طبع.

20. تحفة الملوك:لمحمد بن أبي بكر الرازي (ت666هـ)، ت: الدكتور صلاح أبو الحاج، دار الفاروق، عمان، ط1، 2006م.

21. ترويح الجنان بحكم شرب الدخان:لعبد الحي اللكنوي (1264– 1304هـ)، المطبع المصطفائي، لكنو، 1300هـ.

22. التعريفات:للسيد الشريف علي بن محمد بن علي السيد الزين أبي الحسن الحسيني الجُرْجانيّ الحَنَفِي (740–816)، مطبعة مصطفى البابي، 1938م.

23. تكملة فتح الملهم بشرح صحيح الإمام مسلم: لمحمد تقي العثماني، مكتبة دار العلوم كراتشي، ط1، 1422هـ.

24. تنبيه الولاة و الحكام على أحكام شاتم خير الأنام أو أحد أصحابه الكرام: لابن عابدين، الإصدار: 1، مركز أنوار العلماء الدولي للدراسات، ت: الدكتور صلاح أبو الحاج.

25. العقود الدرية في تنقيح الفتاوى الحامدية:لمحمد أمين بن عمر ابن عابدين الحنفي (1198–1252هـ)، المطبعة الميرية ببولاق، مصر، 1300هـ.

26. تنوير الأبصار وجامع البحار: لمحمد بن عبد الله الخطيب التُّمُرْتاشي الغَزَّي الحَنَفي (ت1004هـ)، مطبعة الترقي بحارة الكفارة، 1332هـ.

27. التوضيح شرح التنقيح: لعبيد الله بن مسعود المحبوبي صدر الشريعة (ت747هـ)، دار الكتب العربية الكبرى، 1327هـ، وأيضاً: المطبعة الخيرية، مصر، ط1، 1324هـ.

28. تيسير التحرير: لمحمد أمين بن محمود البخاري المعروف بأمير بادشاه الحنفي (ت: 972هـ)، دار الفكر – بيروت.

المراجع

29. التيسير بشرح الجامع الصغير: لعبد الرؤوف بن تاج العارفين بن علي بن زين العابدين الحدادي ثم المناوي القاهري (ت: 1031هـ)، مكتبة الإمام الشافعي – الرياض، ط3، 1408هـ – 1988م.

30. الجامع في أحكام اللحية: لعلي الرازخي، دار الآثار، اليمن، ط1، 2005م.

31. الجواهر المضية في طبقات الحنفية: لعبد القادر بن محمد بن أبي الوفاء القرشي (ت775هـ)، ت: عبد الفتاح الحلو، مؤسسة الرسالة، بيروت، ط2، 1413هـ.

32. حاشية الشلبي على تبيين الحقائق: لأبي العباس أحمد بن يونس بن محمد الحنفي المعروف بـ(ابن الشلبي)(ت 947هـ)، مطبوعة بهامش تبيين الحقائق،المطبعة الأميرية بمصر، ط1، 1313هـ.

33. حاشية الطَّحْطَاوي على مراقي الفلاح:لأحمد بن محمد الطَّحْطَاوِيّ الحنفي (ت1231هـ)، ت: محمد عبد العزيز الخالدي، دار الكتب العلمية، ط1، 1418هـ.

34. حاشية العدوي على كفاية الطالب الرباني: لعلي الصعيدى العدوي، تحقيق: يوسف البقاعي، دار الفكر، بيروت.

35. حلية الأولياء وطبقات الأصفياء: لأبي نُعَيْم أحمد بن عبد الله الأصبهاني (ت430هـ)، دار الكتب العلمية، بيروت، ط1، 1403هـ، وأيضاً: طبعة دار الكتاب العربي، بيروت، ط4، 1405هـ.

36. الحلية في إعفاء اللحية لعبد اللطيف البلوشي، المكتبة الشاملة.

37. خلاصة الأفكار شرح مختصر المنار: لقاسم بن قطلوبغا الحنفي (ت879هـ)، ت: الدكتور صلاح محمد أبو الحاج، مركز أنوار العلماء العالمي للدراسات، الإصدار الأول.

38. خلاصة الدلائل شرح القدوري للرازي، ت: د.صلاح أبو الحاج، مركز أنوار العلماء للدراسات، الإصدار1.

39. الدر المختار شرح تنوير الأبصار: لمحمد بن علي بن محمد الحصكفي الحنفي (ت1088هـ)، مطبوع في حاشية رَدّ المُحْتَار، دار إحياء التراث العربي، بيروت.

40. درر الحكام شرح غرر الأحكام: لمحمد بن فرامُوز بن علي الحنفي المعروف بـ(مُلا خسرو)(ت885هـ)، الشركة الصحفية العثمانية، 1310هـ، وأيضاً: طبعة در سعادت، 1308هـ.

41. ردّ المحتار على الدر المختار: لمحمد أمين بن عمر ابن عابدين الحنفي (1198-1252هـ)، دار إحياء التراث العربي، بيروت.

42. الرد على من أجاز تهذيب اللحية: لحمود التويجري، مكتبة المعارف، الرياض، 1985م.

43. رسائل الأركان: لعبد العلي محمد اللكنوي بحر العلوم (ت1225هـ)، المطبع العلوي، لكنو، 1309هـ.

المراجع

44. سنن ابن ماجه: لمحمد بن يزيد بن ماجه القزويني (207-273هـ)، ت: محمد فؤاد عبد الباقي، دار الفكر، بيروت.

45. سنن أبي داود: لسليمان بن أشعث السجستاني (202-275هـ)، ت: محمد محيي الدين عبد الحميد، دار الفكر، بيروت.

46. سنن الترمذي: لمحمد بن عيسى الترمذي (209-279هـ)، ت: أحمد شاكر وآخرون، دار إحياء التراث العربي، بيروت.

47. سنن الدَّارَقُطْنِي: لأبي الحسن علي بن عمر الدَّارَقُطْنِي (306-385هـ)، ت: السيد عبد الله هاشم، دار المعرفة، بيروت، 1386هـ.

48. سنن النَّسَائيّ الكبرى: لأحمد بن شعيب النَّسَائِي (ت303هـ)، ت: الدكتور عبد الغفار البنداوي وسيد كسروي حسن، دار الكتب العلمية، بيروت، ط1، 1411هـ.

49. شرح الزرقاني على موطأ مالك: لمحمد بن عبد الباقي الزرقاني (1055-1122هـ)، دار المعرفة، بيروت، 1398هـ.

50. شرح المنار: لعبد اللطيف بن عبد العزيز الكرماني ابن ملك (ت801هـ)، المطبعة العثمانية في دار الخلافة، 1316هـ.

51. شرح حدود ابن عرفة: لمحمد بن قاسم الرصاع المالكي (ت894هـ)، المكتبة العلمية.

52. شرح سنن أبي داود: لبدر الدين محمود بن أحمد العيني، ت: أبو المنذر خالد بن إبراهيم المصري، مكتبة الرشد – الرياض، ط1،1420 هـ – 1999م.

53. شرح عقود رسم المفتي: لمحمد أمين بن عمر ابن عابدين الحنفي (1198-1252هـ)، دار إحياء التراث العربي، بيروت، ضمن مجموع رسائله.

54. شرح مختصر الطحاوي لأبي بكر الجصاص (ت370هـ)، ت: د. سائد بكداش وآخرون، طبعة دار البشائر، ط1، 2010هـ.

55. شرح معاني الآثار: لأحمد بن محمد بن سلامة الطَّحَاوي (229-321هـ)، ت: محمد زهري النجار، دار الكتب العلمية، بيروت، ط1، 1399هـ.

56. شعب الإيمان:لأبي بكر أحمد بن الحسن البيهقي (384-458هـ)، ت: محمد بسيوني زغلول، دار الكتب العلمية، بيروت، ط1، 1410هـ.

57. صحيح ابن حبَّان بترتيب ابن بلبان:لمحمد بن حِبَّان التميمي (354هـ)، ت: شعيب الأرناؤوط، مؤسسة الرسالة، بيروت، ط2، 1414هـ.

58. صحيح ابن خزيمة:لمحمد بن إسحاق بن خزيمة السلمي (ت311هـ)، ت: الدكتور محمد مصطفى الأعظمي، المكتب الإسلامي، بيروت، 1390هـ.

المراجع

59. صحيح البخاري:لأبي عبد الله محمد بن إسماعيل الجعفي البُخَارِيّ (194−256هـ)، ت: الدكتور مصطفى البغا، دار ابن كثير واليمامة، بيروت، ط3، 1407هـ.

60. صحيح مسلم:لمسلم بن الحجاج القُشَيْرِيّ النَّيْسَابوريّ (ت261هـ)، ت: محمد فؤاد عبد الباقي، دار إحياء التراث العربي، بيروت.

61. طبقات الحنفية: لعلي بن أمر الله قنالي زاده المشهور بـ(ابن الحنائي)(ت979هـ)، مطبعة الزهراء الحديثة، الموصل، ط2، 1380هـ.

62. عقد الجمان في مناقب الإمام الأعظم أبي حنيفة النعمان: لمحمد بن يوسف الصالحي (ت942هـ)، مكتبة الإيمان، المدينة المنورة.

63. العقود الدرية في تنقيح الفتاوى الحامدية: لمحمد أمين بن عمر ابن عابدين الحنفي (1198−1252هـ)، المطبعة الميرية ببولاق، مصر، 1300هـ.

64. عمدة الرعاية حاشية شرح الوقاية: لعبد الحي اللكنوي (1264−1304هـ)، ت: د. صلاح أبو الحاج، دار الكتب العلمية، لبنان، ط1، 2009م.

65. عمدة القاري شرح صحيح البخاري: لأبي محمد محمود بن أحمد العَيْني بدر الدين (762−855هـ)، مصورة عن الطبعة المنيرية، دار إحياء التراث العربي، بيروت.

66. العناية على الهداية: لأكمل الدين محمد بن محمد الرومي البَابَرْتي (ت786هـ)، بهامش فتح القدير للعاجز الفقير، دار إحياء التراث العربي، بيروت.

67. غنية ذوي الأحكام في بغية درر الحكام (الشرنبلالية): لحسن بن عمار بن علي الشرنبلالي (ت1069هـ)، در سعادت، 1308هـ، وأيضاً: طبعة الشركة الصحفية العثمانية، 1310هـ.

68. الفتاوى الخانية (فتاوى قاضي خان): لحَسَن بن مَنْصُور بن مَحْمُود الأُوزْجَنْدِيّ (ت592هـ)، مطبوعة بهامش الفتاوي الهندية، المطبعة الأميرية ببولاق، مصر، 1310هـ.

69. الفتاوى المهدية في الوقائع المصرية: لمحمد العباسي، المطبعة الأزهرية المصرية، ط1، 1301هـ.

70. الفتاوي الهندية: للشيخ نظام الدين البرهانفوري، والقاضي محمد حسين الجونفوري، والشيخ علي أكبر الحسيني، والشيخ حامد بن أبي الحامد الجونفوري، وغيرهم، المطبعة الأميرية ببولاق، 1310هـ.

71. فتح الباري شرح صحيح البُخَاري: لأبي الفضل أحمد بن علي ابن حَجَر العَسْقَلاِني (773–852هـ)، تحقيق: محمد فؤاد عبد الباقي، ومحب الدين الخطيب، دار المعرفة، بيروت، 1379هـ.

72. فتح الغفار بشرح المنار: لإبراهيم ابن نجيم المصري زين الدين (ت970هـ)، مطبعة مصطفى البابي الحلبي، مصر، ط1، 1355هـ.

المراجع

73. فتح القدير: لمحمد بن عبد الواحد كمال الدين الشهير بـ(ابن الهمام)(790-861هـ)، دار إحياء التراث العربي، بيروت، وأيضاً: طبعة دار الفكر.

74. فواتح الرحموت بشرح مُسَلَّم الثُّبُوت: لعَبْد العلي مُحَمَّد بن نظام الدِّين الأَنْصَارِيِّ، دار العلوم الحديثة، بيروت.

75. الفواكه الدواني على رسالة ابن أبي زيد القيرواني: لأحمد بن غنيم النفراوي المالكي (1125هـ)، دار الفكر.

76. الفوائد البهية في تراجم الحنفية: لعبد الحي الكنوي (1264-2304هـ)، ت: أحمد الزعبي، دار الأرقم، بيروت، ط1، 1998م، وأيضاً: طبعة السعادة، مصر، ط1، 1324هـ.

77. فيض القدير شرح الجامع الصغير: لعبد الرؤوف المناوي، المكتبة التجارية الكبرى، مصر، ط1، 1356هـ.

78. قرة عين الأخيار لتكملة رد المحتار على «الدر المختار شرح تنوير الأبصار»: لعلاء الدين محمد بن (محمد أمين المعروف بابن عابدين) بن عمر بن عبد العزيز عابدين الحسيني الدمشقي (ت: 1306هـ)، دار الفكر للطباعة والنشر والتوزيع، بيروت – لبنان.

79. قواعد الفقه: لمحمد عميم الإحسان المجددي البركتي، الصدف ببلشرز – كراتشي، ط1، 1407 – 1986م.

80. كنْز الدقائق: لأبي البركات عبد الله بن أحمد النَّسَفِي حافظ الدين (ت701هـ)، اعتنى به: إبراهيم الحنفي الأزهري، طبع بالمطبعة الحميدية المصرية بالمناصرة بمصر، 1328هـ.

81. اللحية في الكتاب والسنة وأقوال سلف الأمة: لمحمد حسونة، دار الكتاب والسنة، القاهرة، ط1، 2007م.

82. لسان العرب:لأبي الفضل محمد بن مكرم الإفريقي المصري المشهور بـ(ابن منظور)(ت711هـ)، ت: عبْد الله الكبير ومحمد حسب الله وهاشم الشاذلي، دار المعارف.

83. المبسوط:لأبي بكر محمد بن أبي سهل السرخسي توفي بحدود (500هـ)، 1406هـ، دار المعرفة، بيروت.

84. المجتبى من السنن: لأبي عبد الله أحمد بن شعيب النسائي (215- 303)، ت: عبد الفتاح أبو غدة، مكتب المطبوعات الإسلامية، حلب، ط2، 1406هـ.

85. مجمع الأنهر شرح ملتقى الأبحر: لعبدِ الرَّحمنِ بنِ محمد الرُّومي المعروف بـ(شيخِ زاده)(ت 1078هـ)، دار الطباعة العامرة، 1316هـ.

86. مجمع الزوائد ومنبع الفوائد: لعلي بن أبي بكر الهيثمي (ت807هـ)، دار الريان للتراث، 1407هـ، ودار الكتاب العربي، بيروت.

المراجع

87. المحيط البرهاني في الفقه النعماني فقه الإمام أبي حنيفة: لأبي المعالي برهان الدين محمود بن أحمد بن عبد العزيز بن عمر بن مَازَةَ البخاري الحنفي (ت: 616هـ)، ت: عبد الكريم سامي الجندي، دار الكتب العلمية، بيروت – لبنان، ط1، 1424 هـ – 2004 م.

88. المحيط في اللغة: لإسماعيل بن عباد الصاحب (326–385هـ)، ت: محمد حسن آل ياسين، مطبعة المعارف، بغداد، ط1، 1395هـ.

89. مختار الصحاح:لمحمد بن أبي بكر بن عبد القادر الرازي (ت666)، ت: حمزة فتح الله، مؤسسة الرسالة، 1417هـ.

90. المختار:لعبد الله بن محمود الموصلي الحنفي (ت683هـ)، تحقيق: زهير عثمان، مطبوع مع الاختيار، دار الأرقم.

91. مختصر القدوري:لأحمد بن محمد القدوري (ت428هـ)، مطبعة مصطفى الحلبي، مصر، ط 3، 1377هـ.

92. مرقاة المفاتيح شرح مشكاة المصابيح: لأبي الحسن علي بن سلطان محمد القاري الهروي (930–114هـ)، المكتب الإسلامي.

93. المروءة لمحمد بن خلف بن المرزبان، (ت309هـ)، ت: محمد خير، دار ابن حزم، بيروت، 1420هـ.

94. المستدرك على الصحيحين: لمحمد بن عبد الله الحاكم (ت405هـ)، ت: مصطفى عبد القادر، دار الكتب العلمية، بيروت، ط1، 1411هـ.

95. مسند أبي داود الطيالسي: لسليمان بن داود (ت204هـ)، دار المعرفة، بيروت.

96. مسند أحمد بن حنبل: لأحمد بن حنبل (164-241هـ)، مؤسسة قرطبة، مصر.

97. مسند البَزَّار (البحر الزخار): لأبي بكر أحمد بن عمرو البَزَّار (215-292هـ)، ت: الدكتور محفوظ الرحمن، مؤسسة علوم القرآن، مكتبة العلوم والحكم، بيروت، ط1، 1409هـ.

98. مسند الشهاب: لأبي عبد الله محمد بن سلامة القُضَاعي (ت454هـ)، ت: حمدي السلفي، مؤسسة الرسالة، بيروت، ط2، 1407هـ.

99. المصنف في الأحاديث والآثار: لعبد الله بن محمد بن أبي شَيْبَةَ (159-235هـ)، ت: كمال الحوت، ط1، مكتبة الرشد، الرياض، 1409هـ.

100. المصنف: لعبد الرزاق بن همام الصنعاني (126-211هـ)، ت: حبيب الرحمن الأعظمي، المكتب الإسلامي، بيروت، ط2، 1403هـ.

101. المعجم الأوسط: للحافظ أبي القاسم سليمان بن أحمد الطبراني (260-360هـ)، ت: طارق بن عوض الله، دار الحرمين، القاهرة، 1415هـ.

المراجع

102. المعجم الكبير: لأبي القاسم سليمان بن أحمد الطَّبَرَاني (260–360هـ)، ت: حمدي السلفي، مكتبة العلوم والحكم، الموصل، ط2، 1404هـ.

103. المغرب في ترتيب المعرب: لناصر بن عبد السيد المُطَرِّزِيّ (616هـ)، دار الكتاب العربي.

104. مقدِّمة عمدة الرعاية حاشية شرح الوقاية: لعبد الحي اللكنوي (1264–1304هـ)، المطبع المجتبائي، دهلي، 1340هـ.

105. ملتقى الأبحر: لإبراهيم بن محمد بن إبراهيم الحَلَبي (ت956هـ)، مطبعة علي بك، 1291هـ، وأيضاً: بتحقيق: وهبي سليمان غاوجي الألباني، مؤسسة الرسالة، ط1، 1409هـ.

106. المنتقى من السنن المسندة: لعبد الله بن علي بن الجارود (ت307هـ)، مؤسسة الكتاب الثقافية، بيروت، ط1، 1408هـ.

107. منحة الخالق على البحر الرائق: لمحمد أمين بن عمر ابن عابدين الحنفي (1198–1252هـ)، ط2، دار المعرفة.

108. منحة السلوك في شرح تحفة الملوك: لأبي محمد محمود بن أحمد العَيْني بدر الدين (762–855هـ)، ت: محمد فاروق البدري، بإشراف: د. محيي هلال السرحان، رسالة ماجستير، جامعة بغداد، 1421هـ.

109. موطأ مالك: لمالك بن أنس الأصبحي (93–179هـ)، ت: محمد فؤاد عبد الباقي، دار إحياء التراث العربي، بيروت.

110. النافع الكبير لمن يطالع الجامع الصغير: للكنوي، ط1. عالم الكتب. 1406هـ. ص26.

111. نشر العرف في بناء بعض الأحكام على العرف: لمحمد أمين ابن عابدين الحنفي، مسودة مصفوفة ومصححة ومعلق عليها عن المطبوعة القديمة (دار الفكر)، اعتنى بها وعلق عليها الدكتور صلاح أبو الحاج.

112. نصاب الاحتساب: لعمر بن محمد بن عوض السَّنَامي الحنفي (المتوفى: 734هـ)، المكتبة الشاملة.

113. نفع المفتي والسائل بجمع متفرقات المسائل: لعبد الحي اللكنوي (1264–1304هـ)، تحقيق: الدكتور صلاح محمد أبو الحاج، دار ابن حزم، بيروت، 2001هـ.

114. النقاية: لعبيد الله بن مسعود صدر الشريعة (ت747هـ)، مطبوع مع فتح العناية بشرح النقاية: لعلي القاري، ت: محمد نزار وهيثم نزار، دار الأرقم، ط1، 1418هـ، وأيضاً: طبعة مطبع دهلي، 1286هـ.

115. نهاية المطلب في دراية المذهب: لعبد الملك بن محمد الجويني، أبو المعالي، ركن الدين، الملقب بإمام الحرمين (ت: 478هـ)، ت: أ. د. عبد العظيم محمود الدّيب، دار المنهاج.

116. نور الأنوار شرح المنار: لأحمد بن أبي سعيد الصديقي الميهوي الحنفي المعروف بـ(ملا جيون) (ت1130هـ)، المطبعة الأميرية ببولاق، مصر، 1316هـ.

المراجع

117. الهداية شرح بداية المبتدي: لأبي الحسن علي بن أبي بكر المرغيناني (ت593هـ)، مطبعة مصطفى البابي، الطبعة الأخيرة، بدون تاريخ طبع.

118. الهدية العلائية: لعلاء الدين ابن عابدين، ت: محمد سعيد البرهاني، ط5، 1416هـ.

119. وجوب إعفاء اللحية: لمحمد زكريا الكاندهلوي، ت: ابن باز.

Removing the Confusion on the Ruling of Shaving and Shortening the Beard According to the Ḥanafī School

رفع المرية
في قص اللحية
وحلقها عند الحنفية

Rafʿ al-Mirya fī Qaṣṣ al-Liḥya wa-Ḥalqihā ʿand al-Ḥanafiyya

A bilingual treatise

By Shaykh Ṣalāḥ Abū al-Ḥājj

Translated by
Siddiq Adam Mitha

SUNNI PUBLICATIONS

www.ingramcontent.com/pod-product-compliance
Lightning Source LLC
Chambersburg PA
CBHW021425150726
47989CB00001B/109